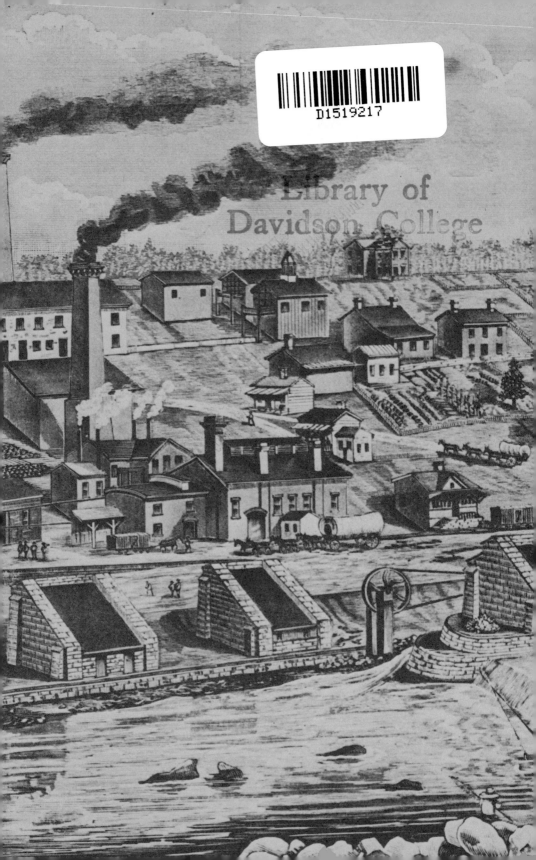

LAMMOT DU PONT

and the

American Explosives Industry

1850–1884

LAMMOT DU PONT

and the

American Explosives Industry

1850–1884

NORMAN B. WILKINSON

Published for the Eleutherian Mills–Hagley Foundation by the
UNIVERSITY PRESS OF VIRGINIA

THE UNIVERSITY PRESS OF VIRGINIA
Copyright © 1984 by the Eleutherian Mills–Hagley Foundation
First published 1984

The Rembrandt Peale portrait of Mrs. Alfred Victor du Pont
is reproduced by courtesy of Mrs. Renée (Carpenter) Draper,
the portrait of Alfred Victor du Pont courtesy of J. Simpson
Dean, Jr. The photograph of the "soda lake" in Wyoming
comes from Lee et al., *Guidebook of the Western United States*
(Washington, D.C., 1916). The wood engraving of the Upper
Yard, 1876, is from Asher and Adams, *Pictorial Album of
American Industry* (1876). All other illustrations are reproduced courtesy the Hagley Museum and Library.

Frontispiece: Lammot du Pont (1831–1884)

Library of Congress Cataloging in Publication Data

Wilkinson, Norman B.
  Lammot du Pont and the American explosives industry,
1850–1884.

  Includes bibliographical references and index.
  1. Explosives industry—United States—History—
19th century. 2. Chemical industry—United States—
History—19th century. 3. Businessmen—United States—
Biography. 4. Du Pont, Lammot, 1831–1884. 5. E.I. du
Pont de Nemours & Company—History. I. Title.
HD9663.U62W54 1984   338.7'6622'0924 [B] 83-21813
ISBN 0-8139-1012-9

Printed in the United States of America

To Marian

Contents

Illustrations

Preface

It was almost "shirtsleeves to shirtsleeves" within two rather than the proverbial three generations for the du Pont family. The black powder company established by Eleuthère Irénée du Pont near Wilmington, Delaware, in 1802 was close to bankruptcy by the middle of the century. Du Pont's eldest son, Alfred Victor, head of the firm since 1837, not a good administrator, preferred working in the mills and laboratory to the tedium and confinement of handling routine office matters and the responsibility of overseeing finances. Accounts had fallen into disarray and the company now faced a half-million-dollar debt, a considerable sum at that time. Alfred's two brothers and four sisters, partners in the business, alarmed at his seeming indifference to this crisis, suggested that he turn over the management of the firm to his younger brother Henry. Alfred resisted, and it was only after months of persuasive pressure—joined in by his wife, who feared for his health and the likelihood of a family schism if he refused—that he yielded to what had become an ultimatum and agreed to relinquish the position of senior partner to Henry at the end of 1850.

Alfred's resignation, however, did not end the participation of his branch of the family in company affairs. Not long before his departure two of his sons, Eleuthère Irénée II and Lammot, began working in the powder yards assisting Uncle Henry and their younger uncle, Alexis Irénée. This coterie of uncles and nephews, later to be joined by other male family members, reversed the company's fortunes, and by the later 1870s had brought it to a position of dominance in the explosives industry. Henry's diligent watchfulness over all fiscal matters restored its financial stability, and his tighter discipline over the work force increased productivity. Surplus funds were shrewdly invested, and the family practice of acquiring agricultural land and farming properties was continued. His daily routine began with a tour of inspection of the mills followed by a trip to outlying farm properties, then back to the company office, where he devoted himself to answering letters, reviewing accounts, and handling financial matters with meticulous care. Only rarely, it seems, did the senior partner leave the Brandy-wine area for any length of time.

Lammot, his younger nephew, a young man of keen mind, gifted with technical and mechanical talents, introduced many improve-ments in the methods and the machinery of mill operations. He devel-oped new types of powder for specific uses, spending long hours in his workshop and laboratory, the results of which gave his firm a competi-tive advantage and affected the entire industry. His uncle early re-ferred to him as "Our chemist," directing all chemical and technical matters to his attention.

Possessed of an engaging and gregarious personality, as well as being a gifted raconteur, Lammot became his uncle's surrogate in dealing with the heads of other powder companies and with ordnance officers of the U.S. government. He was chosen by the Lincoln administration to acquire an ample supply of vital saltpeter from an unfriendly Great Britain early in the Civil War, and in the postwar years he was the powder industry's spokesman before committees of Congress. His skill as a negotiator led to the acquisition of other powder firms during the 1870s, and he was a pivotal figure in getting the industry to regulate itself and abandon suicidal competitive practices in that depressed dec-ade. Aware of the very busy life he led, an observant relative who lived across the Brandywine from the powder mills spoke of Lammot as being "the life of the business."

After thirty years working together promoting the fortunes of com-pany and family, relations between Lammot and his Uncle Henry became strained. His proposals for the reorganization of the company in a manner befitting its much greater size, the delegation of more authority to the younger partners, and the more equitable allocation of ownership and division of profits among the partners brought no satisfactory response from the head of the company. Lammot's sugges-tion that Du Pont enter the burgeoning field of high explosives— nitroglycerine and dynamite—was also ignored. Rebuffed, angry, and hurt by his uncle's adamant refusal to discuss and consider these pro-posals, Lammot withdrew from the firm and in 1880 founded the Repauno Chemical Company at Gibbstown, New Jersey, where he be-gan the manufacture of nitric and sulfuric acids, nitroglycerine, and dynamite.

The new enterprise was begun at a time when discoveries and ad-vances in chemistry and chemical engineering were bringing about changes in many lines of manufacture. Research and development by chemists, physicists, and engineers in the laboratories and machine shops of larger companies were stimulated and underwritten with greater funding. It was in this direction that Lammot channeled future Du Pont company growth when he established the laboratory at Repauno. Later designated as the Eastern Laboratory, this was the prototype of subsequent laboratories and experimental stations from which came the many new and varied products and technical achievements that made possible the remarkable success of the firm in this century under the guidance of Lammot's sons and nephews.

This biography has been written principally from Lammot du Pont's own papers, a large collection of correspondence, memoranda, documents, and drawings hitherto untapped by writers on the Du Pont Company and family. From these materials there emerges an exceptionally competent, vigorous, and innovative man, characterized as possessing the finest intellect of all the members of the du Pont clan. His skill, diligence, and enterprise were devoted to promoting his family's business and enlarging the family fortunes so that the futures of his ten children would be assured. Dedication to hard work, however, did not dull his buoyant, genial personality nor lessen his sense of humor and enjoyment of a good story. His life was replete with exploits, some serious, some humorous, which are recounted here for the light they cast upon his versatility and his personal traits of mind and action.

My gratitude is extended to the Eleutherian Mills Historical Library, Greenville, Delaware, for providing me with study facilities and for many courtesies graciously rendered by the members of its Research and Reference Division, Mrs. Betty-Bright Low, Mrs. Carol B. Hallman, and Mrs. Majorie McNinch. Dr. John B. Riggs, the library's Curator of Manuscripts and his associate Miss Ruthanna Hindes called my attention to newly accessioned materials pertinent to this study which were not included in Dr. Riggs's invaluable Guide to the Manuscripts in the Eleutherian Mills Historical Library, *published in 1970. Daniel T. Muir and Jon Williams of the Library's Pictorials Department helped me select the illustrations, and library photographers Charles A. Foote and George W. Rineer, Jr., made the reproductions.*

Conversations with Dr. Harold B. Hancock added to my understanding of the relations between Lammot du Pont and his uncle

Henry du Pont, and he offered helpful comment on certain chapters closely akin to his own research interests. Dr. Walter J. Heacock, general director of the Eleutherian Mills–Hagley Foundation, encouraged the undertaking of this study, and a critical reading of the text by Dr. Glenn Porter, deputy director, resulted in more precise and felicitous phrasing of some passages. To the Copeland Andelot Foundation and to Rosa Laird McDonald and W. W. Laird I am most grateful for the generous assistance they have given. David T. Gilchrist, director of Foundation publications, has shared his expertise in overall organization of the book.

For her collaboration in all aspects of this work I am indebted to my wife, Marian, particularly for her patient struggling with my idiosyncratic handwriting as she typed and retyped amended and revised drafts of the manuscript.

As biographer I have aimed at the "reincarnation" of my subject, to have Lammot du Pont take on blood, flesh, and bone and become a tangible living person within his family, company, and the industry to which he gave his life. I alone am responsible for whatever flaws, omissions, and misinterpretations may be found in this portrait in words.

LAMMOT DU PONT

and the

American Explosives Industry

1850–1884

Chapter I

As the Twig Is Bent

THE DU PONT COMPANY was approaching its fiftieth year as a manufacturer of black powder when Lammot du Pont, age eighteen, entered the family business in 1849. He had recently graduated from the college of the University of Pennsylvania with a major in chemistry, but the first tasks assigned him by his father, Alfred Victor du Pont, head of the firm, bore little relation to his classroom studies.

On September 5 he began working in the refinery. Here, sometimes on the night shift, sometimes day, under the direction of the refinery boss, Charles Le Carpentier, Lammot was one of a ten-man crew who refined crude saltpeter, the principal ingredient of black powder. Long, monotonous hours were spent dissolving the saltpeter (potassium nitrate from India) in huge iron kettles; repeatedly skimming off impurities that rose to the surface; decanting the hot liquid into vats where it formed crystals as it cooled; giving the crystals successive washings; and then shoveling them into large, shallow copper pans to dry. Whether Lammot made use of the refinery's laboratory during his early apprenticeship is not known, but when night duty sometimes slackened off he did find time to brush up on his chemistry reading by lamplight.[1]

Lammot's home, Nemours, stood on a low bluff a few hundred yards downstream from the refinery and the Upper Yard powder mills that bordered the western bank of Brandywine Creek. The house had been built by his grandfather and founder of the firm, Eleuthère Irénée du Pont, for his eldest son, Alfred Victor, when he married Margaretta Elizabeth Lammot in 1824. Lammot's mother was the daughter of Daniel Lammot, Jr., and Susan P. (Beck) Lammot, member of a prominent Philadelphia merchant family. Margaretta's father was a cotton textile manufacturer with mills in Brandywine Village and on Chester Creek in nearby Delaware County, Pennsylvania. With his daughter he was

Nemours, birthplace and home of Lammot du Pont for fifty years, 1831 to 1881.

Mrs. Alfred Victor (Margaretta Elizabeth Lammot) du Pont (1807–1898), mother of Lammot du Pont. Portrait by Rembrandt Peale.

instrumental in organizing the Church of the New Jerusalem (Swedenborgian) in Delaware, and at Nemours, Margaretta, now Mrs. Alfred Victor du Pont, held family services in accordance with its tenets and ritual. Her husband, deistic in religious outlook, raised no objections to this practice.

Young Lammot's paternal grandmother, Sophie Madeleine du Pont, had died in 1828, three years before he was born, and any memory of his paternal grandfather was very shadowy, for he had died in 1834 when Lammot was only three years old. The grandparents' home, Eleutherian Mills, built in 1802–3, was within voice range of Nemours and connected to it by a short stretch of road. Both residences fronted westward toward the Kennett Turnpike a mile away, looking out upon a large orchard of pear, peach, apple, cherry, and plum trees. Beyond the orchard lay fields of hay, oats, corn, and wheat, and in the distance pastureland where cattle, sheep, and horses grazed.

Closer to the homes were flower gardens, berry and vegetable patches, and a large stone barn around which clustered wagon sheds, stables, poultry runs, pigsties, pigeon lofts, and dovecotes. All this was company owned; the farmhands were company employees and they kept the various du Pont households supplied with foodstuffs, fruits, and flowers from the farm, orchard, and garden.

Lammot's uncles and aunts, the brothers and sisters of his father, had their homes near the powder mills. Uncle Henry, an 1833 graduate of the U.S. Military Academy at West Point, now second to Lammot's father in company affairs, lived with his wife Louisa at the Eleutherian Mills homestead. Residing with them until the early 1850s was Aunt Victorine, Mrs. Ferdinand Bauduy, the eldest of Sophie and E. I. du Pont's seven children, and a childless widow since 1814. The homes of the others, Uncle Alexis, Aunt Eleuthera, and Aunt Sophie were all within a radius of less than a mile, and Aunt Evelina's home, Winterthur, was several miles northwest up the Kennett Turnpike. Across the Brandywine from the powder mills was the Louviers Woolen Mill, operated by cousin Charles I. du Pont, whose home stood near the mill.

Convenient to the mills and neighboring to all the du Pont domiciles were the homes of many of their employees—powdermen, masons, carpenters, wagoners, farmhands, laborers, and domestics—living in scattered banks or double rows of small stone houses bearing such names as Upper Banks, Duck Street, Chicken Alley, Charles' Banks, Free Park, Wagoners' Row, and Squirrel Run Village. Most of these families were Irish or of Irish descent, their number increasing appreciably during the 1830s and 1840s— decades of famine and trouble in Ireland. Fewer in number but generally performing the more skilled tasks of millwright, boss carpenter, master mason, refiner, and cooper were a few Frenchmen, Scots and Scots-Irish, and some Englishmen and Welshmen.

In this paternalistic enclave set amid woodlands, farms, and gardens, within sound of the mills managed by his father and uncles, Lammot spent his boyhood years. It was not a lonely childhood, for he was the fourth of seven children born between 1825 and 1837; two sisters and a brother were older than he, and two brothers and a sister younger. Shortly before the birth of her fifth child, a son she named Alfred Victor after his father, Lammot's mother received from his Aunt Vic a clipping of light verse expressing the frustration of a mother of a large family trying to find time and place to do some quiet reading on Malthus!

Specimen of a Malthusian

My dear, do pull the bell,
And pull it well,
And send those noisy children all upstairs,
Now playing here like bears.

You, George and William go into the grounds,
Charles, James and Bob are there—and take
      your string—
Drive horses, or fly kites, or anything,
You've quite enough to play at hare and
      hounds.

You, little Mary, Caroline and Poll,
Take each your doll,
And go my dears into the two back stair,
Your sister Margaret's there—

Harriet and Grace, thank God are both at
      school,
As far off as Ponty Pool.

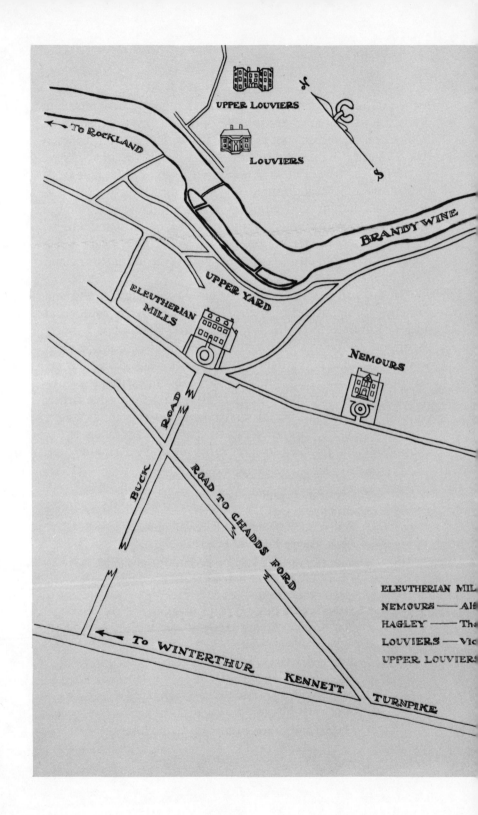

UPPER LOUVIERS

LOUVIERS

To ROCKLAND

BRANDYWINE

UPPER YARD

ELEUTHERIAN MILLS

NEMOURS

BUCK ROAD

ROAD TO CHADDS FORD

To WINTERTHUR

KENNETT TURNPIKE

ELEUTHERIAN MIL
NEMOURS —— Al
HAGLEY —— Th
LOUVIERS — Vic
UPPER LOUVIERS

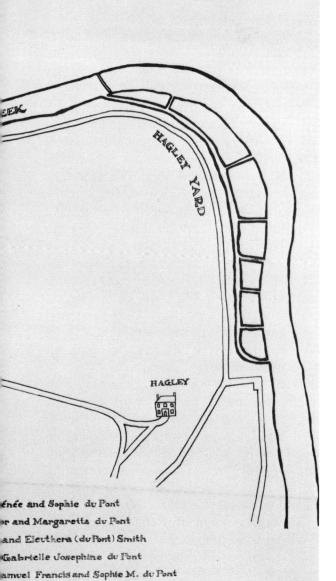

The du Pont residences on the Brandywine.

EEK

HAGLEY YARD

HAGLEY

WILMINGTON →

énée and Sophie du Pont
r and Margaretta du Pont
and Eleuthera (du Pont) Smith
Gabrielle Josephine du Pont
amuel Francis and Sophie M. du Pont

Drawn by W. Fletcher

I want to read, but really can't get on—
Let the four twins—Mark, Matthew, Luke
    and John,
Go—to their nursery—go—I never can
Enjoy my Malthus among such a clan.

Aunt Vic puckishly appended to this, "It struck me how much *you* would sympathize with the author—happily it is not yet come to the four twins with you!"[2] But another daughter and son were born by the fall of 1837, and a new wing was added to Nemours the following year. It may have been that about this time their father had a small, frame workshop erected a few yards from the east side of the house to which he could retreat to design and experiment in peace and quiet. At a later time this became Lammot's laboratory and workshop.

Mrs. du Pont, Margaretta, or Meta to all her relatives and close friends, had the help of a few servants in managing this large and lively household. For companions and playmates outside of the immediate family there were many cousins, eight in Uncle Henry's family, eight in Uncle Alexis's, five in the Charles I. du Pont household across the creek at Louviers, and numerous children of the neighboring workmen's families.

From early childhood Lammot was aware of the dangerous nature of the family business and the hazards of living so close to the mills. His first frightening experience happened at the age of three when a graining mill near his home containing a thousand pounds of powder blew up, killing the lone workman tending it.[3] Years later, in 1859 when he was twenty-eight years old, Lammot recalled this first of many explosions to which he was exposed in a memorandum which he titled "Notes on Accidents": "Mary Simmons was taking care of us children. I was but 3 years old and was sitting in a spot on the upper back piazza when it occurred. I was looking up at the window over the door when, before I heard the noise, I recollect distinctly seeing the whole glass fly out of the window, each pane apparently whole, then break and fall on the piazza. It also broke the article on which I was sitting. I jumped up and ran crying into Polly Simmons. Irénée was in Mother's room before the window glass on that side came in and cut him. He still bears the mark on his face."[4]

Irénée was Eleuthère Irénée II, his older brother by two years, who upon finishing college a year before Lammot had gone into the powder mills where he worked until his death in 1877. Loyalty to family rather than personal choice seems the reason for his becoming a powderman, implied in a comment made by a relative after he died: "Cousin Lina says that Irénée repeatedly told her that he was never made for a powderman and disliked the work."[5]

Primary schooling for Lammot and his brothers and sisters was obtained at home from their mother, with assistance from Aunt Victorine, a cultured, well-read woman who had helped educate her own younger sisters and brothers and the children of the local workmen who attended the Brandywine Manufacturers Sunday School. While too young to be part of the family class made up of the older children, Paulina, Victorine, and Irénée, Lammot listened in on the lessons in reading, French, and English. Brother Irénée's fluency in French inspired him to ask Aunt Vic to teach him the language and for some time he did tolerably well, but initial enthusiasm soon faded. Ruefully his patient instructor noted that after "teaching Lammot six months you would be surprised to see how little progress he has made."[6] His forte was not languages—his spelling was phonetic rather than correct throughout his life—but in mathematics and the applied sciences he developed the keenest interest, along with a liking for history. There is reason to believe this mental mold was set by the time he was twelve years old. In the summer of 1843 his mother gave him the choice of a vacation at Cape May, New Jersey, or a box of instruments. He had no difficulty making a decision. "Of course," he wrote his brother Irénée, who was away at school in Pennsylvania, "I chose to have a box of instruments."[7] What kind of instruments these were was not mentioned, but they were most likely for mechanical drawing.

Lammot was enrolled as a boarding student in 1842 at the Wilmington Classical Institute, a school with a good reputation that had been established in 1832 by the Reverend Samuel M. Gayley, a Scotch-Irish Presbyterian clergyman. The school was a few miles from Nemours, on the Lancaster Pike on a country property named Mantua. The curriculum covered all branches of English, mathematics, and the classics, so taught as to qualify students for admission to college or the business world. Lammot was one of a class of twenty-five boarding pupils admitted, his parents being assured that good study habits and correct moral principles would be inculcated during his stay. Tuition was $150 yearly, payable quarterly in advance, and this fee covered tuition, boarding, washing, fuel, and lights.[8]

No letters, diaries, or memoranda bearing upon these early school years have survived to tell much about his stay there. He got home often enough to talk about school activities. The school's records are gone, so we cannot learn of his academic achievements or his standing in classes, nor do we have any evaluations by teachers or headmaster. Samuel Gayley was learned in classical languages and the literature, history, mythology, manners, and customs of the Greeks and Romans; his teaching style was described as lively and energetic. His effectiveness as headmaster and teacher was not based solely upon his being a scholarly don. He took part in community affairs, promoted the improvement of Delaware's public school system, was a trustee of Lafayette College at Easton, Pennsylvania, and of Delaware College at Newark, Delaware, from which he declined the offer of the presidency.[9]

The only family observation on the quality of instruction offered at Gayley's school was made by Lammot's father years later when it moved from Wilmington to Media, Pennsylvania, after a fire seriously damaged Mantua. Using the testimonials of satisfied parents to announce the opening at the new location, Gayley quoted Alfred Victor du Pont: "I thank you most cordially for your attention to my boys. Their progress in study is highly satisfactory." Here he was including Lammot's younger brothers Alfred Victor and Antoine Bidermann, who followed him at the Classical Institute.[10]

The choice of the University of Pennsylvania as Lammot's college was made because of its proximity to home; Irénée was there, and it had been his father's alma mater though he had had to leave it suddenly in 1818. After a devastating explosion almost totally destroyed Eleutherian Mills, he had been summoned home by his father to help direct the rebuilding of the factory, and he had never returned. During his two-year stay at the college (1816–

18) Lammot's father had been an assistant to Thomas Cooper, the able and controversial English scientist whose utilitarian philosophy had been succinctly stated in the *Emporium of Arts and Sciences*, a publication he edited in 1813: "We teach our youth in vain unless we enable them to keep pace with the improvements of the day." And in another place Cooper had noted the absence of scientifically educated men in industry: "There are few chemists in this country among manufacturers."[11]

Cooper's stay as professor of chemistry and mineralogy (1816–19) had been too brief, and his personality too thorny, to bring about a significant shift from the older attitudes, which regarded the sciences as purely theoretical intellectual pursuits or as adjuncts to medicine. The natural sciences, botany and natural history in particular, were the prevailing enthusiasm during the first half of the nineteenth century, but there were foreshadowings of a shift, a slowly dawning awareness of the need to have theory applied to the useful and practical arts.[12]

By the early 1840s the university was displaying interest in offering a program in applied sciences that would prepare a young man to earn a living in industry. One influence bringing this about may have been the Franklin Institute, founded in 1824 by William H. Keating, Cooper's successor, and Samuel Merrick, where working mechanics were being taught the principles of applied science. Public lectures on popular science were offered, and Keating, in addition to his teaching at the college, taught the applied chemistry course at the institute from 1824 to 1826.

The success of the institute could not have gone unobserved by the university, but the traditional view of educating men only for the "respectable" professions—law, medicine, the ministry, and teaching—in which preparation for industry had no place, still predominated. Another consideration was whether enough upper class families, whose sons made up the student body, would look with favor upon and pay tuition for systematic instruction in the mechanical professions. To many proper Philadelphians this would have been demeaning.

Expansion of the curriculum to include the applied sciences came about slowly, not by planned administrative action but piecemeal over a number of years and largely through the influence of a few individuals. One was James C. Booth, educated at the university, followed by several years studying chemistry in Germany. On his return to Philadelphia in 1836 he had set up a private laboratory where he made analyses and assays, smelted and refined metal for the U.S. Mint, and offered laboratory instruction to a number of interested college students. Booth was the author of several books on chemistry and also lectured at the Franklin Institute.

A second was John F. Frazer, who succeeded Alexander Dallas Bache as professor of natural history and chemistry in 1844, two years before Lammot du Pont became one of his students. Frazer shared the views of Cooper, Keating, and Booth that the sciences should be more utilitarian, that industry could be advanced by college-trained young men who understood the applications of chemistry, mineralogy, and engineering to industrial processes. The content and methods of his classroom teaching reflected this conviction and made their impress upon his students. Lammot was in Frazer's classes when he was introducing the practical emphasis in an innovative, experimental manner on his own, with no formal sanction given by university authorities. Soon after Lammot graduated Frazer formalized what he had been doing informally for half a dozen years by presenting to the university trustees a convincing explanation of how practical scientific courses could be further developed and expanded under his and Professor Booth's direction. His proposals, directed to J. R. Ingersoll, a most influential trustee, resulted in the establishment in 1852 of the university's School of Mines, Arts, and Manufactures.[13]

Lammot was fourteen when he finished the Wilmington Classical Institute, a year too young to be admitted to college. Much of this year, 1845, he spent in Philadelphia receiving private tutoring while living at the home of Mrs. Ann Shapley on Spruce Street below Seventh; brother Irénée, in his freshman year, also boarded with Mrs. Shapley. The college, with a total enrollment of 105 students, was located on Ninth Street between Market and Chestnut streets. Lammot's tutor was a Mr. Johnson, possibly a Walter R. Johnson who lived on Broad Street below Chestnut.[14] It is not known in what subjects Lammot was being tutored, but most likely in his weakest, literature and the classical languages. If efforts were made to improve his spelling, they were only minimally successful; his intense, direct, quick mind remained untrammeled by the rules of English spelling; for example, *weight* was spelled "wate"; *character* became "caracter"; *ceiling* came out "sealing"; and *facsimile*, "fact similar".

The parents' concern for their two young sons away from home at school in the big city is apparent in the letters from their mother inquiring about their health, their diet, their studies, clothes, and laundry, reminding them of social amenities to be observed when calling upon Philadelphia friends and relatives, and sometimes asking them to purchase items not obtainable in Wilmington shops. At a teenage pimply stage Lammot's face broke out, and for this his mother prescribed Rochelle Salts in water, but she cautioned, "Take great care to buy Rochelle Salts and not *poison*."[15] On some of his frequent business trips to Philadelphia their father would notify them to meet him, if they had time from their studies, usually at the Merchants' Hotel on Fourth Street above High Street. One pictures the boys joining their father at the host's table, enjoying a meal quite superior to their usual boarding house fare; recounting for him their school activities while asking for news of family, friends, favorite pets, and things at the mills.

Lammot passed the university entrance examinations in the late fall of 1845 and was admitted to the second term of the freshman class early in February 1846, two months before his fifteenth birthday. Despite starting classes a month late he finished the freshman year in July with an overall average of 10.3 on a grading scale of 7 to 15, an average of 11 or above being considered distinguished.[16]

Parents of out-of-town students could request that a faculty member be named guardian of their sons while attending the college, the guardians to handle their finances and attend to the general well-being of their charges. In practice the students usually lived with their guardians, their room and board payments augmenting faculty incomes, which depended upon fees received from students in their classes. Preferring this to having their sons remain in a boardinghouse, arrangements were made by the parents for Lammot and Irénée to become the "wards" of Dr. John Robertson, an instructor in the classics, whose home was at 119 South Ninth Street.

Lammot's college notes have not survived nor is there much in his letters that tells how he found college life, what subjects appealed and which he found onerous; there are a few mentions of friendships formed, but nothing on what he thought of his teachers and the quality of instruction. Both boys continued to need special tutoring in Greek and Latin, which Dr. Robertson supplied; he helped Lammot struggle through translations of Crito and furnished Irénée with literal translations of passages from other classical writers.[17]

The Zelosophic Society, one of two literary societies at the college, elected Lammot to membership, but his attendance and participation in debates and declamations were erratic. At a meeting in 1847 he presented a paper on the French Revolution, a subject for which family sources could have provided ample firsthand information. At another meeting he successfully debated the affirmative view of the question, "Have Prosperity and Increase of Wealth been a Favorable Influence upon the Manners and Morals of a People?" Brother Irénée was "Attorney General" of Zelo in his senior year, but Lammot's hopes to succeed him in this post were dashed when election results gave him only one vote to his opponent's eighteen![18]

Classes were suddenly interrupted for Irénée in mid-April 1847, when his father requested that he be allowed to come home for a week. On April 14 a very serious explosion in the mills had killed eighteen workmen, the worst accident experienced since 1818, the disaster that had terminated the father's career at the college. Mills and homes were shattered or badly damaged, Nemours was made uninhabitable, forcing the family to temporarily move in with relatives.[19]

Alfred Victor insisted that the emergency absence should not be detrimental to Irénée's school work. He instructed his son to bring home his books, noting what material would be covered while he was away. But, he cautioned, "if you think a week's absence would be of less injury to Lammot's studies than to your

The du Pont brothers Lammot, Alfred Victor II, and Eleuthère Irénée II, c. 1847–50, while students at the University of Pennsylvania.

own you must waive your right of an elder son, and let him come down in your place; this I know would be a trial, yet if best, it must be done."[20] Alfred Victor's words convey the impression he thought Lammot was the abler student whose studies would suffer less by absence from classes.

During the school year the boys got home fairly often; for holidays, vacations, and breaks between terms. They made the thirty-mile trip either by the Philadelphia, Wilmington, and Baltimore Railroad or by the Delaware River passenger boats that furnished regular service between Philadelphia and Wilmington. A family carriage or the company mail wagon would pick them up at the railroad station or boat landing for the four-mile ride home to the Brandywine.

The ties of love and respect that knitted the family together, the warm affection between parents and children, made these excursions happy occasions at Nemours. All too quickly they came to an end, the sons' departures leaving a quieter household and a sense of loss in the family circle. Their mother, devoted but not given to impulsive displays of emotion, expressed the bittersweet sense of separation when they returned to college at the close of the summer vacation in 1847: "Tell Motty I have thought with great pleasure on the second kiss he came back to give me today. Dear boys, how I miss you at every turn. Lex came in tonight and called out 'Mother,' imitating Mott, and he made me start."[21]

Lammot's final examinations in his senior year confirmed that his academic strength was in natural philosophy (physics) and chemistry and that he performed better in written examinations than in oral recitations. Professor Frazer's instruction from the sophomore year on covered a broad range of subjects: physical geography, elements of mechanics and chemistry, equilibrium and motion of solids and fluids, optics, astronomy, heat, electricity, magnetism, sound, meteorology, and experimental lectures on chemistry.

In mathematics his final grade was a distinguished 14.0, and his recitation average 8.2. His instructor was Professor Henry Vethake, reputedly a hard teacher who took his students through algebra, geometry, plane and spherical trigonometry with appli-

cations to surveying and navigation, equations, analytical geometry, conic sections, differential and integral calculus, and analytical
mechanics. Professor Henry Reed, a cultured, versatile, upper
class Philadelphian, Lammot's instructor in English, rhetoric, and
history, gave him a final examination grade of 10.0 and a recitation grade of 9.9. The reading of Greek and Latin authors,
dramatists, poets, and philosophers, and writing compositions
in the classical languages, even under tutelage of the distinguished scholar Professor George Allen, were laborious chores
for Lammot, and his final examination grade of 5.0 showed it;
in recitation he did somewhat better, earning a final average of
8.7. In a graduating class of twenty that received bachelor of arts
degrees in July 1849, Lammot ranked eleventh.[22]

The University of Pennsylvania at that time had the custom
of conferring the master of arts degree upon holders of A.B. degrees "of three years standing." This was an honorary degree for
which no additional graduate study was required; there is no
evidence that Lammot returned to his alma mater for further
study, yet the university's commencement program of 1852 lists
him and all his classmates in the Class of 1849 as recipients of
the M.A. degree.[23]

According to his son Pierre, later in life Lammot expressed
some doubts about the effectiveness of book learning and high
achievement in the classroom: "I have observed that those who
stand at the head of the class at school and college rarely amount
to much in their after life."[24] In his own class he had ranked
midway.

First thoughts on what Lammot would do after finishing
college seem not to have included working in the powder mills.
The discovery of gold in California had spread like an infectious
fever impelling thousands of men, young and old, to go west in
search of their El Dorados. Two of Lammot's half uncles, Henry
and Robert Lammot, were among the gold trekkers, and briefly
he too was tempted to become a "forty-niner."[25] Possibly his father's declining health and his mother's persuasion kept him from
leaving home. Being of the third generation, he may have assumed that it was expected he should go into the family business,

as brother Irénée had done. If initially it was solely family custom and loyalty that prompted him to join his brother, this tall gangling youth of eighteen displayed such technical, experimental, and administrative talents that twelve years later he was spoken of as "the life of the business."[26]

The predominance of the du Ponts in the black powder business at midcentury was noted in a popular scientific journal: "The most extensive powder-mills in the world are those on the Brandywine, Delaware, and the best powder is made at these mills. They manufactured last year 2,500,000 pounds."[27] A month earlier, on June 18, 1850, Wilmington's *Delaware Gazette* in a burst of local pride had headlined a column, "Delaware Beats the World," followed by the above statement, which the *Scientific American* apparently lifted verbatim from the local newspaper.

Lammot began his career at a time that coincided with an increasing demand for black powder. Canal building, though diminished from the boom era of 1815–40, needed it for blasting out rock and hardpan in digging canal beds. Streams were being cleared of obstructions to river traffic; foundations for bridges, dams, and buildings were excavated by powder, and it was used for boring tunnels through hillsides. The burgeoning extractive industries needed it in quarrying and in coal and mineral mining. Trappers, migrants, and traders moving westward took along powder and rifle for protection and survival, and it was a valuable barter item in the Indian fur trade, as Jacob Astor's American Fur Company, long a Du Pont customer, had learned to its profit.

In the boom period from 1850 to 1855 the major powder consumers were the railroad contractors who laid down 20,348 miles of new track between 1851 and 1860; the copper mines that increased output 1,000 percent during the decade; iron mines whose production rose 40 percent; and the gold miners who were having to dig and blast deeper for the 2,225,000 ounces of the precious metal taken from the earth in 1860. Locally, the major newly expanding market was anthracite coal mining in Pennsylvania, where annual output by 1860 was exceeding 9,000,000 tons.[28]

Powder sales of the Du Pont Company are an index to the

quickening pace of these aspects of the economy, as the following figures indicate:

Year	Sales	Percentage increase	Production (25-lb kegs)
1850	$258,586	23	93,417
1851	309,929	20	109,419
1852	342,863	10	143,037
1853	411,530	20	170,695
1854	551,890	34	179,979
1855	694,814	26	202,367[29]

Some of the powder sold in 1854 and 1855 was military powder furnished to both belligerents in the Crimean War, the Russians and their British and French opponents. In these same years Du Pont expanded its overseas sales and began shipping powder to Mexico, South America, the West Indies, the East Indies, and Africa, markets formerly dominated by British powder merchants who could not supply them during the Crimean War years.[30]

Keeping production ahead of demand began at the refinery, where Lammot first worked. The crude saltpeter refined and the sulphur sublimated here were distributed among four powder yards—Eleutherian Mills (or the Upper Yard), Upper Hagley, Lower Hagley, and the Lower Yard on the opposite bank farther downstream. Each yard had its own complement of mills in which the refined saltpeter was mixed with pulverized charcoal and sulphur, usually in proportions of three-quarters saltpeter and one eighth each charcoal and sulphur, but this formula was subject to some variation depending upon the kind of powder being made.

After thorough mixing and grinding in a rolling mill under heavy cast-iron rollers, the mixture, or "powdercake," which was kept moist all the time, next went to a press mill. Here a screw, or hydraulic, press squeezed it under heavy pressure to make it hard. When taken from the press the "presscake," which looked like a sheet of slate, had to be broken into small chips. This was done in a granulating, or corning, mill, in earlier times by hand mallets and later by running the presscake through a series of toothed zinc rollers. The chips were then passed through an arrangement of sieves of specified mesh size. Undersized grains and the powder dust created in this operation were sent back to the press mill to be added to the next batch of powder coming through.

The grained powder was then glazed by being tumbled in barrels. Tumbling rounded off the grains into ball-like pellets, and the friction of the tumbling action created heat that eliminated some of the remaining moisture. An innovation made about the time Lammot entered the firm was the addition of a small quantity of graphite, or black lead, toward the end of the glazing operation. This gave the grains a high gloss and made them pour more easily. The coating of graphite sealed the grains so that the powder did not readily disintegrate into its component parts in long storage or during transportation. From the glazing mill the powder went to the drying tables on which it was spread in thin layers to dry in the sun, or it was taken to a heated building, a dry house, heated with hot air or steam, where it was placed on trays to dry. Powder dust created in the graining, glazing, and drying operations was screened out by running the powder through a sieve of fine mesh, the dust being returned to the press mill. The finished powder grains were packed in barrels, kegs, or canisters that were labeled and then stored in a magazine, usually in an isolated location some distance from other mills. Knowledge of the complete process was a closely guarded secret known only to the directing members of the firm and to a very few trusted workmen of long service who were promoted to foreman or became assistants to the yard superintendent, who was always a du Pont.

After working some months in the refinery, Lammot received his first promotion in a rather unusual manner. On the morning of April 1, 1850, his father told him to take his fishing pole and walk toward the creek, ostensibly to do some fishing, instead of going immediately to work. As he passed the refinery he was to look in to see if Le Carpentier, the superintendent, was about his usual duties. If he was, Lammot was to continue on to the creek and fish for a while; but if not, he was to lay aside his pole, go in and take charge of operations. Lammot followed his father's instructions, and not seeing Le Carpentier anywhere about, went in and assumed charge of the work crew, two weeks short of his nineteenth birthday. He was then receiving an annual salary of five hundred dollars.

Le Carpentier's absence apparently did not surprise Lammot's father. Though a longtime employee, since 1829, and a family friend, now earning $1,000 annually, more than double the average wage paid to powdermen, for some time he had shown dissatisfaction and on several occasions threatened to quit. Reasons for this are not known, but death had brushed him very close in the severe explosion of 1847 that had killed eighteen men in the dry house and pack house near the refinery. The senior du Pont, despite his outwardly dour mien, was a sensitive man, paternalistic in dealings with his employees by which he had earned their loyalty and affection. Possibly he knew and respected the causes of Le Carpentier's dissatisfaction, and to avoid an unpleasant "on the carpet" confrontation he had decided upon this unobtrusive maneuver for Lammot to move into his position.[31]

Le Carpentier's naming one of his sons Alfred Victor after his employer is indicative of his respect and affection. His departure also coincided with a move by the other company partners to ask Lammot's father to step down as senior partner and turn over direction of the company to his brother Henry. If Le Carpentier knew of this, and as a confidant of Alfred's probably he did, his loyalty, and disgust at what he may have considered unfair action, may have prompted his sudden, unannounced quitting company employ.

During his first four months as boss of the refinery Lammot's health suffered as a result of long hours, overwork, and possibly from worry and the inner tension created by feeling that he had to prove he could handle his new responsibility; his weight dropped from 180 to 149 pounds. Some of the work he did in the laboratory may have been deleterious to his health. Soon after his promotion his father had him make a small quantity of guncotton, cautioning him that in the process he might blow himself up![32] Guncotton was a new form of explosive recently developed in Europe but still in the laboratory stage as methods of stabilizing it for safe use in firearms had not proved successful. A request for a sample of guncotton had come from the Washington Arsenal, but why his father asked young Lammot to make this highly hazardous chemical compound is not clear. Possibly he had confidence in his son's laboratory skill; perhaps he wanted him to become aware of the need to always be extremely careful when working with explosive materials. The sample was made, presumably with the father at his son's side, and grains of it test-fired before the sample was sent to the Washington Arsenal. The father complained that he had been made ill for several days by this experiment, and probably Lammot suffered equally bad effects.[33]

In these beginning years Lammot routinely made analyses of samples of crude saltpeter and sulphur; tested them for purity after refining; calculated costs of refinery operations; and determined whether red or black charcoal made a better powder. He was impatient with and annoyed by interruptions and delays to experiments he had underway. On one occasion he appealed to his younger brother Alfred Victor (Fred), then a student at the University of Pennsylvania, to hurry up a Philadelphia supply firm that was repairing a spirit lamp he needed for analyzing powder residuum: "I have at present to analyze some of the residuum left by our Eagle gunpowder, so I have been flashing it for the last 2 days as hard as I have been able. I keep 2 wires red hot in the stove and touch it off at the rate of 15 grains every ten seconds, but I have got done this operation. That is, I have 500 grains of residuum and can't proceed any farther for want of my *lamp* as I am afraid to boil it on the stove for 8 hours without boiling it over."[34]

As he gained experience and confidence Lammot's health improved and he began to put on weight. His mother observed the change, informing his sister Sophie, who was away from home, that "Motty is hard at work now & powder brisk, working night and day. Bishop [Lammot's brother Irénée] & Motty both getting fat and in good spirits."[35] His Aunt Eleuthera provides another glimpse into his appearance and personality in a letter to her husband's nephew, Lt. Richard S. Smith, on the staff at West Point Military Academy, which Lammot was going to visit in

August 1850. Her letter of introduction read: "I know you will introduce Lammot to a minute inspection of the place, which notwithstanding his apparently imperturable demeanor, he will greatly enjoy. Under his quiet parlour face he is full of fun, but is not easily drawn out."[36]

New Year's Day was customarily a festive time for the du Ponts when all members of the family gathered for dinner, usually at Eleutherian Mills. Gifts and gossip were exchanged in an air of fun and conviviality. The younger people played games, put on skits, and sometimes engaged in horseplay. On one occasion Lammot was the star of a hilarious bit of impersonation when his brothers and sisters dressed him up as a woman, a veritable giantess six feet tall and large in proportion. No dress could be found that was long enough, so he donned a woman's riding habit, the skirt of which "hung very low over the saddle" to reach the floor and was stuffed with a pillow for a tonneau—a ludicrous sight. Several young female cousins were afraid of the "giantess," and when Lammot was introduced to Victor and Charles du Pont as a "Miss Jackson," these gentlemen bowed to the "lady," not recognizing Lammot beneath the disguise. Their formality broke his reserve and he had to burst out laughing, shattering the impersonation. "A little nonsense now and then is relished by the wisest men" was one of Lammot's favorite aphorisms, his son Pierre remembers.[37]

Happy times such as these helped the elder circle of family members forget for a time their growing dissatisfaction with the way Lammot's father was managing the business. Lammot was unaware of this, for he was not yet privy to the discussions of his aunts and uncles on such sensitive matters.

Chapter II

An Ultimatum and
Reorganization

THREE YEARS AFTER E. I. DU PONT'S death in 1834, his sons and daughters and son-in-law James A. Bidermann, husband of his daughter Evelina, had reorganized the powder firm into a copartnership for a period of ten years. Its capital was fixed at $182,000 divided into twenty-six shares, each valued at $7,000. As the eldest son, Alfred Victor became senior partner, holding eight shares; and as directing manager his annual salary was $3,000. His two younger brothers, Henry and Alexis, junior partners, each held five shares and were paid $2,000 annually. His four sisters were silent partners, each holding two shares of stock, receiving no salaries, but sharing proportionately in whatever profits were earned.

Alfred Victor's accomplishments during his thirteen years as senior partner were considerable. Annual sales rose from $213,000 in 1837 to $306,000 in 1849.[1] New markets had been opened, particularly in the fast-growing midwestern states with the establishment of new powder agencies. He had erected the company's first office building in 1837 near his parents' home from which his father had conducted the business since its beginning. A new, complete set of mills had been built between 1839 and 1841 farther downstream on the opposite side of the Brandywine and given the simple designation of the Lower Yard. In the Hagley Yard and the Upper (or Eleutherian Mills) yard, additional buildings had been erected and older ones refitted. One new structure was a large keg mill across the stream from the Hagley Yard, where a gang of coopers under the direction of a master cooper made wooden kegs and barrels according to Alfred's specifications and using machinery he introduced.

As a result of comparative efficiency tests between the older wooden waterwheels and newer metal turbines, Alfred had the more efficient turbines installed in some of the mills. To speed up movement of materials, he laid a narrow-gauge rail track between the mills, and on this men pushed flatcars and horses pulled heavier boxcars carrying raw materials or finished powder. At Edgemoor on the Delaware River, just outside Wilmington's city limits, he had erected a powder magazine and wharves for storage and shipment by boat.

Despite prolonged bad times in the 1830s and early 1840s, Alfred's relations with his workmen were good. He advanced money to pay for the passage of workmen's families and other relatives from the British Isles, principally Ireland, deducting small amounts monthly from their wages to pay off the advances. He sometimes acted as executor settling the estates of deceased workmen. Pensions were paid to widows whose husbands had been killed in powder mill accidents and medical care was furnished powdermen's families by a company doctor, the patient paying only for the medicines prescribed.

The goal of many Brandywine millworkers, powdermen, and others was to save enough money to buy a piece of land and become farmers. Some went into farming locally, but the appeal of cheap, arable land in the Midwest led others to head toward the Mississippi Valley and beyond. Parting words from their employer warned them of the sharp practices of land speculators they should guard against. Their accumulated wage balances plus interest at 6 percent were paid them, but sometimes Alfred transferred their funds to the Du Pont Company agent located in the town nearest to where the workmen intended to settle. With the funds went a letter introducing the newcomers and a request that since they had had little experience handling large sums of money, and none whatsoever in real estate matters, the agent should act as their advisor and make it his business to see that they were not cheated. In all, this personal concern for his employees and their families, many of whom he had grown up with, sharing boyhood pleasures and working experiences, was enlightened paternalism that lessened some of the harshness of this dangerous business.

By inclination, and from lack of experience, Alfred was not a skilled administrator. His interests and achievements were manifestly in production. He preferred to be in the mills or the laboratory, leaving much of the office and financial paperwork to his younger partners and a small office staff. When his father died he had not immediately become head of the firm. This position was held for the three years 1834–37 by his brother-in-law James A. Bidermann, who had assisted E. I. du Pont with management duties for nearly twenty years. Alfred may have felt, and his brothers and sisters possibly concurred, that in 1834 he was not prepared to assume executive direction of the business. Between 1834 and 1837 Bidermann had put its finances in order, paid off the last nonfamily shareholders, helped draw up the 1837 partnership agreement, and had then gone off to Europe with his wife Evelina for a two-year stay, leaving Alfred in the top post.

During the ten-year span of the partnership agreement, 1837–47, there was no openly expressed dissatisfaction with Alfred's leadership. His achievements were evident to his brothers and sisters, and, in retrospect many years later, to some of the younger du Ponts. One of these was Henry Algernon du Pont (1838–1926), a nephew, the elder son of Alfred Victor's brother Henry. Late in his life he confided to another member of the family his boyhood impressions of his Uncle Alfred and what had undoubtedly been told to him by his elders: "Uncle Alfred was the only man I ever knew who possessed both literary and scientific ability. He was a good chemist and machinist; could work with his hands at most trades and was a very learned student of history. He was not a very able business man, and when he retired in 1850—at the written suggestion of his brothers and his wife— the firm was $500,000 in debt."[2]

It was this aversion to bookwork, the routine handling of accounts, and the drawing up of balance sheets that first drew criticism from the other partners. It began with the expiration of the ten-year partnership agreement at the end of 1846, when it was expected that Alfred would have had all the accounts closed out and a balance sheet ready to submit to them. This he failed to do, an omission that caused his brothers and brother-in-law to call upon him early in January 1847 and issue a mild reprimand. They were disappointed at not being furnished a statement showing the company's financial condition; it was important

Alfred Victor du Pont (1798–1856), father of Lammot du Pont, senior partner and head of Du Pont Company 1837–50.

that the accounts of the old partnership be settled. They agreed to a renewal of the partnership for another year, with the proviso that Alfred have a statement ready for all the partners by March 10. The youngest brother, Alexis, was optimistic that the "determined manner in which we insisted that the business should be settled will induce Alfred to attend to it." But older brother Henry was doubtful; he feared that "the day will come and find us as we have been for the last few years, without a balance sheet."[3]

Henry's surmise was correct; Alfred repeatedly put off the distasteful chore, and his partners did not push him. Their patience may be explained by the heavy demands to produce powder for the Mexican War, their concern over signs of his failing health, stomach disorders which he self-diagnosed as dyspepsia, and anxiety over the very damaging explosion that had taken such heavy toll of lives and property on April 14, 1847, which disrupted operations and ate up months of time in rebuilding. The stalemate continued until the end of 1849, when his partners finally requested Alfred to turn over the financial direction and handling of company correspondence to his brothers. Apparently, Alfred yielded little, for in July 1850, in a polite but firm reminder, they demanded that he step down. They hoped he would see the justice and wisdom of this move, but if he failed to surrender authority they would be compelled to publicly announce a change in the partnership, and this, coming suddenly, would have a bad effect upon the company's credit, and upon Alfred's reputation. Unless he forced it earlier, they would wait until the end of 1850 to formally reorganize the partnership, and he could be assured that his great services to the company and the obligations he had conferred upon them individually would be borne in mind by his affectionate brothers and sisters.[4]

What rejoinder or defense Alfred made to this ultimatum is not on record. The close-knit nature of the business had the brothers seeing each other every day in the small stone office building that was headquarters, and this letter may have resulted in heated discussions not committed to paper. It is unlikely that Alfred talked about this to either of his sons, Irénée or Lammot; they were new to the business, and the father's pride and self-esteem might have prevented a frank discussion of the embarrassing position in which he now found himself. Concerned about his health, his wife, Meta, also fully aware of Alfred's dislike and neglect of routine office management, and wholeheartedly wanting to avoid a serious family rift, may have sympathetically and diplomatically advised her husband to step down for his own good. He was not a well man; at the last family New Year's Day gathering he had had to excuse himself from dinner and had returned home aided by Meta, Lammot, and Irénée. He rebelled at being considered really sick; he had never been ill, refused to take the prescribed medicines, and was very imprudent in caring for his health.[5]

Meta kept her children who were living away from home informed about their father's health: "Papa is not well, quite sick indeed, very miserable night and day, and is fretful, so that I have to be running after him up and down stairs incessantly. He is so restless that he cannot stay long in one place. He is not throwing up as he did last winter but he don't eat and suffers pain all over."[6] Another letter to her daughter, written three months after Alfred had received the ultimatum to resign, pictures him morose and depressed, maybe feeling some self-pity tinged with bitterness, but faced with a decision he could not avoid: "Your father has been twice to Phila. since you left us, and the rest of the time he sits in the house, rarely goes into the yard, never any further, so that I feel obliged to do ditto."[7]

Retirement came about quietly at the end of the year with no fanfare or publicity, and no discernible acrimony. "We have at last induced him to resign the management of the most fatiguing part of the affairs to his brothers," wrote his sister Eleuthera. "His eldest son, Eleuthère Irénée, is now in the business, and the second, Lammot, has charge of the refining of the saltpetre. He is a good chemist and fond of his employment." Lammot's only written observation on his father's forced retirement is found in a chronology of company history which he compiled some thirty years later: "On the 31st of December this year [1850] father retired from the business having entered in 1818 and having made during that time 1,283,610 kegs [of powder], and having built every building then standing on the place or furnished the drawings of them."[8] There is here a note of restrained filial pride in his father's achievements.

A new five-year partnership agreement went into effect January 1, 1851, with Henry du Pont succeeding Alfred as the senior partner. Their younger brother, Alexis, and Alfred's eldest son, Eleuthère Irénée, were junior partners. An analysis of the firm's financial structure covering the years 1840 to 1849—capital invested, profits earned, and dividends paid out—preceded the drawing up of the new partnership. It was probably prepared by Bidermann, the most experienced and financially astute of all those connected with the firm. The analysis showed that the firm's capital (20 shares at $21,000 each, totaling $420,000) was overvalued for the income it yielded. If the annual 6 percent dividend continued to be distributed, there would not be enough working capital left to cover operating expenses, and the firm could not carry on. It was therefore recommended that instead of a 6 percent dividend a 3 percent dividend be paid the shareholders. This was the most important proposal of a number that were considered and incorporated into the new partnership agreement.[9]

In final form the agreement kept the capitalization at $420,000; the number of shares was tripled from twenty to sixty, but the value of each share was reduced from $21,000 down to $7,000, the valuation in the 1837 partnership agreement. The sixty shares were distributed among the active and silent partners in this manner:

Henry du Pont	18 shares
Alexis I. du Pont	15 shares
Mrs. Victorine E. (du Pont) Bauduy	6 shares
Mrs. Sophia du Pont	6 shares
E. Irénée du Pont	6 shares
Collectively	9 shares
Total	60 shares

The nine shares held collectively were owned on a pro rata basis according to the number of shares each partner held in his or her own right. Alfred Victor was nominally no longer a shareholder, but the six shares in his son Irénée's name were possibly regarded as a fair equity in the business to be held by Alfred's branch of the family. They may also have represented acknowledgment by the other partners, as they had indicated in their letter requesting his resignation, of his valuable services to the company in years past.

A provision of the agreement assured continued family control of the firm by stipulating that shares could only be sold to another shareholder, the active managers being given the first opportunity to purchase, the silent partners second. To guard against what had been cited as one of Alfred's failings, the managers were enjoined from using their signatures or the company's name to borrow money or to endorse loans except for the proper use and benefit of the company. If earnings warranted, dividends were to be paid July 1 each year, but from the profits a suitable sum would first be set aside for the "speedy extinguishment of accommodation paper" (meeting notes due and paying off other loans), and only after a sum of not less than $20,000 was put into a permanent sinking fund. Insurance companies would not insure high-risk powder mills, so this last was a self-insurance fund to cover costs of rebuilding and equipping after explosions and fires.

As a means of recouping a portion of the losses caused by Alfred Victor's alleged mismanagement, he and Meta were required to transfer ownership of twenty-two pieces of property located in Brandywine and Christiana Hundreds and several tracts of land outside Delaware to his brothers, Henry and Alexis, in trust for the benefit of the company. And as surety for the loans made to their cousin across the Brandywine at the Louviers Woolen Mill, all the real estate owned by Charles I. du Pont and Company was transferred to Henry and Alexis, also to be held in trust for the powder company.

Lammot, four months away from his twentieth birthday, witnessed the signatures of all the partners to the agreement.[10] Whether the witnessing was only a formality or whether he read and understood each provision is not known. But with Irénée now a junior partner it would seem obvious that the brothers would have discussed the reorganization and the bearing it had on their future role in company affairs. The forced retirement of their father, difficult as it must have been for his sons to accept, could have been justified to them by either Uncle Henry or Uncle Alexis as necessary to clear the company debts, put it in sounder financial condition, and give it firmer, more efficient management. Their fortunes, too, were tied to the fate of the family business.

EXPERIENCE, AND A QUESTIONABLE EXPLOIT

Supervising refinery and laboratory operations continued to be Lammot's major responsibility for the next five years. He enlarged the refinery building, put in more saltpeter boiling kettles, and installed the first steam engine in the powder yards. The engine with its boiler was placed in a small building adjacent to the refinery and used to furnish a plentiful supply of distilled water needed in purifying the saltpeter. He consulted his father on these changes and also outlined for him some ideas he had about better methods of making charcoal.[11]

The pace at which he drove himself was often noted by his mother in letters to his sisters away from home: "Lammot is busy at the refinery tearing down boilers, etc., and [is] over head and ears in work." Another read, "Polly and I went to church yesterday without Lammot, who had furnaces under blast trying an experiment on a large scale & did not like to leave them."[12] His younger brother Alfred Victor II and his cousin Charles I. du Pont, Jr., had moved to Louisville to open a powder agency and to operate a paper mill. They sent samples of their paper to Lammot for analysis to determine what percentage of clay it contained. Lammot made the analysis and apologized for his tardy response: "As up to Friday night I had been up for 65 hours with four hours sleep, and spent 57 out of the 65 hours in the Refinery, besides having to work the Refinery during Sunday, so I have about as much to do as keep my mind occupied, besides [having made] analyses of 4 samples of saltpetre yesterday."[13]

On occasion he pressed woman and children of the family into performing light but necessary chores such as cutting labels to be pasted on powder containers. His mother spoke of their spending an evening with relatives: "We had a grand cutting match last evening, all of us, and got through a famous pile. I suppose all is going on right on the place for Irénée and Mott are both in good humour."[14]

But there were other occasions when all was not well. His father's continued illness worried Meta and the children. Periods of confinement to bed when he was devotedly nursed by his wife were interspersed with spells of fretful convalescence. Still only in his early fifties, Alfred Victor had been blessed with vigorous good health through most of his life and had actively engaged in every aspect of the powder mill operations for thirty-two years. Now to be relegated to the shadows as a semi-invalid brought on a moodiness of disposition.

Mending books, repairing small items around the house, reading, and feeding the chicks and young turkeys occupied some of his time. Chess became a favorite game, and for a time he played every afternoon, sometimes with his wife or daughter Paulina, and sometimes with Lammot, who took time from work to compete in what developed into a family tournament. Lammot found it hard to admit that his parents were better players than he, a flash of youthful conceit that amused his mother: "Chess is the present mania. . . . It was a great bore to play at first, for I had lost my taste for the game completely, but now I am getting interested in it. Tis amusing with Motty. We had never played together until this week, when he coolly informed me that I did not play as well as he by any means! So, I beat him; yesterday the same thing. 'Well, you may beat me, I grant,' said he, 'but I play the best.' The same in checkers; he confesses I beat, but he plays the best! Your papa plays better than I do, but it requires his utmost to do it."[15]

There were accidents and crises both on and off the du Pont domain that tested her son's quick thinking and courage. Fires usually followed the explosion of a powder mill, but at 2 A.M. on a Sunday in March 1851, when the mills were not operating, everyone was awakened by brother Irénée's cry, "Dr. Smith's house is on fire!" This was Aunt Eleuthera's home a few hundred yards away. It was the Smith barn and haystacks, not the house, but a shift of wind could quickly engulf the residence in flames. Bucket brigades were formed, women manned the household pumps, Wilmington fire companies were sent for, and Irénée dragged cattle by their tails out of the barn. Wet blankets were laid on the roof of the Smith home, valuables were quickly thrown into baskets and boxes and rushed to Nemours, where Lammot's mother felt it was her duty to stay to "guard this house for I knew hundreds of people would come from Wilmington and might plunder or fire our home if they found it vacant." Of her second son she wrote, "Lammot did wonders, of course, nearly killed and burnt to death, clothes on fire and the men had to throw water on him and he fell on a fence and broke three of the railings." Evidence strongly suggested arson, but fortunately the barn and its contents were insured.[16]

An accident that came close to inciting mob action against the du Ponts occurred on the morning of May 31, 1854. Three large wagons, each loaded with 150 kegs of powder, passing through Wilmington on their way to a wharf on the Delaware River blew up as they neared 14th and Orange streets. The three wagoners, all the horses, and two residents of the neighborhood were instantly killed; fifteen persons were injured, a number of houses shattered, others badly damaged, and fires started. The total property loss was estimated at between $75,000 and $100,000, an enormous amount of damage.

Alexis I. du Pont was the first to arrive at the scene of the holocaust. In its immediate aftermath, as realization of its devastation took hold, an aroused crowd of angry Wilmingtonians surrounded him. Lammot tells of his own fast ride into town and the tense scene he came upon: "I ran to the barn, jumped on horseback and arrived at the scene 22 mins. after. George Gordon was haranguing the populace saying the *Duponts* ought to be lynched, etc. But as soon as he saw me he stopped. I suppose he thought that it was too late, that the men [powder mill workmen] were coming in behind me. Even Uncle Alexis began to think there was some danger on account of mob law. His expression was of satisfaction when I put my hand on his shoulder, and turning he saw me."[17] We can only surmise whether Lammot's tall, confident, commanding presence halted a brewing riot.

The company made as complete restitution as possible; it expressed its sympathy and compensated the bereaved families, and paid for the rebuilding and repair of all damaged property. The cause of the explosion was never determined. Guesses were that powder had leaked from a keg, fell onto stones in the road, and was sparked when a horse's shoe struck it; or that a wagoner smoking a pipe or cigar was careless with a match or butt. It was established that the wagons were traveling too close together in violation of a company regulation that they remain a quarter of a mile apart when traveling in caravan. Wilmington's city council promptly passed an ordinance prohibiting the transportation of powder within city limits. The Du Pont Company then built a road (Du Pont Road) outside the city limits from the mills to Middleburgh, a marshy, isolated spot on the Christina River where it erected a wharf from which it loaded vessels.

The erection of a new shipping facility in 1854 was timely, for the following year the Du Pont Company began supplying powder to the warring powers fighting in the Crimea. Russia's historic aim to obtain a warm-water port, to gain access to the Mediterranean Sea, had brought on war with Turkey. France and England allied themselves with Turkey to safeguard their possessions and spheres of influence in and around *Mare Nostrum.*

Both belligerents turned to neutral nations for supplies of black powder, and buying missions were in the United States in the fall of 1854. Through the New York merchant house of Grinnell, Minturn & Company, the Russians made large purchases from the Du Pont Company and from the Hazard Powder Company at Hazardville, Connecticut. The first of the Du Pont contracts, January 30, 1855, was for 18,000 25-lb. kegs of cannon and musket powder at 16½ cents a pound; the second contract in April was for 5,000 100-lb. barrels at 17 cents a pound; and the third in November was for 10,000 100-lb. barrels at 16 cents a pound. Du Pont agreed to furnish the powder with the proviso that the needs of the United States should take precedence if this government called upon it. Hazard and Du Pont had consulted with each other before bidding on the first contract and both agreed the price would be 16½ cents a pound.[18]

For the English, also through Grinnell, Minturn & Company, Du Pont furnished 22,036 25-lb. kegs in 1855 and 20,000 kegs in 1856. The war orders in 1855 boosted powder sales for the year to $694,814, the highest thus far in company history.[19]

Getting the powder into the custody of Grinnell, Minturn & Company on schedule was Lammot's task, and shipments left

the Du Pont wharves on the Delaware and the Christina in May,
July, and September of 1855; but it was the New York firm's
responsibility to deliver the powder to the warring nations. England, sovereign of the seas, was unwilling, however, to acknowledge the traditional American position that neutral ships meant
neutral goods, and were therefore not subject to seizure by a
belligerent. Her warships patrolled the Atlantic and Mediterranean ready to intercept all vessels suspected of carrying munitions or other contraband to the enemy.

A reputed feat of daring, but one not publicized until after
his death, cast Lammot as the hero of an almost unbelievable
hare-and-hounds pursuit by English patrol vessels of a vessel laden
with powder for Russia. Obituary accounts in Wilmington and
Philadelphia newspapers told of Lammot sailing on one of the
powder vessels destined for Sebastapol on the Black Sea. It eluded
English frigates all the way across the Atlantic, slipped through
the Straits of Gibraltar, and sailed unmolested the length of the
Mediterranean. It navigated the Bosporous into the Black Sea,
and as it was approaching Sebastapol it was hailed by British
warships and ordered to heave to. At this critical moment—the
captain wavering—Lammot took command and ordered full speed
ahead. The British fired two broadsides, some shot going through
the rigging but missing the hold with its explosive cargo. Hotly
pursued, Lammot brought the powder vessel between offshore
rocks and beached it safely under the protecting guns of the massive fortress. For the safe delivery of the shipload of powder the
Russian government reportedly paid three million dollars.[20]

There are good reasons for doubting that Lammot ever participated in an exploit of this kind. His papers and those of other
members of the family, as well as company papers, make no mention of it. He had no reason to be on board as supercargo, for
the agents, Grinnell & Minturn, were responsible for its delivery.
And, so far as is known, at age twenty-four Lammot had had no
experience navigating a seagoing vessel. In 1858, three years after
this event supposedly took place, he went to Europe on a combined business-vacation trip, and in his travel journal he noted
that this was the first time he had crossed the Atlantic Ocean.

Piqued by this tale of his father's derring-do, his son Pierre,

many years later, made a thorough check of his father's movements and prepared a calendar showing his whereabouts during
the years of the Crimean War. This careful accounting shows no
period of time when Lammot could have been out of the country
long enough to sail to the Black Sea and return. Where the newspapers of 1884 picked up this story or for what reason the account was fabricated remains unexplained. It is possible that a
reporter garbled the chronology and facts of a Civil War mission
in 1861–62 in which Lammot did play a leading role. This will
be discussed in a subsequent chapter.[21]

Chapter III

First Patent:

"An Improvement in

Gunpowder"

THE CRIMEAN WAR made apparent once again the dependence of American powdermakers upon the British for their supplies of saltpeter, in the form of potassium nitrate, which came from India, the brightest jewel in Victoria's imperial crown. Fortunately the Du Pont Company had placed large standing orders with its supplier, Ashburner and Company in Calcutta, and shipments had been received fairly well on schedule, though at rising prices as the war progressed. Shipments were permitted to the United States by the British only on condition that American purchasers, with a certificate authenticated by a British consul in this country, swore that the saltpeter would be used in making powder solely for domestic consumption, not for export to any other country. Du Pont readily agreed to this stipulation. But when saltpeter tripled in price within two months, from six cents to eighteen cents a pound, efforts were revived to find a substitute material.[1]

A substitute for Indian saltpeter had been sought sporadically in this country for decades. During the War of 1812 caves in Kentucky and Tennessee had been the source of cave saltpeter, but the high cost of extracting and transporting it was prohibitive except under emergency wartime demand. Another type of saltpeter, sodium nitrate, had been found in the coastal regions of Peru and had been exported during the 1820s and 1830s, principally for use in the manufacture of acid and the making of soap and glassware. Attempts had been made to use it in place of potassium nitrate in making black powder, but with no success for it was too hygroscopic, or prone to absorb moisture from the atmosphere.[2]

In September 1855 Lammot began experimenting with Peruvian nitrate, making small quantities of powder and discussing his methods and the results obtained with his father. Working on the theory that varying the proportions of saltpeter, sulphur, and charcoal might give better results, he made up a number of slightly different batches and then tested them for their flammability and deliquescent qualities. His father suggested that a considerable increase be made in the proportion of sulphur because of the greater strength it imparted, its flammability at a low temperature, and its binding qualities. Acting as a varnish, the coating of sulphur sealed the powder grains, making them more impervious to moisture.[3]

Lammot's routine work and the special assignments given him by Uncle Henry did not allow him the luxury of uninterrupted research at this task. He continued to enlarge the refinery, improving its operations and those of the charcoal burning houses. These duties absorbed much of his time, and they were accomplishments that pleased the head of the firm, who spoke favorably of Lammot's work to other members of the family. His Aunt Evelina (Mrs. James A. Bidermann) congratulated him: "Your uncle has given me quite a fine account of all your improvements in the Refinery. For my part I had to content myself seeing the outside from Aunt Louisa's windows (Eleutherian Mills residence overlooked the refinery), and still I found a great many alterations. It now looks quite picturesque and I think Bidermann ought to take a drawing of it."[4]

The experiments using sodium nitrate had to be an off-and-on project extending over many months, and it was not until January 1857 that he submitted his patent application papers with a sample of the "improvement in gunpowder" to the U.S. Patent Office. In his application Lammot stated that limited supplies of Indian saltpeter, plus its high cost, had long prompted the search to find a substitute. He had combined powdered Peruvian sodium nitrate (72%) with powdered sulphur (12%) and powdered charcoal (16%) and granulated the mixture; he had given it a hard glaze by adding a small amount of black lead (graphite), and had then tumbled it in a barrel for nearly twelve hours. Glazing the powder in this manner, he claimed, prevented it from absorbing moisture from the atmosphere to any injurious extent and made it a satisfactory explosive for blasting and analogous purposes. Significantly, it could be produced more cheaply than powder made from Indian potassium nitrate. Specifically, he requested a patent for the invention of a process for the first time using sodium nitrate in combination with the glazing operation.[5] Lammot did not claim his new powder was suitable for military, hunting, or sporting purposes. For these the traditional powder based on potassium nitrate was superior.

The significance of sodium nitrate, or soda powder, was that for the first time in 600 years an explosive made solely for industrial use had been developed. It was both less costly to make yet more powerful than the inferior grades of gunpowder that had heretofore been used for blasting purposes. And the source of sodium nitrate being South America gave greater assurance that it would not be subject to restraints or embargoes in time of imperial or military crisis as was the case with saltpeter from British India.

Lammot's satisfaction at obtaining his first patent would have been greater if his father had lived to congratulate him upon his success. After six years of recurring illness, oddly diagnosed by his wife as "gout [that] stays in his stomach and won't go to his feet," Alfred Victor had died on October 4, 1856, at the age of fifty-eight. No written expression of grief at his father's death has been found; Lammot's first concern would be to console his mother; grief would have been controlled, confined to the family circle of brothers and sisters who returned home for their father's funeral.

The loss of another close relative occurred within a year when Uncle Alexis I. du Pont was killed in an explosion in the Hagley Yard in August 1857. With his sons Eugene and Alexis and some workmen, Uncle Alexis was dismantling a mill when a tub of powder sweepings ignited and exploded. He was blown onto the road his clothes ablaze, but he leaped into the raceway, dousing the flames. Looking up, he saw flaming debris falling on the roof of a nearby press house in which was some powder. Alexis ran from the race and was clambering to the roof of the press house to kick off the flaming embers when it blew up and hurled him onto some drying tables adjacent to it. Burned and broken he was carried up the hill to his home, Hagley, and after a day of intense suffering this devoutly religious man, here an exception to his other male relatives, died with grieving family and workmen at his bedside. Four workmen were killed in this accident, and Alexis's sons barely escaped injury or death because they had left the scene only a few minutes before the mill exploded.[6]

The death of Alexis was a tragedy to his family and a severe loss to the company, for he was one of its three active partners and was directly in charge of the Hagley Yard. The obvious person to replace him as a junior partner was Lammot, and this came about formally when a new partnership agreement went into effect in 1858. On the books he was credited with three shares, each worth $17,000, and to this $51,000 was added the sum of $6,200 in accumulated interest, bringing his total investment in the business to $57,200. From his own assets he could only raise enough to pay for one share, so he borrowed $17,000 from his mother for the second share, and from each of three aunts he borrowed $5,666.67 to pay for the third share. Uncle Henry raised his "yearly allowance," or salary, from $2,500 to $3,000.[7]

In the summer months 1857 before Uncle Alexis's death there had been occasional talk of Lammot going to Europe to visit powder mills in the British Isles and on the Continent. This was soon after he had obtained his patent for soda powder, so the trip at company expense may have been Uncle Henry's way of showing his appreciation for this accomplishment. Or the journey may have been Lammot's own idea, for he told a friend that he was interested in improving "myself in the manufacture of gunpowder by seeing what was being done abroad."[8]

Had seniority determined who should make the trip it should have been brother Irénée. But Irénée's horizons seem to have been circumscribed to the routine supervision of a set of mills. There is no evidence that he shared his brother's questing attitude toward better methods of manufacturing powder and improving mill operations. His attachment to the business was from

a sense of obligation to the family, not enthusiasm for or enjoyment of the work he was doing. And, coincidentally, at the time
the trip abroad was being contemplated, he was courting a
southern girl, Charlotte Shepard Henderson of Virginia, and the
thought of a long absence from her was not to be considered.
Clearly, Lammot should be the one to go.

His Aunt Eleuthera endorsed the idea, for her nephew was
overworked and needed a vacation: "I am very anxious he should
go. His life is a very arduous one and he is, I think, overtasked.
He superintends the department of Saltpetre Refining and Burning the Charcoal, and if I could remember the number of pounds
of each required in our manufactory weekly I am sure it would
amaze you. . . . He is 26 years of age and a most exemplary young
man." Lammot would certainly call upon his relatives in France,
one of whom was the recipient of this letter; and though he read
and understood their language perfectly well, his aunt suggested
that they all speak English for she doubted if he would have the
courage to converse in French.[9]

Lammot prepared himself by going over his itinerary with
Uncle James Bidermann and reviewing the memoranda his uncle
had written in connection with visits he had made to a number
of European mills in 1827–28 and again in 1837–39. Uncle James
gave him letters of introduction, as did several officers of the
U.S. Ordnance Bureau. Through a friend, J. Buchanan Henry,
nephew of President James Buchanan, letters were given him by
the president to the U.S. ministers in Paris, Berlin, and St.
Petersburg, instructing them to facilitate Lammot's mission by
making available all sources of information within their power.
Passage was booked on the Collins Line steamer *Adriatic* for an
early September sailing by his sister Victorine's husband, Peter
Kemble, in New York, but this was canceled and the trip postponed indefinitely when Uncle Alexis died on August 23.[10]

Toward the end of the year, after the shock had diminished
and factory operations were running smoothly, plans were renewed for Lammot to go abroad early in the new year. During
these intervening months an English powder manufacturer named
Henry E. Drayson of the Maresfield Powder Company in Sussex
visited the Du Pont mills in early November. Lammot was ill in

bed so did not get to meet him, but Uncle Henry showed the Englishman through the yards and learned something about the procedures used in English mills, the substance of which he later related to Lammot. Drayson's father had been superintendent of the Royal Gunpowder Factory at Waltham Abbey for forty years, and the younger Drayson averred that he was familiar with all the principal English mills. He would be glad to escort any member of the Du Pont firm who visited England through any mill he might wish to see. Drayson was impressed by what he observed in the Brandywine mills, and upon departing he assured his host that there really was no reason for a du Pont to make such a visit as nothing new could be learned in the English mills, an implied compliment that Du Pont technology was superior to the English. When this was related to him by his uncle, Lammot's rejoinder was, "This was a piece of Blarney which might be interpreted into stupidity." He was to learn more about Drayson when he got to England.[11]

Lammot was well aware that Europeans had been making black powder for six centuries, Americans for scarcely a century. It was a technology transplanted from the Old World to which some New World innovations had been made, but despite America's technological "leap forward" that had begun in the 1830s, Lammot fully appreciated that long experience could be an excellent teacher. Going to Europe in 1858, he was atavistically repeating the trip his grandfather E. I. du Pont had made in 1801. In preparing himself to launch his enterprise, the company's founder had returned to France to observe the latest methods of powdermaking, to visit mills and arsenals, to consult with the heads of the government's powder bureau, and to acquire drawings and machinery that would be useful in his own undertaking. This "borrowing" of technological information had continued through correspondence, the purchase of treatises and books, the acquisition of patent descriptions, by hiring experienced French powdermen, and from the visits of such observant kinsmen as Uncle James Bidermann.[12]

Lammot's purpose, a half century later, was the same: to get a broad but in-depth view of European technology, to study its operations on the spot, and to note those features that could be adopted advantageously in the family mills. Coupled with this general, ostensible purpose was another more pressing, specific reason to make the trip.

In this country experiments had been underway for some time to perfect both smooth-bore and rifled cannon of larger caliber. The standard cannon powder had not proved satisfactory when tested in these new guns, often bursting them by the high pressure created in the breech at the instant of ignition. Secretary of State Abel P. Upshur and Secretary of the Navy Thomas W. Gilmer had been killed in such an accident on board the warship *Princeton* in February 1844 while witnessing the test of a new gun. Ordnance Bureau officials urged Du Pont and other powdermakers to formulate a slower, progressively burning propellant powder that expended its energy uniformly throughout the length of the barrel yet still gave the desired velocity to the projectile it was hurling from the cannon mouth. Officers of the Ordnance Bureau, particularly Capt. Thomas J. Rodman, who developed the large gun that bore his name, conferred with the Du Pont Company on the problem and collaborative work had already begun before Lammot left for Europe.[13]

British powdermakers had also been trying to develop a powder that could safely and effectively be used in the newer British ordnance, in 10- and 12-inch cannon and in the giant mortars constructed for use in the Crimean War. Lammot believed that the English had achieved some success in this effort, hence his particular wish to visit England's Waltham Abbey Mills and Woolwich Arsenal, the centers of developmental work on ordnance and powder. It was important to the military capability of the United States that it keep abreast of munitions developments elsewhere in the world.

THE "RANSACK" OF EUROPE

Lammot sailed from New York February 19, 1858, on the Cunard liner *Arabia*, a converted Crimean War troop transport. Passage had again been booked for him and a stateroom selected by his brother-in-law Peter Kemble. Kemble thoughtfully chose quarters on the port side, "near the center of the line of motion, hoping that the location may enable you to retain sufficient of your meals to sustain your big self."[14] Another person concerned about his well-being and his demeanor—he must not appear a gauche American to the British—was his mother. Meta wrote him two days after his departure with this counsel: "Try, my son, not to make mistakes in spelling, or in grammar when you converse. *Those two*, correctly done, show to others that you are well bred and born. If you go to a *regular dinner* party you must wear white gloves. I hope you get an umbrella and gum shoes, articles you must have in England's wet clime."[15] She knew her son's weakness for spelling phonetically, and his impatience with stuffy Victorian etiquette.

Lammot was one of thirty-eight passengers, some of whom he described in brief vignettes written in a journal he kept. On legal-size sheets of blue notepaper he scrupulously made entries every day except when suffering miserably from bouts of mal de mer, but for most of the voyage he had his sea legs and retained his appetite. He recorded the distances traveled each day, latitude and longitude readings, the heights and troughs of waves, high winds that almost blew off his spectacles, amusement at the antics of porpoises, amazement at the size of whales that came close by, and the identities of passing vessels bespoke by the *Arabia*. He dined at the captain's table, and it was in a conversation with the captain about the roughness of the passage that Lammot replied he was unable to judge whether it was a smooth or rough crossing as this was his first trip across the Atlantic. This comment seems clearly to refute the account of his role in taking a ship laden with Du Pont powder to the Russian stronghold at Sebastopol in the Crimea in 1855.

Hours were whiled away playing games—blitz, whist, and chess—and indulging in gambling for very limited stakes. "Even the ladies gamble," he noted with some surprise: "Mrs. Dutihl, who's a High Church Episcopalian [from Philadelphia], goes to a dollar on a game of whist." His skill as a chess player soon became evident, bringing on challengers whom he usually beat. With the captain he established an easy camaraderie, and shared with him the good-quality Cuban cigars he had brought along. One can imagine the captain's consternation, possibly choking on his cigar, when one day Lammot matter-of-factly mentioned that he had four pounds of black powder in his luggage! Immediately the captain ordered it removed and placed in the ship's magazine. This was powder Lammot planned to give in exchange for samples he hoped to obtain from the European mills he would be visiting. On the tenth day a pilot came aboard off Holyhead and in early evening the *Arabia* docked at Liverpool. Customs inspection was so perfunctory he called it a "farce," and he was soon on his way to the Adelphi Hotel, where he spent his first night.[16]

During the next two months, from early March until he embarked for home on May 5, Lammot visited powder mills in England, Scotland, Ireland, France, Belgium, and Prussia, but he did not get to Russia as he had hoped. With varying degrees of openness and hospitality he was shown about by the owners, their managers, or their master workmen, and in the government mills and arsenals by ordnance officials. His journal entries cover a multitudinous number of details of powder manufacture; types of power, waterwheels, turbines, and steam engines; saltpeter refining, sublimation of sulfur, and charcoal-making processes; methods and machinery for incorporating ingredients, pressing, granulating, glazing, drying, and packing powder; and types of containers in which it was stored and shipped.

In the third week of his tour he wrote Uncle Henry: "I am a poor hand at describing, but I have taken notes of all I have seen and can explain it when I return." At this stage he seemed ready to confirm the assertion of the English powdermaker Henry Drayson that it would be a waste of time for a du Pont to visit English powder mills, for he concluded, "From what I have seen of the mills here they are far behind us."[17] This was a premature judgment, for in the time remaining he was to record much that was new to him.

On the borders of his journal pages he drew crude, hurried sketches made on the spot, or soon thereafter, of building profiles, machines and machine parts, gearing and power trains, refining equipment, tools, vehicles, and testing and safety devices. Later, on large, separate individual sheets of paper he made careful, finished drawings of general plant layouts, refinery interiors, charcoal houses, machinery, and the like, that attest to his skill as a draftsman.

He witnessed some comparative test firings of several brands of English powder with Du Pont Superfine Eagle powder—"which I saw weighed and loaded fairly"—and recorded that a 68-pound cannon ball was hurled 662 feet by one English brand but only 430 feet by Du Pont powder, though the latter made more noise!

Morley's Hotel was Lammot's London headquarters, and soon after settling in he went to the U.S. Ministry seeking its assistance in gaining admission to Woolwich Arsenal. Here he was received by the secretary of the legation, Benjamin Moran, who penned this brief impression of the caller: "Lammot du Pont of Delaware, one of the powder family, called to see us for a pass to Woolwich, but we could not give it. He is a tall young fellow wearing spectacles, walks clumsily, but talks well and is gentlemanly."[18] Irked at bureaucratic delay, Lammot initiated requests through private channels and a week later obtained permission to visit Woolwich and the Waltham Abbey mills through the good offices of a Henry Byham in the War Office. Meanwhile, by train, carriage, boat, and sometimes on foot, he was journeying to powder mills, usually located in remote, isolated parts of the country.

Between trips and business calls Lammot did some sightseeing in London: Westminster Abbey, the Tower of London housing the crown jewels and armor, Holborn Theatre, Greenwich Observatory, and Sydenham Palace, where some exhibits remaining from London's 1852 Crystal Palace Exposition were on display. These last were a "humbug" he thought; except for a gold crusher and some steam engines, all the rest were washing machines, etc., "and Yankee notions put there as advertisements." He took a boat ride on the Thames from Westminster Bridge to London Bridge, then climbed the 311 steps of the "fire monument" hoping to get a bird's-eye view of the city, "but London was too smokey to see anything." St. Paul's Cathedral, which he attended, was grimy and needed "washing amazingly."

Time for sightseeing was ample, for the English business day began at 10 A.M. and ended at 4 P.M., and no callers were seen before 11. Usually he could make only one call a day unless his appointments were near one another. Putting some free time to profitable use he stopped at Her Majesty's Patent Office, where he learned that copies of patents, including drawings and specifications, could be obtained for a shilling each. Scanning the register, he selected twenty gunpowder patents and had them copied, noting that though some might be of no use, "there are some curious ideas patented and it will give the various patents under which the English manufacturers are working."

Permission for a limited tour of Woolwich Arsenal finally came, but only after being "cross questioned as to my *pedigree*" and after "I confessed I was a barbarian from the States." Happily the superintendent, Maj. Gen. Edward M. Boxer, was an affable person, indeed complimentary, for he informed Lammot that Du Pont powder and Belgian powder were the only foreign powders that gave satisfaction at Woolwich. As they toured parts of the five-mile arsenal property, Lammot was struck by the great bustle of activity; twenty-two vessels were loading and unloading simultaneously at the wharves; great stores of ammunition and weapons were being moved about; and lined up in one long row were 600 8-inch mortars, the largest guns in English service. Lammot was especially interested when his escort showed him what probably had been designed as England's "secret weapon," the Monster Mortar, made to batter down Russian fortifications during the Crimean War. This was a 3-foot mortar fashioned to hurl projectiles weighing 2,600 pounds a distance of five miles when fired by a massive powder charge. When tested, however, it had proved to be a failure. This visit was too brief. There was much more he wanted to see, but certain areas were closed to foreigners. Major Boxer generously offered to give him a letter of introduction to the commanding officer of the Royal Gunpowder Factory at Waltham Abbey. Lammot was learning that red tape could be cut—if scissors were wielded by the right person.

His next call was at the Maresfield Powder Works near Lewes to which he had been invited by Henry Drayson, the English visitor to the Du Pont mills the previous November. Drayson was not on hand to greet him, his absence being quickly explained by the manager and part owner of the works, a Frederick Spray. Spray told his visitor that Drayson had had no connection with the Maresfield works for the past eighteen months and had spent time in prison for forgery and other misdemeanors. When in America, Drayson had tried to sell the Du Pont Company a powdermaking process he had developed; when Spray revealed that it had not been his to sell, Lammot excoriated Drayson as "A Damn rascal!"—his strongest written epithet—and wrote him off with the remark, "Altogether I think him small potatoes." Time was not altogether wasted, however. Spray discussed a method he had recently patented in which the ingredients of powder were incorporated by being boiled in a vacuum pan. As Spray described it, Lammot recognized some similarities to a vacuum process he had experimented with four years earlier but had discarded as uneconomical. A firing demonstration proved that the vacuum-process powder was very powerful, but Lammot became wary when Spray stated that if the Du Pont Company wanted to purchase the American rights to it, all negotiations had to be with him personally, not with the Maresfield Company. "This looks bad," Lammot noted in his journal. Later he obtained some samples of the Maresfield powder from that company's London office.

His letter of introduction from the superintendent of Woolwich Arsenal got him into the Waltham Abbey mills, but here also certain areas were off-limits without special permission from the government's Ordnance Board in London. Beginning in the refinery he noted some minor differences in the refining of saltpeter; sulfur was doubly refined, the second time by a process of distillation altogether new to him. Wood was charred in cylinders loaded into horizontal ovens above the furnaces, the cylinders being moved to the ovens on rail cars and maneuvered into place by a hoist suspended from the ceiling. He writes as if this were a novel technique, something not seen elsewhere.

He admired a dozen new rolling mills powered by a 30-horsepower double-cylindered high-pressure steam engine. This turned a single drive shaft that passed beneath the floor of all the mills and geared vertically into each pair of the five and a half ton rolling wheels that crushed and incorporated the ingredients. Lammot was not given to superlatives, but here he broke custom, labeling the mills "beauties." Always alert to safety, he went on to describe a safety device that caught his eye: "They have an arrangement so that when one mill of the set blows up it loosens a catch and upsets about 3 cubit feet of water on the platform of each of the mills that did not blow." Among the individual large drawings he made is one showing in careful detail the arrangement of this dousing device.

Time was spent in a well-equipped workshop examining lathes, boring machines, and tools used to construct and repair all types of powder mill equipment. Whether he then realized the wisdom—the economy, control, and time saved—of having such a machine shop in the Brandywine mills we do not know, but two months after his return home a large machine shop was under construction in the Hagley Yard.[19] In the press house he found that the trays on which powder was spread to be compressed by a hydraulic press were made of gunmetal, a material the English had found to be more durable than wood. The sorting of powder into the desired sizes of grain was done in a remarkable granulating machine, "decidedly the best granulating machine in England or Europe," he declared, and subsequently made a large drawing of it. Upon leaving, he surreptitiously was given samples of rifle, musket, and cannon powder, the last a forerunner of what developed into the large-grain English "Pebble" powder used to fire the new, large-bore cannon. One of the major purposes of his trip had been accomplished. Nine pages of his journal are crammed with notes and sketches that give a meticulous technical description of what he saw at the Waltham Abbey mills. Summing up, to his brother Irénée, he confided that his stay in the British Isles had been very profitable and he had seen more than he anticipated.

Next on his itinerary was France, the family homeland, the birthplace of his father and his aunts Victorine and Evelina. In his baggage were gifts from Aunt Evelina (Mrs. James A. Bidermann) to her son James I. Bidermann and his wife Camille, who resided in Paris. Cousin James was a railway construction engineer. Travel on the boat train from London to Dover and on the Channel steamer to Calais was extremely light. Lammot noted that he had an agreeable traveling companion named "Mr. D'Israel, nephew of the lord of that name . . . not only had we a

whole train but a steamer to ourselves." The uncle was Benjamin
Disraeli—Lord Beaconsfield—then Conservative leader in the
House of Commons and chancellor of the exchequer.

Lammot's trip to France ended almost before it began, at
the customs house in Calais. As he handed the key to his valise
to the customs officer he told him he would find some gunpowder samples and cigars in it, and received a response which he
interpreted as "It would be all right." Not having eaten breakfast,
he went to a nearby dining room and had hardly tasted his food
when the customs man rushed in, white as a sheet, and excitedly
ordered him to come with him at once. Lammot protested, saying he would like to finish his meal, whereupon two gendarmes
moved in and escorted him back to the inspection area.

Here he found his luggage spilled open, his clothes on the
floor, Aunt Evelina's packages lying about, the powder samples
off to one side, and an officer trying to read his gunpowder notes.
Lammot snatched the precious papers from him, angrily demanding to know what the duty on *writing* was, at which the
officer charged him with being a conspirator, a plotter against
the life of Emperor Napoleon III![20] Amused at the ludicrousness
of the situation, Lammot mustered up his "fractured" French
and exclaimed, "Oh, yes, je voulez prie L'Empereur!" ["I wish to
appeal to the Emperor"], and, mockingly asserting he was a dangerous character, invited the gendarmes to go through his pockets and search his person. More expostulations followed but the
officer gradually cooled down and, finally convinced that the
American was not an assassin, gathered up Lammot's belong-
ings, rammed them into his valise, and charged him duty on
nothing. This contretemps was resolved favorably for Lammot,
but it and later like incidents, which he considered vexing and
petty, made him warily critical of French officialdom.

In Paris he dined with the Bidermanns at their home, No. 4
rue de Berczy, delivered his aunt's hastily rewrapped gifts, and
received Cousin James's assurance that he would do what he could
to get Lammot into some of the government powder mills. Formally armed with a letter of introduction from President James
Buchanan to the U.S. minister to France, John Y. Mason, he
presented himself at the ministry seeking its good offices to have

him admitted to the Paris Arsenal and some of the mills. When told it would take at least three days to get an answer to his request, he decided to go to the Wetteren powder mills near Ghent, Belgium, and to the Spandau mills near Berlin. But this too could not be done immediately, for his passport had to be visaed in turn by the Belgian, Dutch, and Prussian consuls, then by the American minister, and finally by the Paris prefect of police, who, Lammot noted in frustration, "closes his door at 2 o'clock, so I cannot start, and I lose 3 days by this infernal passport system."

During these days of enforced waiting he went to the shop of "a great apparatus man," a M. Bianchai, with whom he placed an order for a mercury densimeter to be taken home, for "there is not one in our country." He obtained drawings of a new method of drying powder and of a glazing barrel used in Turkish powder mills. When he tried to buy some powder made at the Esquerdes mill he was refused because he did not have an official permit to make the purchase. All was not business, however; this was Paris, the most beautiful city in the world, and for the first-time visitor it offered a thousand attractions. The tomb of Napoleon was barred to him because he did not have his passport with him. If he gave thought to it he may have recalled that the signature of his great-grandfather, Pierre Samuel du Pont de Nemours, had been on the document that had sent Napoleon into exile on the Isle of Elba in 1814. His forbear's hasty departure to America the next year had been occasioned by Napoleon's triumphant return to France during the 100 Days.

With no appreciative or critical comment Lammot went "through the galleries of paintings" in the Louvre, did the Assyrian and Egyptian museums, and the Musée d'Artillerie, "which is worth seeing." He toured the Plâce de Vendome; stood before the Egyptian Obelisk; walked through the Arc de Triomphe; gazed at the Bastille monument; and dropped in at the Library of the Institut National, the prestigious learned society of which his great-grandfather had been a member. He heard *The Magician* sung at the Grand Opera, but rather than appraising the musical performance his attention focused on the interior decor of the building, which suffered by comparison with other theaters he had been in: "The Opera House cannot compare to many of the

London theatres nor to the Philadelphia Opera House, and the 'brag' of scenery turns out to be not much better than the old Walnut Street Theatre." As he saw the sights of Paris the advice given by his brother Alfred Victor may have come back to him: "When you once get over there go and see everything. There is no use hurrying back as it is not likely you will be over the pond again soon."[21] Neither brother could then foresee that America's greatest internal crisis would send Lammot hurrying back to Europe on a very important secret mission three and a half years later.

At the Wetteren mills in Belgium, the superintendent was "a very gentlemanly Dutchman" named Charles Van Cromphaut. He could not speak English, which forced Lammot to converse in French—"I had to jabber away, with such success that he finally showed me his mills." The plant was almost a hundred years old, established in 1760, and only two explosions had occurred in all that time. One of these had been caused by some powder captured from the French at Waterloo in 1815! It was a complete tour, his host taking Lammot into all the buildings, explaining fully his operations from the refining of the raw materials to storing the finished powder in the magazines. Some of the technology was familiar, other techniques differed in some details from those in the Du Pont mills and those he had seen in Britain. There was greater use of steam to power the mills; steam heat was used in charring wood and in drying powder, yet some rolling mills were still turned by horsepower.

In America women were rarely employed in powder plants. Sometimes they peeled the bark off wood before it was charred—but always at a safe distance from the mills—and sometimes they cut and pasted labels on canisters and kegs. Here at Wetteren Lammot saw women pushing wheelbarrows loaded with saltpeter from storage bins into the refinery. The total work force numbered 180 persons, and their average daily output was 500 pounds of good sporting powder and 8,800 pounds of blasting powder. After discussing prices and market conditions, Lammot took leave of his gracious host, carrying several samples of Mr. Van Cromphaut's powder and extending a warm invitation to him to visit the Du Pont mills if he should ever come to America.

From Wetteren he went to Brussels, where he spent the night, and the next day traveled to Spandau, on the western side of Berlin. A letter of introduction from Capt. Alfred Mordecai of the U.S. Ordnance Bureau to the director of the Prussian government's Spandau works, a Major Otto, readily opened doors. He arrived on a holiday so the mills were not running, but Major Otto took him in tow. As they walked through the grounds Lammot's immediate impression was one of orderliness and neatness. Well-kept tanbark paths connected the two-story brick mills, each surrounded by a massive earth embankment as high as the eaves. Some mills had white marble steps with brass or mahogany handrails. Ingrain carpet covered the mill floors, and where traffic was heavy sheep hides were laid on top of the carpeting. There had not been an explosion at Spandau in twenty-one years.

The refining process was much like that in the Brandywine mills but not as economical, for the discarded salts still contained about 35 percent saltpeter. A slight profit was made by selling the refuse salts to chemical processors who extracted some potassium nitrate and other chemicals from it. The varieties of wood for charcoal were named in German, which Lammot did not understand, but he was given some samples of each and told that all wood was aged for six years before being charred. Separating the powder dust from the powder grains before packing was done by a complex arrangement of bags, a procedure Lammot had never seen at any other plant.

On leaving he was given samples of several kinds of Spandau powder, Major Otto making him swear he would not reveal how he had obtained them, for it could mean his dismissal from the Prussian Army if the gift became known. Lammot reciprocated by promising to send him samples of Du Pont's cannon and musket powder through the American consulate in Berlin.

Train travel on the Continent Lammot found very slow; it took two days and two nights to get from Berlin back to Paris, traveling some stretches at fifteen miles an hour, a speed that put him "very much out of humour." His exasperation doubled when going through customs at the Gare du Nord, where all his powder samples and a pistol-type eprouvette in his luggage were seized and impounded; transporting powder by train was illegal. Explanations were futile; a proferred bribe of forty francs was rejected; and equally futile was his attempt to bluff the elderly guard with whom he argued for the better part of an hour. Lammot had foreseen the possibility of this happening, so he had first filled all his pockets with the powder samples; but he saw that the suspicious bulges would lead to an examination of his person and the likely loss of all the powder. So he had kept only five pounds, evenly distributed, in his pockets, and put the balance in his bags, and now this had been confiscated.

Determined not to return home without his "booty," he immediately took steps to get it back, going first to higher ranking customs officials, then to officials of the railway, to a local magistrate, to the Paris commissioner of police, and finally to the French minister of war. To gain the ear of the last he first called at the American legation and asked U.S. Minister John Y. Mason to intercede with the war department and request the return of the samples to him. Mason declined to do so unless instructed by his superiors in Washington, which instruction would take weeks to come through. But Mason hinted there was another way to gain his objective—cross certain palms with *douceurs* and the powder would be released. Drawing on his letter of credit, Lammot sent Mason a £100 Bank of England note, "which I hope will be readily disposed of in Paris . . . hoping it will answer every purpose." Some days later he was informed the "dangerous articles" would be awaiting him at the customs office in Calais upon his return to England. The young man was learning the real meaning of what sometimes lay concealed beneath the ambiguities of diplomatic parlance.

During his second stay in Paris, Lammot visited the government refinery where his grandfather, E. I. du Pont, as a teenager in the late 1780s had served his apprenticeship. Instead of the customary Indian saltpeter the French were now using sodium nitrate, but with poor results, M. Maurau, the refinery director, informed him. He was queried as to whether the Du Pont Company had tried using sodium nitrate, and with what results. "In fact he pumped me, but I kept quiet," Lammot noted. The French did not yet know about his success in adapting sodium nitrate for blasting powder, which he had patented a year earlier, and he did not see fit to disclose it. Maurau confided to Lammot that the French were experimenting with a new method of producing saltpeter from the air and from ocean water. Nitric acid extracted from the air was being combined with potash evaporated from seawater to form potassium nitrate. The project was still very much hush-hush, and rumor had it that Napoleon III was a heavy silent investor in a company capitalized at four million francs to produce this synthetic saltpeter.

Lammot obtained passes admitting him to three of the government's eleven powder plants, one at Bouchet near Marolles in the department of Seine-et-Oise, the second at Ripault, nine miles from the city of Tours, and the third at Esquerdes, six miles from St.-Omer. His reception at Bouchet was cool; M. de Hubert, the superintendent, at first was reluctant to show him around, but after careful examination of his credentials and some conversation that made it clear that Lammot was not a curious novice, he was escorted through the mills. Here he noted that the large charcoal house had twenty-two charring cylinders; the gasses that accumulated in the cylinders as the wood charred were tapped off and fed into the furnaces as supplemental fuel by a piping arrangement. Wood for certain grades of powder was also charred in brick-lined pits covered with cast-iron lids luted, or sealed with sand, an outmoded rule-of-thumb procedure but one still required by government regulations.

Balls of gunmetal, samples of which were given to him, were used to pulverize the charcoal and sulphur into the "dust," which was then mixed with saltpeter. Bouchet still had the older stamping mills, an arrangement of mortars and pestles, for mixing the raw materials, but it also had rolling wheels, somewhat smaller than Du Pont's, for incorporating the best grade sporting powder. Blasting powder was made by a machine Lammot had never seen before, so he made a rough sketch of it and jotted down its specifications as de Hubert explained its operations and lauded it as the quickest and most economical way to make blasting powder. The tour ended with Lammot having lunch with the superintendent at his home, and then walking to Marolles to catch his train, accompanied by de Hubert most of the way.

In most respects the mills at Ripault were like those at

Bouchet. There were slight variations in some machines but not of such significance to warrant noting and sketching. Daily production could go as high as 4,000 kilograms, but actually it was half that amount. The few observations on Ripault suggest that Lammot was becoming surfeited—it was time to think of returning home. As he rode through the Touraine countryside on his way to Paris, he thought this part of La Belle Patrie was "the garden of France, in reality . . . a most beautiful country." Beneath his usual stoical demeanor was a sensitivity, seldom evident, to what was aesthetically appealing.

His last few days back in Paris were spent with the Bidermanns, picking up the laboratory equipment he had ordered from Bianchai the instrumentmaker, packing the "booty" accumulated from the mills he had visited, and buying gloves to be taken home as gifts to the ladies on the Brandywine. On his way to Calais he stopped at St.-Omer to make his last call at the mills at Esquerdes, six miles distant. His reception here was cordial, for the superintendent had been advised of his coming, but all the Frenchman wished to talk about was a technique he had recently patented for charring wood with superheated steam. After "a cross-fire of five hours" discussing different charring methods, he was shown the superintendent's process and was permitted to sketch and note its specifications. Powder was tested at Esquerdes, Ripault, and Bouchet with both cannon and musket eprouvettes, devices "we must get" Lammot reminded himself. In the packing house at Esquerdes he saw the best grade of powder being packed in varnished (japanned) canisters, an improved type of container. When he asked his host for samples of powder, he was again told these could be given only upon government order, which led Lammot to conclude that "the French officers are afraid of their shadows!" Embarking for England at Calais this time he had no difficulties in customs; but the powder samples for which he had paid £100 "ransom" to the U.S. minister were not there. This necessitated a hurried return trip from London to Calais some days later, and arousing the French customs men at 2 A.M., but finally he was escorted back on board the ferry with the powder safely in his possession.

Ireland was not on Lammot's itinerary but his curiosity about

some powder mills at Ballincollig on the River Lee near Inniscarra, not far from Cork, had been sharpened by a conversation
with a Henry Unkles of Cork whom Lammot had met in London. The English government had erected some new mills here
during the Crimean War, patterned after those at Waltham Abbey, and had installed "the best machinery in the *World*," according to Unkles, partner in a company to which the mills were now
leased. Unkles could not accompany him to Ballincollig and when
Lammot introduced himself to the superintendent there, Thomas
Tobin, he was courteously refused admission. This was disappointing, but Tobin, later Sir Thomas Tobin, willingly discussed
the powder business and some aspects of Ballincollig's operations, and finally took Lammot on a carriage ride around the
outside of the establishment while he described its operations.

The River Lee, comparable in size and flow to the Brandywine, provided power to the Ballincollig mills, turning the largest stone rolling wheels Lammot had yet seen, each weighing ten
tons. Materials moved from mill to mill via boats on the raceway,
a novel means of transport to the American. Finished powder
was hauled from the mills in large wagons, each holding about
200 25-lb. kegs, about the capacity of the larger Conestoga wagons that Du Pont used for overland deliveries. He had opportunity to examine the wooden kegs made by Ballincollig's coopers,
describing them as "smaller than ours but they put in full weight."
On first thought this suggests that Du Pont shortweighted its
customers, but Lammot may have meant that Du Pont kegs were
a little larger to allow some free space for the powder to tumble
about in when kegs in storage were periodically rolled to prevent
powder from caking. Tobin gave him samples of the Irish powder and also a new kind of powder that had the texture of saw-
dust. He was told it sometimes performed very well, at other
times poorly, but he considered it worth looking into, "for from
its appearance it might be made cheap enough to supersede powder." His Irish visit ended with a jaunt to Blarney Castle, but he
fails to say if he kissed the stone.[22]

Passage home was booked on the *Fulton*, sailing from
Southampton on May 5, expected arrival in New York May 20.
Final days in London were taken up in a flurry of activity: visit-
ing England's largest privately owned saltpeter refinery; looking

into the costs of sheet metal for the manufacture of metal kegs at home; getting more information on the strange new powder given him at Ballincollig; trying to interest a merchant house to become the English agency for Du Pont powder, and writing thank-you notes to those who had opened doors and facilitated his "ransack" of Europe. Typical of these, with none of the spelling or grammatical errors cautioned against by his mother, was a note of May 4 to Henry Byham of the War Office, who had secured him admittance to the Woolwich Arsenal and the Royal Gunpowder Factory at Waltham Abbey: "With the permit that you had the kindness to obtain for me I have visited both establishments and found myself amply repaid. I cannot sufficiently express my thanks for your trouble, particularly when letters of introduction to Col. Askwith, Major Baddeley, Captain Boxer and Mr. Anderson, with a letter from our President to the American Minister had failed to obtain it. If you in any way could make use of my services they are at your command."

When he boarded the *Fulton*, which he dubbed a "slow tub," his baggage contained samples of raw and refined materials, finished powder of many types, copies of patents, technical books, mill and machinery drawings, pistol eprouvettes, canisters, labels and advertising cards, laboratory apparatus (with some special pieces ordered to follow), and the 104-page journal in which he had recorded all that he had observed visiting the European mills. One can assume his head teemed with suggestions and ideas that he was impatient to talk over with Uncle Henry and brother Irénée. Unfortunately no summary evaluation of Lammot's journey has been found in his surviving papers or in those of the company or family members. The only direct mention of it occurs in a letter written by his Aunt Eleuthera to a French relative a week after his return: "In the three months he was absent he has contrived to see more than I ventured to hope, besides accomplishing successfully the object of his journey."[23]

INNOVATION, INVENTIONS, AND EXPANSION

It would be highly conjectural to state what specific changes were made in the Du Pont mills as a direct consequence of Lammot's stay in Europe. His customary thoroughness had him noting and sketching what was familiar as well as what was novel, for Uncle Henry and brother Irénée would be interested in similarities as well as differences in the two powdermaking technologies. With some exceptions, his terse, unadorned style of writing makes it difficult to determine what *really* impressed him, what methods and equipment were probably superior to Du Pont's and therefore worthy of closer examination and possible adoption. But despite the absence of emphasis and contrasts, a number of subsequent developments in Du Pont operations seem clearly to stem from Lammot's journey abroad.

His persistence had won him admission to the Waltham Abbey Mills where he had spent four days—the longest stay at any powder mill. Here he learned something about the English development of a slow-burning, large-grain propellant powder suitable for firing large caliber cannon. Soon after his return home, bringing samples of this powder for analysis, he resumed collaboration with Capt. Thomas J. Rodman of the Ordnance Bureau working on an equivalent powder for the Rodman, Dahlgren, and Parrott large guns. An Ordnance Bureau officer at the Watertown, New York, Arsenal was informed by Lammot that he had learned how the new type powder was made by the English, and that as soon as samples were ready some would be sent to him.[24]

Sometime later he and Rodman successfully test-fired their creation and named it "Mammoth" powder. The ballistics secret here was that the initial maximum pressure of the powder (the explosive or bursting force in the gun's breech when ignited) was proportionately diminished as the size of the grain was increased. Large grains of densely compressed powder burned at a slower rate than the small grain powder, thus propelling the projectile along the path of least resistance—throughout the gun's barrel, rather than instantaneously expending its force within the breech of the gun, too often the cause of fatal accidents. Accordingly, Mammoth powder, in subsequent refinements, was made in various sizes ranging from that of a walnut to that of an apple, tailored to the caliber of the gun in which it was to be fired. The new powder hurled the ball or shell at greater velocity and over longer distances than the small-grain powder customarily used. Lammot modestly credited his collaborator for the success of their effort: "To Rodman belongs the *Honor* of the introduction of large grain powders with an idea of controlling combustion."[25] The first real test of the new powder came in the Civil War when Union gunners firing Rodman and Dahlgren guns generally outgunned Confederate batteries.

Lammot's work in his laboratory gave him an appreciation of the value of refined scientific apparatus in eliminating the older, traditional rule-of-thumb practices in experimental and quality-control work; thus his satisfaction at receiving several pieces of equipment he had ordered when in Paris from Bianchai. He was particularly pleased to obtain a mercury densimeter to measure the specific gravity of gunpowder, to his knowledge, the first in the United States. He had learned of the instrument while at Waltham Abbey, but it had not been shown to him nor had the name of its maker been mentioned. But after persistent inquiry he had found out that it was called "Mallet's Apparatus" and that Bianchai, who made them for the French powder mills, was the only source from which one could be obtained.[26] Most immediately the densimeter proved valuable in determining the specific gravity of the new Mammoth powder. Subsequently Lammot designed an improved instrument for measuring the specific gravity of solids and a better hydrometer for determining the specific gravity of liquids.

Lammot's restless, searching mind, seldom satisfied with the accepted, routine ways of getting something done, was constantly alert to improvement through innovation. He realized that the Du Pont Company's near sixty years' experience as a manufacturer of powder gave it a decided advantage, but he was well aware that success could spawn self-satisfaction, placing too great a reliance on what was customary. His perception is cogently stated in this observation: "We, the present proprietors inherit in our business, all the good done by our fathers, as well as those things done badly; and with the march of improvements, one family in a business is more apt to fall behind the world than to be able to keep in the advance. For while improvements are spread far and wide, the errors and mistakes remain as permanent investments."[27] Here he is also saying that perpetual control and direct management of a business in all its operations by the members of one family is short-sighted and damaging. It excludes capable and ambitious outsiders who could help keep it "in the advance" rather than "falling behind the world." This attitude is in direct contrast to his Uncle Henry's, which held that since all the planning, engineering, building and operations had always been satisfactorily done by du Ponts, no help was needed from outsiders.

With his zeal for new ideas and innovations Lammot combined a sense of history, which gave him a perspective on the past, and an appreciation of the successive steps that had brought powdermaking technology to its present high level. This prompted him to set about locating and bringing together all the sketches and drawings of mills and machinery that had been made since the company's beginning. If he did not do this he feared they could be lost as a historic record and as a reference sought by some future generation. "So," he wrote, "I think it would be time well expended to devote a few hours to it. . . . Moreover, I will arrange the drawings so as not to injure them, and if hereafter anyone of good will wishes to arrange them I will have done no harm, and perhaps may be of some use."[28] This archival impulse resulted in a collection of informative drawings of mill structures and machinery in use for more than fifty years of Du Pont Company operations. They are contained in a large binder labeled "E. I. du Pont's Book of Mill Drawings" which has served as a valuable guide in the restoration of some of the structures by the Hagley Museum now located on the old powder mill property.

The prime sources of power in the European mills Lammot had visited were waterwheels, turbines, and steam engines. Despite the likely hazard they posed, there was greater use of steam engines than in American powder mills. In the early 1850s he had installed a small steam engine in the refinery, the only one in all three Du Pont yards, but a summary prepared by him in 1874 listed ten engines in operation, producing an aggregate of 202 horsepower.[29] Obviously the conversion had not been rapid, but what had been done could well have been the result of Lammot's convincing his Uncle Henry that steam engines could function safely and more efficiently. At a time when steam was supplanting waterpower throughout industry, one can understand the hesitancy of powdermakers to install furnaces that could emit sparks and boilers that might explode in close proximity to powder buildings. But Lammot had given impetus to a changeover that resulted in the construction of a large steam power plant in 1884 that drove many of the mills in the Hagley Yard.

Between 1861 and 1865 there were an inordinate number of explosions caused by the increased pace of production to meet the powder demands of the Union forces during the Civil War. Some accidents, however, may have been successful acts of sabotage; others could have been the consequence of having to employ inexperienced mill hands. Lammot supervised the extensive rebuilding of the mills and the replacement of machinery made necessary by these explosions, introducing some of the features he had admired while abroad. One was to move the power train—gears and shafts—in the rolling mills from an overhead connection so that it ran under the floor of the mill. When a powder mill "blew," the force of the explosion usually vented itself upward and outward, carrying chunks of shattered wheels, gears, shafts, stones, wood or sheet metal roofing, and sometimes human bodies. The explosive force seldom vented downward, so that by running the power train from the waterwheel or turbine beneath the floor rather than through the upper wall of the mill, there would be less destruction of costly machinery and it could be repaired and put back into production in a shorter time.

At the Waltham Abbey Mills Lammot had been so impressed by a granulating machine that he had described it as "decidedly the best granulating machine in England or Europe." Just when he constructed one similar to it is uncertain, but he did erect a vertical granulating machine equipping it with elevators, adding levers to rollers and installing shaker shoes, all features of the English machine.[30]

Two patents were granted to Lammot in 1865 for improvements in gunpowder presses. One was for the substitution of hard, indurated rubber as the material for layboards or plates in place of wood, leather, or metal. Apparently the hard rubber soon proved unsatisfactory, for company inventories of 1866 and 1867 show a stock of discarded broken rubber press boards on hand, and, for the first time, the inventories list press boards made of gunmetal. We can only guess whether this change was influenced by the presses he had seen at Waltham Abbey, where press boards made of gunmetal were used. His second patent was for the invention of a horizontal press that could be operated by either hydraulic or steam power.[31] At several of the British mills he had seen horizontal hydraulic presses at work and had remarked upon their superiority over the older vertical screw presses. Again the question arises, Had the inventive, or "improvement" spark, unavoidably delayed in execution by more pressing matters, been kindled by his observations made in 1858?

One could speculate at length on other possible benefits that resulted from Lammot's notes, sketches, copies of foreign patents, acquisitions, and the conversations he had had with his powdermaking hosts. To expand upon the specific instances already enumerated would only belabor the obvious. His knowledge of the industry and his grasp of the numerous facets of its operations had been greatly enlarged by his stay in Europe and had given him a confident mastery of its technology. Within a short time after his return home he was placed in charge of all technical, chemical, and construction matters in the home mills. Uncle Henry recognized his abilities and relied upon his skills as chemist, inventor, designer, engineer, and builder.

Lammot's foresighted approach to improving Du Pont operations is evident in a proposal he made to his partners for a series of regular monthly meetings—what today would be "brainstorming" sessions. He requested that on one Saturday each month a paper be presented by a member of the firm on some new idea connected with the powder business. Illustrations and drawings should be used where appropriate and kept for future reference, and all those present should take notes. At each meeting a subject should be selected for the next session, and assignments should be equally undertaken by all the partners. Following the presentation of the paper there should be general discussion, particularly on points where there were disagreements. Any matter of dispute not resolved at the meeting should be given further thought, subjected to observation and experiment, and reported on at the next session. Improvements agreed upon by all members should then be put into effect without delay. To assure company and family unity, and, possibly in deference to Uncle Henry's seniority, all decisions had to be carried unanimously.[32]

If we knew the date of the proposal for such academically structured seminars, we might be able to infer whether the idea had been generated by the broadening influence of his trip overseas; and the response to it would be a measure of its value in helping Du Pont attain its role as the leading American powder manufacturer. But no further mention of these sessions occurs. Before claiming any originality on Lammot's part for introducing them, or implying he was in advance of his contemporaries, one would need to know whether such formally structured meetings were then commonplace at management levels throughout American industry. It will be shown subsequently that he did pioneer in proposing methods to measure industrial efficiency well in advance of those who have become the recognized practitioners in that field.

The introduction of superior features of European powder-making into the family mills would most likely have been more quickly accomplished if there had not been unavoidable interruptions. The continued development of Mammoth powder in collaboration with Rodman demanded a good deal of Lammot's time. Severe explosions in 1859 and 1860 hampered production until mills and machinery could be replaced, and getting this done was primarily his responsibility. Planning and directing the reconstruction of a newly acquired plant in the Pennsylvania coal region and overseeing its operations for many years thereafter was another task that frequently took him away from the Brandywine. Then came the Civil War, postponing any contemplated technical changes that interfered with production of powder for the Union. The war also thrust Lammot into the dual role of home-front defender and as agent for the U.S. government on a highly sensitive mission to Great Britain.

WAPWALLOPEN

The anthracite coal mines in Carbon and Luzerne counties of eastern Pennsylvania were a major market for black powder. With the invention in 1808 by Judge Jesse Fell of a furnace grate in which hard coal would burn satisfactorily, the coal deposits began to be developed. A second stimulus occurred in the 1830s when Frederick W. Geissenhainer successfully burned anthracite in a hot blast furnace for smelting iron, thus ushering in the first stage of America's age of iron and steel.

Coal began supplanting charcoal and wood as an industrial fuel and for heating homes. By the 1850s surface deposits were being depleted, making deep-pit mining necessary to reach the seams buried in the earth, and the most economical and efficient way to extract the coal was to blast it loose with black powder. The lucrative coal mining business was sought after by the Du Pont Company, the Hazard Powder Company, and the Schaghticoke Powder Company, both of Connecticut, and the Laflin Powder Company and the Smith and Rand Powder Mills of New York State. The prospects of good profits also lured a number of smaller companies to erect powder mills close to the mines.

Du Pont's customers in the anthracite region had been served by its agents in Philadelphia and Reading, shipments of powder going up-country first by wagon and canal boat, later by rail. As business increased, agencies were opened in the mining towns of Mauch Chunk, Pittston, Catawissa, Wilkes-Barre, and Scranton. Here the powder sent from the Brandywine mills was stored in magazines from which the agents made deliveries as orders were received from the mines. But shipping costs, delays, damage to powder in transit, and shortages when powder was needed lost customers to the local mills not handicapped by these disadvantages.

By 1858, some months after Lammot's return home, it was thought time to put the Du Pont Company in a stronger competitive position by establishing its own mill to make blasting powder in the mining region. After nearly sixty years at one location, with no previous experience in operating branch plants, this contemplated initial departure from the Brandywine was cause for serious consideration by Uncle Henry and his nephews. The move, however, proved to be a propitious one. Coal production between 1860 and 1870 was to rise annually from 14½ million tons to 33 million tons, an increase of 126 percent, which brought about demand for larger amounts of blasting powder. The Civil

War was soon to put unprecedented demand for military powder on the Brandywine mills, leaving the commercial trade to be supplied in large part from the new Pennsylvania mill. This expansion into the coal fields proved to be a turning point in Du Pont Company history, for it was the first step in the acquisition, absorption, and consolidation of a number of powder mills under its control, resulting in its near monopoly of powder production in the anthracite region within the next quarter century. Lammot was the key figure in this growth. Though final policy and investment decisions were made by Uncle Henry as senior partner, his closest advisor and man in the field carrying out these decisions was Lammot.

The move into the mining region began with the purchase of the powder mills of Parrish, Silver & Company on Wapwallopen Creek in Nescopeck Township on the east side of the Susquehanna River twenty miles south of Wilkes-Barre. An explosion and then a damaging flood had resulted in bankruptcy. Assets were seized by creditors, and at a sheriff's sale in April 1859 the Du Pont Company had acquired the property for $35,000.[33] Du Pont's negotiator for the purchase was William Breck, a relative and company agent in Scranton, but the task of rebuilding the mills and getting them into production fell to Lammot. Named as plant manager to work with him was Charles A. Belin, most recently the company's agent in Davenport, Iowa. Belin had grown up near the Brandywine mills where his father, Augustus M. Belin, and then his older brother, Henry H. Belin, had successively been the company's head bookkeepers since the 1820s. Belin, at forty-three, had no powdermaking experience and possessed few mechanical skills. He was to acquire the first and improve the second under Lammot's tutelage.

Lammot spent the summer months of 1859 at Wapwallopen, with occasional help from his brother Irénée, rebuilding the mills and installing machinery. Workmen's dwellings were put in better condition, and a house for the Belin family was acquired and refurbished. An adjoining property possessing additional waterpower was soon purchased. Workmen, some of them former employees of Parrish, Silver & Company, were hired at $1.00 a day, the majority being of Pennsylvania-German stock with such

names as Hummel, Miller, Fine, Gruver, and Bucher. In this isolated location, where the labor supply was scant, Lammot was
forced to depart from the long-standing company policy of not
hiring men who had worked for other powder manufacturers;
Du Pont preferred to train its workmen in its own methods.

Saltpeter, sulphur, and charcoal were sent up from the Brandywine by way of the Pennsylvania Canal, which paralleled the
Susquehanna River, the average time in transit being two to three
weeks. The canal boats unloaded at Beach Haven on the west
bank of the river and the cargoes were then taken by ferry across
to Wapwallopen on the eastern side. Mail and some materials
came via the Lackawanna and Bloomsburg Railroad to Beach
Haven and then ferried across; letters between Wilmington and
Wapwallopen were usually delivered within three days.

Lammot and Belin purchased teams of horses and delivery
wagons and hired teamsters. Contracts were made with coopers
in Wilkes-Barre and Bloomsburg for kegs and barrels; roads on
the plant property were repaired, and the poor condition of the
public roads around the mills called to the attention of the township road supervisors. When these gentlemen moved too slowly
to satisfy Belin he offered the services of some of his workmen to
speed up road and bridge repairs in return for the lowering of
township taxes levied on the mills.

The Lackawanna and Bloomsburg Railroad was asked to
transport finished powder from the plant. Reluctantly it agreed
only after the Du Pont Company supplied a specially constructed
freight car designed to minimize the danger of an explosion in
case of an accident. Similar caution was shown by canal boat
captains who preferred to carry coal and other less hazardous
cargoes than powder. Scores of details of this kind were handled
by Lammot and Belin, the former making numerous trips up-
state; between visits he was kept fully informed of developments
by frequent letters and telegrams from Belin. Samples of the first
powder made at Wapwallopen were sent to Lammot for analysis,
and at the beginning of October 1859 Belin reported that "the
mills are running full time and we are turning out on an average
about 100 kegs every twenty-four hours." At midyear 1860 he
informed the home office, "I am happy to say the Wapwallopen

Powder is getting a great reputation. I am only sorry I have not the means to turn out twice as much as I do."[34]

The boom in anthracite coal production coupled with wartime demand for both military and blasting powder resulted in Wapwallopen's annual output reaching 78,000 kegs, nearly two million pounds, by 1868. This was accomplished despite floods, droughts, explosions, epidemics, and labor problems that plagued the plant during the first decade of its existence. There were times when frustration and disappointments drove Belin to long to get out of "Powder Hollow," but his confidence was renewed and his spirits buoyed up by Lammot's determined optimism, his understanding, and his skilled leadership in getting operations back to normal. This direct, personal involvement with Wapwallopen was perforce diminished by the coming of the Civil War.

Chapter IV

Confidential Agent
in Crisis

A MONTH AFTER LINCOLN'S election in November 1860 Lammot received a letter from his youngest brother, Bidermann, in Louisville containing this bit of gallows humor: "Tomorrow morning I start for New Orleans by rail and expect to stay there until the 23rd and return here by Christmas, unless they tar and feather me, pack me in a hogshead and start me floating down the river, as they have done sundry persons."[1] This uneasy premonition of Bidermann's, a partner with his brother Alfred Victor (Fred) in the Louisville Paper Mill, was symptomatic of the mounting sectional animosity between North and South. A northerner by birth but now a traveling paper salesman from a border state, Bidermann was uncertain of the reception he would receive as he journeyed deeper into a South inflamed and moving toward secession.

Presidential campaigning in New Castle County, in Wilmington, and in the mill villages along the Brandywine during the fall months of 1860 had been lively and at times heated, with meetings, debates, speeches, parades, torchlight processions, and liberty trees. The local newspapers, the *Delaware Republican*, voice of the Republican Party, and the *Delaware Gazette*, the Democratic paper, mirrored the rampant partisanship in local politicking and kept their readers informed of the fervid electioneering going on throughout the country. Writing to a relative in France, Lammot's Aunt Eleuthera told of the great excitement and talk of politics everywhere, but noted that "we are not very warm politicians in our family, so we shall be glad when it is all over and quiet is restored. In about 4 weeks it will be decided."[2] Characterizing du Pont family members as lukewarm toward politics was a misstatement. If she had reflected she would have remembered that her Uncle Victor (1767–1827) had been a member of Delaware's House of Representatives in Dover in 1815 and then a state senator from 1820 to 1823. Her father, E. I. du Pont, had actively lobbied among U.S. congressmen for protective tariffs in 1816, and in 1828 he had run unsuccessfully for election to Delaware's lower house. He had been a delegate to the National Republican Convention in Baltimore in 1831 where he was a member of the committee that offered the party's presidential nomination to Henry Clay. The du Ponts were admirers of Clay and supporters of his "American System": protecting American industry by tariffs, improving road and canal transportation with public funds, and creating a stable centralized banking system.

As recently as 1857 Charles I. du Pont, Eleuthera's cousin, had sat in the state senate as a Democrat, a maverick in a family now predominantly Whig and Republican; this was a second term, for he had also been a state senator from 1841 to 1845. In the current election Eleuthera must have known that her brother Henry was a presidential elector from Delaware on the ticket of the Constitutional Union Party. Company, community, and personal concerns kept du Pont family members sensitive and alert to political developments at local, state, and national levels, and each generation since then has produced one or more scions who has held elective or appointive office.

Brandywine workmen, predominantly Irish and Democratic, were divided in their support of John G. Breckenridge of Kentucky, the South's Democratic candidate, and Stephen A. Douglas of Illinois, the choice of northern Democrats. Business and professional men, gentlemen farmers, mill owners, and some of their employees were Republicans, some favoring Lincoln and others John Bell of Tennessee, the candidate of the Constitutional Union Party, a compromise third party that appealed for support of the Constitution and preservation of the Union. Most members of the du Pont family were Bell supporters, the candidate seeking to heal wounds and allay sectional differences. Charles I. du Pont, the recent state senator and his elder son, Victor, a Wilmington lawyer, were Democrats. But their loyalty to the Union was stronger than their partisanship; both became members of the local "Committee of Safety" and spoke out against secession.[3]

Lammot supported the Constitutional Union ticket, but there are no indications that he was politically active. On election night, however, with his uncle and cousin Charles, he sat near the Morse telegraph in the company office listening to the returns until 3 A.M. the following morning. Delaware, a border state with strong southern leanings, particularly in Sussex and Kent counties, and with some sympathizers in New Castle County, gave Brecken-ridge a majority vote, as did New Castle County, where he polled 3,003 votes to Lincoln's 2,073 votes. Brandywine and Chris-tiana Hundreds, however, went for Lincoln, giving him 617 votes to Breckenridge's 466; Bell, the du Pont–supported candidate, polled only 116 votes, a poor fourth trailing Douglas, who had 198 votes.[4] When the count nationwide showed Lincoln to be the winner the local Bell people swung into line behind him pledging their support. Uncle Henry believed Lincoln to be a thoroughly honorable man who favored conciliation rather than confrontation with the South. The threats of disunion reported in the press, now that a "Black Republican" had been elected president, he considered merely sensational newspaper ac-counts—all good men and patriots, he was certain, would unite to preserve the Union. Ellen, one of his daughters, had a differ-ent opinion: "I think it is miserable that Lincoln's elected—whenever I think of our having such a president, from such a party, it makes me feel like tasting green persimmons. . . . I wish the republicans and abolitionists were in the Atlantic, then we would be at rest."[5]

The next few months made clear that compromise and con-ciliation could not prevail in this crisis; the sense of separate-ness—southern nationalism—had become too deeply rooted. Led by South Carolina beginning in December 1860, eleven states withdrew from the Union by early February 1861 and formed the Confederacy. An early step taken by individual Confederate states was the seizure of the government forts, military posts, and arsenals within their borders in preparation for armed clash that now appeared inevitable. Delaware, a state with divided loyalties, and controlled by a Democratic governor and legislature, nevertheless rejected the invitation to join the Confederacy and remained in the Union.

The du Pont family had numerous ties with the South. A distant branch of the family, Huguenot exiles from France, had settled in Charleston in the late seventeenth century, and some of their descendants still lived in the Palmetto state. Victor du Pont (1767–1827), elder brother of E. I. du Pont, had been stationed in Charleston as a French consular official during the 1790s, and his first son, Charles Irénée, was born there in 1797. Victor and his wife Gabrielle Josephine had made friendships in that city's French community that were continued by their children and grandchildren. Anthony Cazenove of Alexandria, Virginia, had been among the first of the powder company's agents, a business association that had led to social ties and close family friendships. Cazenove and du Pont children went to the same schools, and over the years there had been a good deal of visiting back and forth in one another's homes. Most recently a southern belle, Charlotte Shepard Henderson, whose mother was a Cazenove, had married Lammot's brother Eleuthère Irénée in October 1858.

In the principal cities and larger towns of the South the Du Pont Company had developed a growing market for its blasting and sporting powder. Business had fallen off during the latter part of 1860, but it experienced an upsurge in the opening months of 1861 as large orders were received from its agents in New Orleans, Macon, Charleston, and other southern points. Shipments went out from the Brandywine mills until April 12, when the Federal garrison at Fort Sumter in Charleston harbor was fired upon by the Confederate batteries of Gen. Pierre G. T. Beauregard. Thereafter no powder was shipped southward. Powder in the magazines of the company's southern agents was seized by military authorities in the Confederate states at the outset of the war. The total amount confiscated by the end of 1861 amounted to 643,000 pounds, worth $110,670. An additional $150,000 in remittances were owed the company by its agents within the seceded states.[6]

News of the bombardment of Fort Sumter shocked the people of the mill villages along the Brandywine from Rockland to Wilmington. Reaction quickly followed with a frenzy of demonstrations, flag raisings, the ringing of bells in church belfries and mill cupolas, and mass meetings in village schoolhouses. Plans were made to organize Home Guard units to protect the region from enemy raids and attempts at sabotage by "traitors." Henry du Pont was appointed major general in command of all state militia by Governor William Burton early in May, and Lammot was named captain of Company A of the Brandywine Home Guards, made up principally of powdermen and workmen from the paper mills at Rockland. He had become thirty years of age on April 13, the day Fort Sumter had surrendered.

The importance of the powder mills to the Union cause and the need for their immediate protection was emphatically stated in a message from Uncle Henry to Secretary of War Simon Cameron a week after hostilities began: "I will remark that the gunpowder mills in this neighborhood, of which I am at the head, are of importance to the Government in these times, from their extent and immense facilities of production. They are wholly unprotected, and there is not a musket or rifle in the place; but we have over 300 good men, true and loyal, and if we could get some 200 or 300 stand of arms from Frankford Arsenal and accoutrements, we could take care of ourselves for the present, as far as mobs and disaffected persons are concerned. If the arms are to be had, it would be prudent to have them soon."[7]

Henry's fears were not unfounded. The day after he made this plea for weapons, word was received that a band of secessionists from Maryland planned to seize the powder stored in the company's magazine at Edgemoor on the Delaware River just above Wilmington. Late that night he and his four nephews, Irénée, Lammot, Alexis, and Eugene (the latter two the sons of Alexis Irénée, who had been killed in 1857), with a dozen workmen, armed themselves. Taking five large freight wagons they went to Edgemoor, loaded all the powder from the magazine, and brought it safely to the mills in the small hours of the morning. Anxious kinfolk who had waited up all night were relieved to hear the rumble of wagon wheels on the powder yard road.[8]

This first alarm, though false, galvanized the Home Guards into drilling and learning the manual of arms, at first without

guns. Parade and marching formations were done in nearby
schoolhouses, at the Rockland paper mill, where ample floor space
was made available, and in the local lyceum building in Henry
Clay Village. Lammot preferred to have no spectators when his
company drilled, for he was embarrassed trying to teach others
what he did not know himself. This was self-deprecatory, for on
a Saturday late in May, in competition with Home Guard Company B, his men proved their superiority in drill, marching formations, and gun handling and won a sword for their captain.
Lammot complimented them on their prowess and thanked them
for winning him the sword, to which they responded by giving
three cheers and hurling their caps in the air. Cousin Ellen, one
of Uncle Henry's daughters, thought Lammot's Company looked
"mighty well in ranks, and drill infinitely better than the 'down
the creekers' or 'red-legs' [Company B] . . . [so called] from the
red stripe down their pants." Late in April, Lammot had purchased fifty muskets for his men in Philadelphia, bringing them
home well concealed in a wagon. And Uncle Frank, Capt. Samuel F. du Pont, now commanding officer of the Philadelphia Navy
Yard, had promised to send more weapons to the Brandywine
Home Guards as soon as they became available.[9]

Constant vigil night and day was kept all along the seven-
foot-high board fence that enclosed the powder yards, and gate
tenders were more watchful than ever of people coming through
the gates, but somehow an evil-looking stranger got into the
Hagley Yard on the last day of April. Workmen picked up clubs
and went after him, yelling, "A spy! a spy!" Lammot and Eugene
happened to be nearby and intercepted him, ordering the man
to stand by. They queried the stranger as to his identity and why
he had come into the powder yard. His explanation evidently
satisfied the du Ponts who concluded he was a harmless vaga-
bond, possibly a little demented, and they had him escorted out
of the yard with a word of warning. This, plus rumors of two
men dressed as women seen near the yards, and a warning from
military authorities in Philadelphia that a "known desperado"
was on his way to Wilmington to blow up the powder works,
heightened fears of sabotage and put the Home Guards on double
alert. The destruction of the Du Pont Mills, now gearing up for

rapid, large-scale manufacture of powder for the Union armies, would cause great exultation below the Mason-Dixon line.[10]

The increased pace of production, plus his Home Guard duties, eliminated the luxury of work in the laboratory for Lammot, except for routine tests of raw materials and analyses of sample batches of finished powder. His trips to Wapwallopen became less frequent. More men were hired, some with no previous experience in powdermaking, and the mills went on a twenty-four-hour schedule to fill the orders the Bureau of Ordnance began placing in May. The first order was for 900 barrels of cannon powder and a 100 barrels of musket powder, a total of 100,000 pounds at eighteen cents a pound, to be delivered to arsenals in Philadelphia by June 15. Uncle Henry shared the belief of many that the conflict would soon be over and thought the demand for military powder was only an emergency that would soon pass. To a Philadelphia correspondent he gave his opinion that "the extra demand for powder for war purposes will not equal the regular demand which would have existed had peace continued without extraneous troubles."[11] But the intensity and spread of the fighting during the summer and fall months proved him altogether wrong. Another 1,000 barrels were ordered in June, followed by orders for 2,000 barrels in September. In dollars, powder purchased by the army and navy during 1861 amounted to $404,405, roughly 40 percent of the company's total output; the other 60 percent going to Du Pont's commercial trade amounted to slightly over $600,000.

Soon after the war began the Du Pont Company calculated that it had a six-months supply of saltpeter on hand and on order with its suppliers. The Army Bureau of Ordnance took stock and reported it had almost four million pounds in storage, an amount considered adequate for the predictable future. By October, however, the supply had dwindled to a point that worried army and navy officials, one of whom was Capt. S. F. du Pont, recently transferred from the Philadelphia Navy Yard to command the South Atlantic Blockading Squadron. He expressed his concern to Assistant Secretary of the Navy Gustavus Fox, following which Fox conferred with President Lincoln. These discussions led to Henry du Pont being summoned to Washington on October 30 to review the saltpeter situation with Secretary of State William H. Seward and Secretary of War Simon Cameron. Convinced there was danger of an impending shortage, these gentlemen then decided that a special purchasing mission should immediately be sent to England to buy all the saltpeter available there and what was enroute from India. The mission was to be kept strictly secret, only they and the person chosen to go as confidential agent knowing anything about it. The agent they selected was Lammot du Pont.

Lammot's experiences during his 1858 visit to Great Britain and the Continent had demonstrated his ability to deal successfully with government officials and with owners and managers of powder companies. His persistence in getting what he went after was a quality recognized by Uncle Henry and other close family members. He was familiar with London; he knew the principal saltpeter brokers; and he was known at the banking houses that would handle the funds for the saltpeter purchases. And, importantly, there was confidence in Lammot's resourcefulness when faced with unexpected difficulty, his quick thinking that could turn apparent failure into success. Optimistic, he sailed for England on the steamer *Africa* on November 6 with instructions to purchase for the U.S. government a year's supply of saltpeter (approximately three million pounds), the purchase ostensibly to be a private one made for E. I. du Pont de Nemours and Company. Funds from the Secret Service Fund of the State Department would be placed at his disposal in London to pay for the saltpeter. His passport, dated November 1, provides a succinct physical description of Lammot at age thirty: six feet one inch tall, medium high forehead, gray eyes, ordinary nose, large mouth, broad chin, light brown hair, light complexion and oval face.[13]

Arriving in London on November 19, he quickly went to work and within four days his agents had bought 22,840 bags of saltpeter, all that was available in England, and he contracted for an additional 10,553 bags on board ships enroute from India, in all, three and a third million pounds. The steamer bringing the funds with which he was to pay for the saltpeter had been delayed, leaving Lammot the holder of nearly all the saltpeter in England but without the money to pay for it! He began knock-

Lammot du Pont in his thirties (photograph probably from early 1860s).

ing on the doors of Anglo-American banking houses, and, according to Samuel Bancroft, Jr., a neighboring Brandywine textile manufacturer, to whom he later reportedly related his venture, he found a banker who "was damn fool enough" to loan him three million dollars "on his face!" This was Baring Brothers; they gave him credit, and forthwith he began making arrangements for the shipments.[14]

Four ships were chartered to carry the saltpeter to New York, and the first of these, the *Moses Grinnell*, was at dockside being loaded on November 30 when the dockmaster abruptly announced that all shipments of saltpeter to the United States were prohibited! Astounded, Lammot asked why, and soon learned he was enmeshed in an international impasse, in the middle of a crisis bordering upon war between the United States and Great Britain. On November 9, three days after Lammot had left New York, the British mail packet *Trent*, in southerly waters homeward bound through the Bahama Channel, was stopped by the U.S.S. *San Jacinto*, Captain Charles Wilkes. On board the *Trent* were two Confederate envoys bound for England, James M. Mason and John Slidell. Considering them enemy agents, Captain Wilkes seized them and their secretaries and had them forcibly transferred to his ship over the protests of the British skipper. They were taken to Boston and imprisoned in Fort Warren. In the northern cities Wilkes was acclaimed for his capture of the prominent Confederates and hailed publicly as a hero for his daring twisting of the British lion's tale.

When England's Foreign Office learned of this insult to its dignity as Mistress of the Seas, it denounced Wilkes's action as a flagrant violation of England's rights as a neutral power. The English press headlined the incident, fueling a war fever among upper class and commercial elements in England who favored recognition and support of the Confederacy. The influential London *Times* trumpeted that the huge saltpeter purchases being made for America were "an outrage to England such as might render it difficult to obtain supplies hereafter," and urged that the "contraband" not be allowed to leave the country. Lammot's purchases had not gone unobserved by the Foreign Office. Lord Russell, foreign secretary, was informed on November 27 that three

thousand tons had been bought, a thousand of which were about
to be loaded for shipment to the United States the next day. A
warning was given: "It is more than a year's supply for that Government even in a time of War, and the very rapid way it is being
shipped off within *three days* of its purchase are altogether unusual, and looks as if the Federal Government, having decided
on a rupture with this country, was desirous of first laying in a
supply of saltpeter." If the shipment was to be embargoed not an
hour was to be lost.[15]

The matter was laid before Lord Palmerston, the prime minister, who discussed it with his cabinet on November 30, at which
time Russell proposed that a ban be placed on the export of all
arms, gunpowder, and saltpeter to the United States. Palmerston
commented on the crisis in Anglo-American relations, charging
the United States with heaping affronts and indignities upon
Britain that could lead to war, even though that might not be
the objective of its present policy. If war should break out, Palmerston asked his ministers, "would it not be weakness and folly
in the extreme to allow them in the interval to draw from our
storehouses and manufacturers those means and implements of
war which they are now scantily supplied with, and which when
obtained by them would probably be turned against ourselves?"
The cabinet unanimously supported his position—no military
supplies should go to a potential enemy—whereupon the Order-
in-Council was issued that stopped the loading of Lammot's first
saltpeter boat, evoking from him the exasperated epithet "The
Devil is to pay!"

Lammot then tried a ruse by which he thought he could
evade the ban. He had the ship's manifest changed to show its
destination as France, planning to have the cargo reshipped from
there to the United States if his stratagem succeeded. But the
English saw through this transparent evasion and forestalled it
by promptly issuing a second Order-in-Council forbidding the
export of saltpeter to *any* place outside the British Isles. Simultaneously Lammot learned that Her Majesty's government was
now going into the market to replenish its own depleted stores
of saltpeter, and that agents for the Confederate States, and for
Russia and Italy, were also placing large orders with saltpeter

suppliers. He calculated that whatever additional purchases he might make would now cost about fifty shillings a hundredweight instead of 36s. 4d. to 40s. that he had paid for the saltpeter now sitting on the dock because of the sudden embargo.[16]

In this deadlock Lammot decided to return home for further instructions. England was demanding that Washington free the Confederate agents Mason and Slidell, that it repudiate Wilkes's illegal seizure of them, offer apologies for his conduct, and that it acknowledge his stopping the *Trent* as a breach of international law that violated England's rights as a neutral power. Until these demands were met, the embargo would remain. In the days just before his departure Lammot noted active preparations for war. English arsenals and shipyards were working night and day; troops were being readied to be sent to Canada; and Lord Lyons, Britain's minister to the United States, had been instructed to close his legation in Washington and prepare to return home if this country did not soon resolve the *Trent* affair to England's satisfaction. Lammot was convinced the English wanted war and was using the *Trent* crisis as a pretext to provoke it. It was his opinion that the English aristocracy longed "to see us split into two or more nations." Also, he had heard Englishmen say that "we *must* have the northern part of Vermont and New Hampshire, and all of Maine—we want them for a railroad communication with our Provinces."[17] With these forebodings auguring ill for the success of his mission, he sailed from England on December 7 and arrived home on the Brandywine on Christmas Day.

Christmas was spent with his mother and other members of the family at Nemours, and with Uncle Henry to whom he recounted the details of his mission. Uncle Frank was receiving the plaudits of a grateful Union for the capture by his squadron in November of Forts Beauregard and Walker, Confederate strongholds guarding Port Royal on the South Carolina coast. Lammot had arrived home too late to witness the wild celebrations in the villages near the commodore's home—the ringing of church and mill bells, a 100-gun salute at the keg mill, the flag raisings, and the flood of congratulatory messages that poured into Upper Louviers. His neighbors were preparing a hero's reception for him and plans were afoot to raise money to present him with a ceremonial dress sword. More large orders for powder had recently been received, and work had begun on these when the euphoric mood of the community was shattered by a deafening explosion.

Midmorning on November 20 four mills in the Upper Yard at the creek's edge below Eleutherian Mills and Nemours blew up with a thunderous concussion. Three workmen were instantly killed and a number of others injured by hurtling stones, broken machinery, and flaming debris. Homes in the area had doors torn off their hinges, windows shattered, plaster shaken loose, and chinaware and other household items flung wildly about. Lammot's mother was hit on the head by a large parlor lamp and cut by glass, but was not seriously injured. Several of his cousins were cut and bruised; guests staying with Aunt Sophie at Upper Louviers and others at Cousin Charles's home were badly shaken and frightened; both homes had been extensively damaged. Lammot was filled in on these events and saw that the damaged homes and mills were being repaired and rebuilt. Aunt Sophie, a devoutly religious woman, thankful that no more lives had been lost, and grateful for the speed at which repairs were made, exclaimed, "I feel as though I could say all day long, 'Bless the Lord, Oh my soul! and forget not all his benefits!' . . . There is certainly a dauntless energy in the du Pont blood that ought to make its mark!"[18] These qualities of dauntlessness and energy were soon to be tested in Lammot, a favorite nephew.

The day after Christmas, Lammot was in Washington, closeted with Secretary of State Seward discussing the failure of his mission. This was a critical day in the diplomacy of the Civil War. It was the last of seven days of grace which England had given the United States to respond to its ultimatum on the *Trent* incident. If the United States failed to give satisfaction, diplomatic relations would be severed! Britain, the world's number-one power, would then certainly become an ally of the Confederacy, probably joined by France, which had expressed support of England's position toward our breach of neutrality. Such a powerful alignment against the North could not be allowed to take place. Lincoln, Seward, and the other cabinet members considered this ominous situation in meetings on December 25 and 26. It was evident to them that Wilkes's act had been a violation of international law, one that this country had repeatedly demanded the British observe in previous conflicts when they had been the belligerent and the United States the neutral. In the face of overwhelming public sentiment that had applauded Wilkes, his seizure of Mason and Slidell was repudiated, diplomatic apologies were offered, and Mason and Slidell were set free. This assuaged England's pride; its war fever subsided, bringing about a more favorable climate for the continuance of friendly relations, which presumably would include lifting the embargo. Without the saltpeter Lammot had purchased, the Union forces could not long effectively fight the South, possibly three months at the most.

During his conference with Seward on December 26 following Lincoln's meeting with his cabinet, Lammot, as agent for the Du Pont Company, was instructed by Seward to write him a letter recounting fully his mission to England and its present status. This he did, informing Seward that he had bought £80,000 worth of saltpeter but had been forbidden to ship it home. As to the reasons for this, "real or pretended," he would make no reference, but he requested the secretary of state to instruct the U.S. minister to England, Charles Francis Adams, to do what he could toward having the embargo lifted. In response, Seward then gave Lammot a letter addressed to Adams containing his instruction that Adams use his office "towards the relief of that firm." Again he cautioned Lammot not to mention the government as party to the transaction. Prudently, the secretary of state sought to maintain the fiction that the saltpeter purchase had been made by a private business firm, not by the government.[19]

Lammot spent the few remaining days between Christmas and New Years at home. Then on New Year's Day, as other members of the family were gathering for their annual fete and gift giving, he set sail once again for England. By ironic coincidence the released Confederate agents, Mason and Slidell, were passengers on the same vessel. One wonders what shipboard conversation might have passed between them and Lammot. Upon arrival in London on January 13 Lammot delivered Seward's letter to Adams. It can be assumed that the minister was fully informed of the embargo, and it can also be assumed that Lammot respect-

fully reiterated to him the serious consequences that would follow if the saltpeter did not soon get to America.

To hasten the phlegmatic British, Lammot tried another tack,
a bit of economic pressure that he counted on to get quicker
action. His purchases had cornered virtually all the saltpeter
available, so he "confidentially" informed his London agent that
if the embargo was not soon lifted he would quickly unload all
his saltpeter, taking whatever price he could get for it. A sudden
glutting of the market would send prices plummeting, a drop
damaging to brokers in the business. As this "confidential tip"
spread through the trade, these gentlemen used their considerable influence in government circles and with the press to have
the embargo lifted. The *Times* reversed its former jingoistic
thumpings—America had apologized, albeit rather ambiguous
fashion, for the *Trent* incident—and it ran a series of articles calling for the lifting of the ban. The ban was lifted on January 18,
and the chartered boats began loading a total of 30,000 bags of
saltpeter at London, Liverpool, and Greenock.[20] To what extent
this maneuver affected governmental decisions can only be surmised. The most that might be claimed for it is that it possibly
hastened the deliberations of Palmerston and Russell, resulting
in an earlier removal of the embargo that might otherwise have
been the case.

A writer for the *Times*, however, sought recognition—and
compensation—for his alleged influence with the government on
Lammot's behalf. For the articles he had written favoring the
release of the saltpeter he sought out Lammot and asked for
£1,000! Lammot must have been surprised, then amused at the
request. He mulled it over for a few moments, then agreed to it,
but only on condition that the *Times* man first settle a claim Lammot had against him! The encounter is best told in Aunt Sophie's
words to whom Lammot later laughingly recounted it: "'How
so, sir? I don't understand you—what do you mean?' Lammot
then with his naive, good-natured tone and manner commenced
recapitulating all the *Times* had said to inflame England against
America & bring on the stopping of the saltpetre—then the loss
of time, expenses and inconveniences of every sort to which this
had subjected *him*, winding up with, 'I am willing to be satisfied

with an estimate of about *two* thousand pounds for all this, and when it suits you, sir, to settle this little claim, I'll be very much pleased to hand you over the thousand pounds for your claim.' Of course the representative of the *Times* could do nothing but laugh and shake hands and leave."[21]

The only official, and indirect, recognition of Lammot's successful negotiations is found in a letter written by Gen. James W. Ripley of the Ordnance Office to Secretary of War Edwin M. Stanton three months after Lammot had returned home and after all the saltpeter boats had arrived and unloaded. He reported that the government now had on hand 7½ million pounds of saltpeter, sufficient to make 94,445 barrels of gunpowder, enough to carry on the war on its present gigantic scale for another three years. The Du Pont Company, furnishing about 40 percent of all the powder used by the Union forces, had an additional million pounds of saltpeter in storage.[22]

No formal expression of thanks to Lammot by the United States government for his successful completion of this mission at a time of international crisis has been found, though this may have been done personally by someone in the Ordnance Bureau or the War Department. The nearest to any official acknowledgement is contained in a memorandum from Secretary of War Stanton to the Committee on Ordnance of the United States Senate in which he noted that "Mr. Lammont [*sic*] du Pont conducted the affair satisfactorily and advantageously, and has rendered a full and formal account of the funds intrusted to him."[23]

Chapter V

Captain Lammot Du Pont

SHORTLY AFTER HIS RETURN from England, Lammot was again in Washington, this time as spokesman for the powder industry. Faced with the escalating costs of carrying on the war with the Confederacy, the House Ways and Means Committee was considering a variety of taxes on industry. When the proposed taxes on explosives became known to the powder manufacturers, they considered them excessively burdensome and discriminatory. Representatives of the larger companies and a number of smaller companies, in all about seven-eighths of the industry, met in Washington and drew up alternative proposals to be submitted to Congress. Lammot was chosen to present their case.

On March 18, 1862, he offered the industry's recommendations, prefacing his remarks by reminding the congressmen that the explosives business was a vital industry in both war and peace, that it was a hazardous business at all times, and that it sold its products on long-term credit, usually six to nine months, yet the producers were required to pay their taxes in cash on a monthly basis. The bill presently before them was discriminatory because it taxed powder at a 29 percent rate, whereas the tax on many other manufactured products averaged only three percent. As proposed, the tax bill would result in fraud because it would encourage mislabeling the various grades of powder; the tax fell too heavily on the cheaper grades such as blasting powder, and this would bring about a decline in their consumption. He then offered this amended tax schedule showing the industry's estimated annual production, the prices for different grades of powder, the tax rate per pound, and the yield of revenue to the government:

17,500,000 lbs. valued at 18¢ and under @ ½¢ lb.	$ 87,500
10,000,000 lbs. valued at 19¢ to 30¢ @ 1¢ lb.	100,000
875,000 lbs. valued at over 30¢ @ 6¢ lb.	52,500
	240,000
Plus the existing tax on imported saltpeter @ 1¢ lb.	200,000
Total	$440,000[1]

Lammot convinced the Ways and Means Committee that the amended schedule was a more equitable one, and it was adopted without change on March 28.

The spring months of 1862 were extremely busy ones in the Brandywine mills, which worked round the clock to keep pace with war orders and an increasing demand for blasting powder from the commercial trade. Members of the du Pont family noticed the nighttime activity in the mills below their homes. Cousin Sallie (Sara), one of Uncle Henry's daughters, described the scene to her brother Henry Algernon, now stationed at Fort Hamilton in New York Harbor: "They have night work all the time now in the refinery, and it is all lit up with kerosene lamps; the illumination is quite splendid all night from the back windows. Cousin Lammot and Gene work there, night about; and *both* are there all day, so never visible." Aunt Sophie across the creek at Louviers, childless, but with a loving maternal attachment to all her nieces and nephews, deplored what the pressure of work was doing to two of her nephews: "Lammot is killing himself in the refinery, working day and night, and Eugene the same. With the latter it is not quite so injurious to health as he can't attend to all Lammot can, and he's younger and stronger [Eugene was twenty-seven]. . . . Lammot's time is all engrossed with innumerable cares, for Lammot plans all new inventions, overlooks buildings, etc., etc., Indeed is the *life* of the business." In this letter to her husband stationed on the flagship *Wabash* she stated that Lammot should get away from the mills for a time and pay him a visit at his headquarters at Port Royal, South Carolina, but she doubted if their nephew could be spared. The refinery could not keep pace with the mills; in a rare departure from practice it had had to buy *refined* saltpeter, because, despite "Lammot's clever inventions to simplify work . . . they could not refine it fast enough."[2]

Supervision of the mills at Wapwallopen continued to be Lammot's responsibility. Within a short time after returning from England in February he had gone there to confer with manager Charles Belin. The mills had been damaged by an explosion in January, so their rebuilding first demanded his attention. But the home plant required most of his time; his trips upcountry had to be reduced, but Belin after three years' experience as manager was displaying more confidence in handling some aspects of operations. His weekly letters, sometimes more frequent, reflect a conscientious man determined to please his employers by keeping them well informed and by seeking their guidance on myriad matters on which he needed advice. Uncle Henry was, of course, kept informed of all activity at Wapwallopen, and he and Irénée visited it on rare occasions, but it fell to Lammot to see that its operations were efficient, that it ran at minimum expense, and produced a profit. Wapwallopen was the first of a number of powder mills acquired by the Du Pont Company in the anthracite region by the latter 1870s, all of which came under Lammot's supervision.

It must have come as a welcome respite in a work-filled day for Lammot in early June when an unexpected visitor from Ireland presented himself. This was Sir Thomas Tobin, director of the Ballincollig powder mills near Cork, which Lammot had visited in 1858. He was pleased to be host to this genial, knowledgeable Irishman. Accompanied by his brother Irénée, Lammot took him through all the yards, a visit which, though it was raining, lasted four hours. Tobin was impressed by what he saw: the numerous buildings scattered through an extensive wooded creek valley of great natural beauty, the strong, well constructed mills, the railroad and cars on which ingredients were moved between them, the wonderful machinery, the superior methods used in the refinery, and the large amount of powder being produced—"There was nothing like it in Europe," declared Sir Thomas.[3] Lammot no doubt would have liked to know if this was honest opinion or courteous flattery.

It was an honor of sorts not long after this for him to be taken into the confidence of his illustrious uncle, soon to be promoted to Rear Adm. Samuel Francis du Pont. In March of 1862 Fernandina on the Florida coast had been captured; in April, Fort Pulaski in Georgia capitulated. From these engagements Uncle Frank had acquired two souvenirs, a Confederate cannon shell found on the beach at Fernandina and another, which had been fired from the *Wabash*, penetrating the solid walls and thick timbers of Fort Pulaski. He wrote Lammot advising that these were enroute home addressed to him because "I want you to keep them in your Chapel or in the office until my return, for I did not care to send such emblems of war to your Aunt Sophie during my absence. But if it pleases God to spare my life I should like to see them some day on my back piazza."[4] Knowing his aunt would recoil in horror from these emblems of war, Lammot must have kept them well concealed until Uncle Frank came home to claim them.

Union victories by sea were balanced by a series of Confederate triumphs on land during the summer of 1862. As strong southern forces moved up through Virginia and into Maryland, isolating Washington on their drive northward toward Pennsylvania, Lincoln called for 300,000 recruits to replenish the falter-

Mrs. Samuel Francis (Sophie Madeleine) du Pont (1810–1888), "Aunt Sophie," mistress of Upper Louviers and chronicler of family and local happenings.

ing Union armies. For this first draft Delaware's quota was 3,440 men, and by late August nearly two-thirds of this number had been raised, some men responding out of loyalty, others induced by bounty payments. After forty-seven men from the powder mills had enlisted, Henry du Pont requested that the remaining workmen be exempted; if they were not he would have to shut down the mills. Washington responded favorably to this request within three days.[5]

Before the exemption was received, Lammot and Irénée had considered volunteering, a probability that greatly dismayed their mother and Uncle Henry and brought this strong objection from Aunt Sophie: "Lammot, it seems, has been wanting to go for a good while, but the consciousness that he was absolutely needed here withheld him from volunteering. It is perfectly absurd, for he serves his country far more usefully here, not only in making powder but in many other ways. Any Irishman could be drilled to make as good a soldier in the ranks—but there is not one man in a thousand with Lammot's scientific genius and knowledge, and his acute mind. Lammot is a man calculated for eminent usefulness, if he is spared and given grace to use the talents entrusted to him."[6] Of the eight du Pont men of military age it is obvious that Aunt Sophie perceived Lammot as the one of greatest promise; to have him go into the ranks as potential cannon fodder would be a reprehensible waste of rare talent.

Exemption did not mean Lammot and the powdermen saw no military service. The two companies of Brandywine Home Guards created at the outbreak of the war were reorganized and incorporated into the Fifth Regiment of Delaware Volunteers for nine months service as Companies B and D. Company B, made up almost entirely of ninety men from the powder mills, was captained by Lammot, and Company D, principally of men from the Rockland region upstream, 83 in number, was commanded by Hugh Stirling, a Du Pont Company carpenter. A Company B memorandum listed the names of about thirty men who refused to join the company, or were rejected. Typical of the reasons stated opposite their names were these: "secesh [secessionist]," "left state," "too old," "no age," "preferred upper company," "would not swear," "refused the oath—secesh," and opposite the name of his Quaker friend Samuel Bancroft, "religious scruples."[7] The services of Companies B and D were to be limited to Delaware, specifically to the protection of the industries in the valley above Wilmington up to the border with Pennsylvania. They were to be outfitted and equipped by the government, but paid only when in actual service; meanwhile they could continue working at their regular occupations, subject to two drill sessions a week.[8]

Drilling had been underway but a short time and the men not yet fully outfitted when near panic seized the people of northern Delaware. Newspaper headlines blazoned the fall of Harpers Ferry and the seizure of massive stores of war matériel by the Confederates. Lee's forces had moved rapidly through Maryland as they pushed on toward Harrisburg, threatening to cut off northern Delaware and leaving it exposed to attack by hard-riding raiders. This was the closest the enemy had yet come to the Brandywine, and Henry du Pont was certain that the powder mills would be their first target. Other objectives would be the shipyards on the Christina River making transports, tugs, supply vessels, and monitors; railroad car and wagon shops; foundries and machine shops; and the tanneries and textile mills making shoes, knapsacks, harness, ponchos, and uniform cloth for the Union armies.

A rumor spread that 3,000 Confederate cavalrymen were preparing to make a lightning dash into New Castle County to destroy the mills—a severe loss to the Union if successful—and the raw volunteer defenders would not be able to stop them. A reassuring word, maybe a bit of bravado to offset undue concern for the folks at home, was written by Mrs. Henry du Pont to her soldier son Henry Algernon still on duty at Fort Hamilton, New York: "We have been thrown into much alarm and anxiety during the past week—though I think as a people and family we du Ponts are not easily frightened."[9]

Lammot was sent at once to Washington to meet with War Department officials to plan a defense, and was soon joined by Uncle Henry. Their meeting resulted in Secretary of War Stanton instructing Maj. Gen. Henry W. Halleck, general in chief of the army, to get troops without delay in position to "protect the powder mills of Messrs. du Pont on the Brandywine. You are aware that a large portion of the Government ammunition is made there, the works being the largest in the world. I have been informed that in the last war with Great Britain [War of 1812] a guard of 4,000 men was kept there. It seems to me that an equal force is now necessary." Halleck promptly telegraphed Brig. Gen. John Reynolds in Harrisburg to despatch a body of Pennsylvania militia to the mills. In the early morning hours of September 17 an advance force of 500 men belonging to the Third Regiment Pennsylvania Reserve Brigade, arrived near the Buck Tavern on Kennett Pike, a half mile from the mills, and pitched their tents at what soon came to be called Camp Brandywine. Lammot had been delegated to meet the leaders of the brigade at the campsite but they would not deal with him, presumably because he was a civilian. This meant that Uncle Henry, Maj. Gen. Henry du Pont, commander of all Delaware state forces, was routed out of bed at 4 A.M. to issue encampment instructions to the new arrivals.[10]

The crisis peaked with the battle of Antietam, fought near Sharpsburg, Maryland, on September 17, the bloodiest battle thus far of the war, with extremely heavy casualties on both sides. Lee's forces were repulsed, and with their retreat toward Virginia the immediate danger passed and Delawareans breathed more freely. But there persisted lingering fears of sabotage or possibly a swift sortie by mounted raiders, so the Pennsylvania brigade remained until the end of September when it was relieved by the Fourth Regiment of Delaware Volunteers. Meanwhile Lammot and Hugh Stirling had increased the number of weekly drills for the men in their Companies B and D. It was not until early November, however, before the men were fully outfitted and armed. Only for dress parade, scheduled every Saturday, were they required to report in full regalia.

Officers received the same basic clothing items as privates, but they had to provide their own dress uniforms, swords, and other ceremonial paraphernalia. This irked Lammot, not because of the expense—he purchased uniforms, swords, sashes, and belts from a Philadelphia outfitter—but because he disliked military trappings, the distinctions between rank they emphasized, and for the very obvious reason that conspicuously dressed officers made easy targets for the enemy. His dislike of military flummery

Lammot du Pont's appointment as captain of Company B, Fifth Regiment, Delaware Volunteers.

WAR DEPARTMENT,

Washington, Octr. 31st 1862.

Sir:

You are hereby informed that the President of the United States has appointed you **Captain, in the 5th Regt. Delaware Volunteers** in the service of the United States, to rank as such from the thirty first day of October, one thousand eight hundred and sixty= two. Should the Senate, at their next session, advise and consent thereto, you will be commissioned accordingly.

Immediately on receipt hereof, please to communicate to this Department, through the ADJUTANT GENERAL of the Army, your acceptance or non=acceptance; and, with your letter of acceptance, return the OATH herewith enclosed, properly filled up, SUBSCRIBED and ATTESTED, and report your AGE, BIRTHPLACE, and the STATE of which you were a permanent RESIDENT.

You will report for duty to

Capt. Lamot Dupont
5th Regt. Del. Vol.

Edwin M Stanton
Secretary of War.

was amusingly discerned by his teenage cousin Ellen: "Lammot behaves too stupidly for anything about his uniform. The orders are that the 9 mos. volunteers raised for service in the State are to be equipped as U.S. troops and their officers to wear the regulation uniform. This makes Capt. Lammot furious; he said, 'uniforms were humbugs, and officers were nonsense. . . . A little man comes rushing for the colonel and can't find him unless he jumps away up in the air to see the top of the colonel's shoulders! Where was the sense of a man's wearing his rank where nobody but himself could see it? Officers were shot at and every thing else.' You know how Lammot talks—like an old goose."[11] Her brother Henry, after four years at West Point a lieutenant very respectful of rank, distinction, and protocol, may have managed a little smile at this lampoon of his older cousin, but he did not share Lammot's egalitarian attitude toward things military.

The chilling reality of sabotage came uncomfortably close on the very night of the battle of Antietam, September 17, when two strangers were seen in Rising Sun Village, across the creek from the Lower Powder Yard. They were closely watched, and toward midnight their actions seemed suspicious enough to warrant their arrest and interrogation. One was a Thomas O'Keefe, a former Brandywine resident who had gone into business in Memphis some years ago, and his companion was his partner named Patrick R. Ryan. Both vigorously denied they were spies, O'Keefe stating he was visiting his estranged wife and child living in the village, and Ryan producing documents attesting that he was a merchant who had been licensed by Union officials in Cincinnati to carry on business in the north.

Suspicions sharpened when they used the term *Confederates* instead of *rebels*, and spoke of the war as a *revolution* and not a *rebellion*. On O'Keefe was found a promissory note for $470 drawn on a well-known Baltimore secessionist, and a large sum of money, reputedly a thousand dollars in gold. This, it was believed, was to bribe a powderman to sketch them a plan of the mills showing the approaches where detection would be least likely. As captain of the local military unit charged with the security of the mills, Lammot may have participated in the apprehension and interrogation of O'Keefe and Ryan, but nothing is recorded to confirm this. The suspects were held at the prison camp at Fort Delaware on Pea Patch Island in the Delaware River until mid-December and then released for lack of any positive incriminating evidence.[12] This was one of several suspected attempts at sabotage that kept the people of the neighboring villages in chronic watchful uneasiness, constantly fearful they were living on top of a "powder keg" that might explode any moment.

Another worry for many families, particularly those with men in service, was the rising costs of food, clothing, and other essentials, most of which had doubled in price since the war began. Periodically appeals were made for funds to alleviate the hardships of those suffering the most. Published lists of contributors appeared in the newspapers showing the amount given by companies, their employees, and by individuals. On the lists for the Relief of Families of Delaware Volunteers the Du Pont Company was shown as having contributed $300; Uncle Henry $500; Lammot and his mother $100 each; Uncle Bidermann and Aunt Eleuthera $100 each; brother Irénée $50; and sister Paulina and cousin Eugene $50 each. Lammot's income for the year 1862 was $39,556, on which he paid a flat 5 percent tax amounting to $1,977.80 to the Internal Revenue Service to satisfy the wartime income tax laws recently passed by Congress. The company's powder sales for the year totaled $1,531,347, a 52 percent increase over 1861, a figure exceeded only once in the next ten years, that being in 1864, when sales amounted to $1,625,305.[13]

The war that Henry du Pont had optimistically predicted in 1861 would be over within a few months entered its third year amid a pervading malaise, a weariness, and surfeit with bloodletting and killing on battle fronts, suffering and sorrow on home fronts. Morale in the North was weakening as more and more people came to believe it better to let the South secede—the cost being demanded to preserve the Union was becoming intolerable. The experiment with federalism had failed; let there be two Americas. The recruiting system was not working, and there was diminishing enthusiasm for volunteering as disillusionment became widespread. To many it seemed that this was "a rich man's war, but a poor man's fight."

Washington's birthday 1863 was used by Wilmington

Unionists to inject some vigor into the flagging fighting spirit by holding a dress parade of the Fifth Regiment Delaware Volunteers. All companies assembled at a field on the Kennett Pike in full dress and arms, where they went through formations and inspection and then marched in smart array through Wilmington heralded by a 100-gun salute. The Brandywine companies led by Lammot and Hugh Stirling, in the sharp eyes of the reviewing officer, Maj. Gen. Henry du Pont, made a very good appearance and were the best drilled of all the units participating.[14]

Shortly after noon on Wednesday, February 25, eleven thousand pounds of finished powder in the pack house at the upper end of Hagley Yard exploded killing thirteen men and injuring others. Tremors from the blast were felt as far away as Baltimore, Philadelphia, and New Jersey. Lammot feared that Irénée was in the pack house at the time. First reports had it that he lay in the blazing ruins, information which Lammot sadly passed on to Uncle Henry, "Uncle, Irénée is gone!" And he sent word to their sister Paulina to prepare their mother for the shock. In a short time a second messenger arrived with word that Irénée was safe; he had been detained at home after lunch to sign some legal papers and was not in the pack house when it exploded. Relief that one of their own was spared was mingled with sadness and concern for the victims and their families. A few days before the accident Lammot had been in the pack house and had noticed that twenty-three men, considerably more than usual, were at work there. He had spoken to Uncle Henry the night before the explosion, telling of his intent to transfer some of them to other mills, but too late.[15]

As he tried to console the bereaved families of the victims, Lammot felt remorse, and possibly a measure of guilt, because he had not acted quickly enough in reducing the number of men at work in the pack house; if he had, some of them would not now be among the dead. In severity, loss of life, and damage to property—to other mills, to homes on both sides of the creek, and to Christ Episcopal Church overlooking Hagley Yard—this accident was only slightly less destructive than the explosions of 1818 and 1847.

Not explosions but rumors of a prison break by the 4,000

Confederate prisoners held at Fort Delaware on Pea Patch Island in the Delaware River brought the mills to a standstill on Saturday, June 20. All the men of the Fifth Regiment, including the two Brandywine companies captained by Lammot and Hugh Stirling, were suddenly ordered to the prison camp to strengthen the inadequate guard force of 175 regular troops. Confederate armies were moving up the Shenandoah Valley meeting only moderate resistance as they again drove toward Harrisburg, the capture of which would be a telling blow to Northern morale. It was believed the rumored break-out was timed to coincide with the arrival of the rebel armies at some nearby point in Maryland where the escaping prisoners, many recently taken in the Vicksburg campaign, would join up with them.

The Delaware companies left for Fort Delaware from Wilmington on the steamboat *Ariel* in such a hurry they took few supplies with them, and Lammot's first move after reporting to his superiors at the fort was to requisition rations, blankets, canteens, ponchos, cooking and eating utensils, coats, hats, boats, and tents for the 97 men in his company. His first real taste of military life came the first night when he was put in temporary command of the regiment, containing nearly 100 drunken men, and not relieved for twenty-four hours. The next day his company had to set up tents for the regiment, helped by "green" men who had never pitched a tent before. He was up all the second night, twenty-four hours as officer of the guard. The third night he got some sleep, but the following day he was appointed officer of the day, another twenty-four-hour stint which, he informed his mother, "gives me the fort to look after as well as 4,000 prisoners. So you see my hands are full." He thought he might be on Pea Patch Island until August.[16]

Concerned about her son's health and comfort, Meta wrote him asking what he needed: an overcoat? [it could be damp and chilly on Pea Patch Island even in June] a mattress and blanket? and would he like a ham? In a short time a large package came from home containing an overcoat, a cot [too large for his tent] some woolen shirts, a valise with other clothes, but no cigars! Accompanying the package was a note of motherly advice to her thirty-two-year-old son—he should sleep more, work less, and smoke less! And he was to be sure to sleep on his cot, the ground down there was too damp.[17]

The departure of the home guard units had left the Brandywine desolate and almost without any able-bodied men. Exposed and defenseless, the powder mills would be easy prey for rebel raiders if protection was not soon forthcoming. Uncle Henry informed the War Department of this, urging that Lammot's and Stirling's companies be sent back home. While Washington officialdom was pondering this request Lammot witnessed the suffering and privations in a prisoner-of-war camp. Some of his own men had become sickened or bored with guard duty after a few days and wanted release. Lammot and his lieutenant listened to them, entering on company records such reasons as:

Irvine	Disabled—cannot perform military duty
Beaty	Attack of hemorrhoids
McKendrick	Needed at home—wife in confinement

Another had to leave on *urgent business*; Samuel Bancroft needed the services of one of his workmen; a third said he had to haul willows; a death in the family took the lieutenant away; and Lammot's Aunt Joanna (Mrs. Alexis I. du Pont) appealed to him to grant leave to a Richard Hunter because he was the only man who could "doctor" a sick horse she owned.[18]

Crowded onto Pea Patch Island, inside the fort and in tent camps around it, the 4,000 prisoners were divided into four classes: Union deserters and soldiers who had been court martialed; Confederate officers; rank and file rebel soldiers; and political prisoners; each group quartered separately. At first their Union guards communicated freely with them, but this was considered bad discipline, Lammot informed his mother, and it was soon stopped. In his eyes the prisoners were "a dirty set of dogs. . . . Day after day their only amusements appear to be playing cards and picking lice. At any time between 11 and 4 o'clock you can see from 100 to 300 of them sitting on the bank of the river, stripped off and picking the lice off their bodies. But they will not bathe nor wash their clothes without being ordered to do so." The only good drinking water came from a well within the fort, yet they were too lazy to carry it from there to their tents and instead drank ditch water which gave them diarrhea—yet they persisted in doing so.[19]

Five physicians looked after the prisoners, and ministers from nearby towns were permitted to visit and comfort them, but "the poor creatures are dying off rapidly," Aunt Sophie wrote her husband, relaying what she had been told by a member of Lammot's company who had come home on a day's furlough. Burials numbered between nine and twelve a day. And of Lammot—"We hear glorious accounts of Lammot's popularity there. They say he is the best officer down there (volunteer), and the '*best fellow.*' His company was the *first* ready after the call, and marched into Wilmington ready to be transported to the Fort before the Wilmington companies were mustered even!"[20]

To her delight Lammot got home on a twenty-four-hour pass a few days later, but he had little time to talk about rebel prisoners. In these last days of June the Confederate armies were only forty miles away in Maryland; once across the Susquehanna River they would be only a few hours by horse from the Brandywine. Lammot believed they would make a raid on the mills. He had come home on emergency leave to aid his harassed Uncle Henry ship off all the finished powder and see that the rest was dumped in the creek when the rebels attacked. He advised his Aunt Sophie to pack all her valuables and her husband's papers and send them at once either to Philadelphia or to some isolated farmhouse out in the country, for sacking the admiral's home would be sweet revenge to the gray-clad raiders. His mother at Nemours was preparing to evacuate, ready to throw the contents of the wine cellar into the pond "less the marauders should increase their appetite for destruction by drinking it." Aunt Joanna had her younger children ready to send off at a moment's notice, her jewelry and papers packed, and a collection of coins hidden in a hole down the hillside, where she would also bury her silver at the last moment. Uncle Henry and his wife Louisa were terribly apprehensive; he had again appealed for troops, but none could be spared; and Henry and his wife would not leave Eleutherian Mills because their daughter Louisa was too ill to be moved. She died on July 2. Fearful of what might befall their home and the surrounding properties, in near hysterical indignation Louisa's sister Ellen wrote to their brother Henry, "We shall be left a set of helpless beggars in the midst of our despoiled Delaware! I think it is a scandal when this State has always been loyal and done its utmost for it to be left to destruction."[21]

As these angry words were being written, the commandant at Fort Delaware, Brig. Gen. A. F. Schoepf, received orders to detach Captains du Pont and Stirling with forty men from their companies and send them at once back to the Brandywine to give some protection to the mills. Here they remained on watchful guard as the Confederacy mounted its greatest effort, rising to near victory on July 3 at Gettysburg, but then, falling back, defeated, and retreating southward into Virginia. So many prisoners taken at Gettysburg were sent to Fort Delaware that by August the grim prison was overcrowded with nearly 13,000 men. The small contingent of men from Lammot's and Stirling's companies that had guarded the mills were ordered back to the fort soon after the Union victory to strengthen the guard force against this new influx of prisoners. Their responsibility to protect the Brandywine was delegated to the Sixth Delaware Regiment of Volunteers.

Mortality among the prisoners at Fort Delaware was high, dysentery and chronic diarrhea from contaminated drinking water being suspected as the major cause. One step taken to combat it was to bring down fresh supplies of water from the mouth of the Brandywine daily. A second was to purify the local water supply by running it through a condenser. For this, on July 6 Commandant Schoepf instructed Lammot to go to Philadelphia to purchase a condenser, fixing $600 as the limit he could pay. Two days later Lammot reported that a brass-tube condenser with a daily capacity of 500 gallons of water could be bought for $400; another type, better made, and with a 3,000 gallon daily capacity would cost $600. Neither price included a boiler to generate steam, which Lammot estimated would add another $600, or a total of $1,200. He calculated the cost of producing pure water by this means would be about a half-cent a gallon. Displaying a thrifty trait common to the family, that of "making do," he sug-

gested to the Commandant that the island be scoured for an old
boiler still in serviceable condition and put it to use, thus saving
six hundred dollars.[22] There is no evidence that the condenser
was ever installed, so drinking water continued to be brought to
the fort from the Brandywine daily.

But Lammot's quality Cuban cigars, La Rosa Conchose and
Imperial Cabanas, were always acceptable to the commandant,
who enjoyed a good cigar. In the brief time they had known each
other he had come to admire the young captain. Mrs. Schoepf
confided to Amelia (Amy) du Pont, a cousin of Lammot's who
visited the fort in August, that Lammot had become one of their
household gods: "Every time the General smoked one of the
segars he had given him, he said, 'God bless du Pont.'" The twenty-
one-year-old Amy was mistakenly introduced to the Schoepfs as
Mrs. du Pont, and they assumed she was Lammot's wife. Before
she could make correction General Schoepf launched into the
"greatest eulogies" of Lammot, and because of their love for him
"devoted themselves to Amy."[23] Lammot was no doubt amused,
and maybe flattered, when he learned this, but at thirty-two he
remained a bachelor, devoted to job and family. Two more years
were to pass before he fell in love with a neighborhood girl,
much to everyone's surprise.

Guard duty at the fort for Lammot's and Stirling's companies ended on July 15, when they were ordered back to the Brandywine, a move that pleased the 135 men in the contingent and
relieved Uncle Henry's worry about the lack of protection for
the powder mills. From the Wilmington dock the two companies marched through the city before turning westward onto the
Kennett Turnpike, a bit of ceremony that caused a local editor to
speculate, "The intention may be to intercept stragglers, or it
may be to overawe persons disposed to resist the draft, which,
we presume, will be made within a week or two."[24]

A step taken to relieve the overcrowding at the fort was to
free those prisoners who would take the oath of allegiance to the
United States. They were derisively labeled "Galvanized Yan-
kees" by local Confederates, and they were held suspect by Union
people despite their oath of allegiance. While at the fort Lammot
or other powdermen in his company may have talked about

working in the mills to these presumably "rehabilitated" prisoners. Upon release a number of them did find their way to the
Brandywine and applied for jobs. This aroused the local newspaper to caution against hiring them, warning that "they might
be more useful to the rebels there than in the ranks. . . . all the
approaches to Du Pont's might be made known to rebel raiders"—they would need to be watched.[25] If Lammot had been
willing to take a chance on hiring these men, it is unlikely that
Uncle Henry would have approved; the company payroll records
for 1863 give no indication that any were hired even though the
mills were running short of hands.

Soon after their return from Fort Delaware five men in
Lammot's company came down with typhoid fever and two of
them died. In early August, Lammot felt symptoms of illness
which he thought may have been caused by striking his head on
some rocks while diving into the Brandywine. Soon after he had
been thrown from a buggy drawn by a fractious horse on a ride
to Winterthur. Though feeling below normal he went up to
Wapwallopen and there was taken ill, but not so badly that it kept
him from going on to New York. Enroute he fainted three times
and fell in the railroad car. On arrival home he went to bed with
a high fever which his doctor diagnosed as typhoid.[26] He remained delirious, intermittently lucid for the next six weeks, cared
for by his mother and sisters aided by brother Bidermann, who
came up from Louisville, and by cousin Alexis Irénée, soon to
take up the study of medicine. Lammot's homeopathic doctor,
August Negendank of Wilmington, allowed him no visitors, not
even Uncle Henry, on whom now fell the burden of most of
Lammot's duties. At a time when the fever ravaged him so terribly that it was feared he would not survive, his Aunt Joanna
(Mrs. Alexis I. du Pont) exclaimed to her daughter, "The thought
of losing him crushes me, for he is the only one I have to appeal
to here, and the idea of that valuable life being sacrificed . . . is
distracting."[27]

One of his first callers while he was recuperating was Aunt
Sophie, who stopped at Nemours on a Sunday on her way home
from church. She found him sitting up in bed, quite thin, but
bright and cheerful and talking a great deal. His appetite was

returning; his mother informed her he was now eating six meals a day but was still hungry, and he was slowly gaining weight.[28] Charles Belin at Wapwallopen had been informed of his tremendous appetite and he cautioned Lammot about getting too fat. Belin could not refrain from describing a delectable coon dinner he had recently eaten and wished he could have shared it with Lammot. On his next trip to Wapwallopen, he promised Lammot, he would have Mrs. Belin prepare one with "boiled acorns and the usual fixings." Lammot was advised of all the recent happenings at the Pennsylvania mill, Belin hoping their enumeration would not prove tedious to the sick man. He wrote at length because, "as I look upon Wapwallopen as your adopted child, and suppose you take an interest in her welfare, these details will probably be read with satisfaction."[29]

During Lammot's illness the subject of guncotton was again revived when the Bureau of Naval Ordnance sent some technical summaries of its manufacture by an Austrian, Baron von Lenk, to the Du Pont Company for its opinion about the process. Had he been able Lammot would have handled this query, but he was fighting to survive the ravages of a devastating fever. Either his brother Irénée or Uncle Henry responded, returning the literature sent by the Ordnance Bureau, with the suggestion that the government spend a few thousand dollars and conduct some experiments of its own; the company's authority on such matters was too ill to be bothered.[30]

Another query came from a New York City acquaintance who had done some experimenting with substitute materials for making black powder. G. A. Lilliendahl had made powder using aloes in place of sulphur, and he believed it left the gun cleaner and was less corrosive; but he asked Lammot if he would investigate this further and let him know the results of his experiments. Lammot replied, expressing interest in the idea, but illness would keep him from doing anything at present. Lilliendahl's acknowledgement bore this comment, "My mind and personal observation had fancied you to be one of those who never get sick but live to a ripe old age without having made the acquaintance of a doctor's bill."[31]

As he grew stronger during November, Lammot made some

batches of powder containing aloes instead of sulphur and test-
fired them. The results reported to Lilliendahl were negative:
extremely high heat was necessary to sublimate the aloes, and
powder made with it had a slower combustion rate than that
made with sulphur; it also left more residuum in the gun. He
would have to postpone testing the projectile force of the two
powders until he felt better, but he would give Lilliendahl his
results at the earliest opportunity.[32] Getting back to his laboratory while convalescing was no doubt good therapy for Lammot.
There is no further correspondence on this matter, but it is likely
he subsequently acquainted Lilliendahl with the final results of
his tests on one of his frequent trips to New York City.

A get-well letter from General Schoepf congratulated him
on his recovery and advised that he forget the powder business
until he was altogether better. When Lammot could manage the
trip the commandant would be happy to have him visit Fort
Delaware, where many changes had taken place since he and his
men had left. Their tour of duty had been short said Schoepf,
"but I remember with pleasure the few weeks of their stay." Enclosed, as a token of the general's esteem, was a photograph of
himself. Lammot acknowledged the letter and photograph, apol-
ogizing for the delay because of illness—"42 days delirious without intermission"—and still unable to get out. Of the general's
photograph, he thought it a very good likeness, with a happy
expression, but the eye was rather stern. Candor was a marked
trait of Lammot's and he expected it from other people.[33]

As he regained strength and writing became easier, he gave
some time to winding up the affairs of Company B; filling in
numerous War Department forms, settling accounts, certifying
return of arms and equipment, completing muster roll data, and
seeking overdue pay for some of his men. Together, his and Stirling's company had a surplus of unexpended funds amounting to
$445. This sum was divided among the widows of four of their
men who had died while in service, prorated according to the
number of children in each family. A number of Wilmington's
prominent citizens, appalled at the plight of war orphans and
abandoned children, late in the year appealed for funds to establish a "Home for Friendless and Destitute Children," and to this
good cause Lammot contributed twenty-five dollars.[34]

Persons who presumed upon his friendship, or sought compensation which Lammot thought undeserved, got short shrift for their efforts. James Peoples and Samuel Brown were both clerks in the Du Pont Company office. Peoples had joined Company B, had done home guard duty, and had served at Fort Delaware. The Du Pont Company paid him his salary while in service. Brown had been conscripted but had paid $250 of his own money for a substitute and had continued clerking all during 1863. He had considered joining Lammot's company, but, he said, he had been dissuaded by Lammot because it would have left the office without an experienced clerk, and Uncle Henry would disapprove of this. So for most of the summer all the office chores had fallen on him, sometimes keeping him at work until midnight and later, and for all this extra work he had received only his regular salary, $67.00 a month. Comparing his lot with Peoples, who had received both office and military pay, Brown thought he had not been sufficiently compensated, and he put it to Lammot, "feeling that you are my friend," asked for his opinion. What opinion Lammot had is not recorded, but on the reverse side of Brown's letter when filed was written the simple notation, "Brass." From which we conclude that Lammot thought hardships endured by Peoples in military service outweighed the extra hours civilian Brown had spent by oil and candlelight keeping books and writing letters; it was "brassy" on his part to presume upon Lammot's friendship to try to obtain extra compensation for himself.[35]

Lammot's rejection of Brown's appeal is in contrast to the assistance he extended to a number of men in Company B after they returned to civilian life. To some he lent money, and for others, including one Nicholas McCartney, he cut through official delay and red tape in obtaining properly certified discharge papers and military pay due them. McCartney wrote him this letter of thanks for his efforts: "When I consider the many difficulties which had to be surmounted in obtaining the amount due me, if it had not been for your assistance I know not how I would have obtained it. I am under obligations to you for all the kindness which you have shown to me."[36]

As the end of 1863 drew near Lammot felt well enough to make a trip to Wapwallopen, where he may have enjoyed the promised raccoon dinner with all the fixings prepared by Mrs. Belin. From there he went to New York City on business and to visit his sister Victorine and her husband, Peter Kemble, who had urged him to forget business and come spend some time with them. His absence from the Brandywine the week before Christmas delayed a trip Uncle Henry was contemplating to Martinsburg, Virginia, to see his son Henry Algernon in winter encampment. Lina, his daughter, pressed her father to go—"I think a change would stir him up and be good for him," but Papa could not leave until Lammot returned.[37]

The year ended with the Du Pont Company posting sales amounting to $1,373,169, of which over a million were sales to the army and navy. This total was a decrease of 10 percent from 1862, but sales for the latter year had included very large military orders, boosting its total sales to over $1,500,000, a 52 percent jump over sales for 1861.[38] Now the federal government, represented by Deputy Collector John P. Hilyard, Internal Revenue, requested the citizens of Delaware to calculate their special wartime tax: 5 percent on incomes, licenses, carriages, silverplate, billiard tables, and yachts, which should be paid to him beginning January 12, 1864. If not paid within a month, a penalty of 10 percent should be added.[39] Lammot's tax bill on an income of $26,372 amounted to $1,318.62; brother Irénée paid $1,073.86 on an income of $21,477; and Uncle Henry, reportedly with the largest income of all Delawareans, $117,985, was taxed $5,899.25.[40] By this modest levy on civilian wartime earnings the government sought to finance an increasingly costly war that had continued far beyond early predictions, and the end of it seemed ever more distant.

Chapter VI

"Uncle Big Man"

NEW YEAR'S DAY festivities for the family gathered at Eleutherian Mills were muted, the usual good cheer and high spirits diminished. The reality of war had come very close during the old year, and what 1864 would bring weighed on everyone's mind. The family circle had been diminished by two deaths, that of Aunt Evelina (Mrs. James A. Bidermann), elder sister of Uncle Henry and mistress of Winterthur, in her sixty-seventh year. Her husband, going blind, was preparing to return to his native France to live out his last years with their son James Irénée. Louisa, the eighteen-year-old daughter of Uncle Henry and Aunt Louisa, had died on July 2 when it was feared the Confederates would sweep into the valley putting the torch to homes and mills.

Three days after Louisa's death her brother, Lt. Henry Algernon du Pont, had been put in command of an artillery battery, and at year's end was stationed at Martinsburg, Virginia, moving closer toward his first test under fire. Over the creek at Upper Louviers, Uncle Frank, Rear Adm. Samuel Francis du Pont, under a cloud for failing to capture Charleston in early April, was marshaling his defenses for a pending investigation by the Navy Department. A number of devastating explosions in the mills had killed workmen, injured others, damaged nearby homes, and delayed production. And when Uncle Henry sorely needed him, Lammot had been laid up for the last four months of the year with nearly fatal typhoid fever. He had returned home from his year-end visit to New York City with sister Victorine and her husband and was with the family on New Year's Day looking well and apparently once more in good health.

But there lingered some bad aftereffects, particularly with his eyes, which became so inflamed he could not use them for any close work, and his back became stiff and painful. He drove himself but found he was able to do less than a half day of work.

At Uncle Henry's urging he spent more time in the powder yards
away from the laboratory and office to rest his eyes, but intermittently throughout much of the year he had recurring attacks
of inflammation of the eyes and what his doctor diagnosed as
spinal rheumatism.[1]

A serious problem demanding Lammot's prompt attention
was the rejection of large quantities of defective powder by the
Ordnance Bureau. Sample batches from each order were customarily test-fired at the Cannon House before being shipped out,
usually to the Frankford Arsenal in north Philadelphia. Further
tests were made by Ordnance officers at the Arsenal, and in the
latter part of 1863 they were finding decided fluctuations in the
performance of Du Pont's cannon and mortar powder. Hundreds
of barrels had been sent back to the mills.[2] Incoming mail from
company agents selling powder to commercial customers contained similar complaints about the quality of blasting powder.

This was obviously due to the greatly increased speed of
production, the unavoidable hiring of inexperienced mill hands,
the poorer quality of raw materials, or the failure to prepare them
adequately. There was also a feeling that the Ordnance Bureau
officer who condemned the powder was excessively rigid in ap-
plying inspection standards to Du Pont powder. He was criti-
cized for giving "all manner of trouble & is just as disagreeable
as he can be," by Lina, the observant eldest daughter of Uncle
Henry, who was privy to some of her father's worries. In mid-
August this officer was replaced by Lt. Col. Stephen V. Benét, a
change welcomed by the Du Pont partners. The Ordnance Department subsequently noted that 42 percent of all powder it
purchased was made by Du Pont, and that during two months
in late 1864, 2,500 barrels (250,000 pounds) of Mammoth,
mortar, cannon, and musket powder that had met all specifications had been supplied by the Brandywine mills.[3]

Business trips to New York City were made with some regularity by Lammot, generally to confer with Furman L. Kneeland, the company's principal agent, whose office was at 66 Wall
Street. When in New York he usually took time to visit his sister
Victorine and her young family, who lived on Ninth Street. On
one such trip early in April he took along his cousins Victorine,

fifteen years of age, and Sophie, thirteen, Uncle Henry's younger daughters, to see the sights of the big city. This may have been their first visit to New York without their parents, and they were delighted to be escorted about by their knowledgeable big cousin, "Mott." Dutiful correspondents, their letters home bubbled with high spirits in telling of all they were seeing and doing. Family news was unfailingly relayed by their mother to their brother Henry Algernon, away in camp, and in her weekly letter she told her son that "Vic and Sophie are in New York. They went there last Monday with Lammot and are having a fine time going through a course in sightseeing which they enjoy vastly. The elders stay at home and the infants are launched into the whirl of New York."[4]

Lammot enjoyed the company of young people. Rapport with them came easily for he retained a boyish zest in the things they liked to do—playing games, fishing, swimming and boating on the creek, bathing at Cape May, riding, sleighing, partying, walking through the woods, and putting together collections of many kinds. At an early age he had begun collecting Indian artifacts—spear points, arrow heads, bannerstones, pendants, some of which were local Lenni Lenape or Delaware Indian in origin; other items from more distant Indian cultures he acquired as gifts or by trade and purchase. This was a hobby he pursued through his adult life, building up a respectable collection that was given to the University of Delaware many years later. Croquet was a new game locally in the early 1860s, and the first court in the family domain was laid out at Nemours, where it became a favored pastime of the younger family members and of some of their elders.

During the hot summer months the Kemble children were brought from New York to spend weeks at Nemours with Grandma Meta, Aunt Paulina, and Uncle Mott. The Louisville du Ponts, Bidermann and his wife Ellen with their brood of five, also visited fairly often. When Nemours grew overcrowded, some of the youngsters were farmed out to Uncle Irénée's and Aunt Charlotte's at Swamp Hall on Breck's Lane downstream, where there were more cousins to play with. Counting all these, and including the children of the Victor du Pont line across the creek and her own offspring, Aunt Louisa in 1868 enumerated just the young females in the family and found there were now "twenty-one Miss du Ponts." To nieces and nephews alike, and to his younger cousins, the tall, bespectacled Lammot with the kindly eyes was affectionately known as "Uncle Big Man."[5]

Working daily in hazardous surroundings where injury or death could strike with tragic suddenness might harden one to gruesome pain and agony. It could develop an attitude of philosophic resignation and enforce a degree of disciplined dispassion to the suffering of the victims of accidents. Not so with Lammot; his concern for the men he worked with was genuine and spontaneous. An instance of this occurred when the upper press mill in the Hagley Yard exploded on May 10, 1864, killing two men instantly; three died a few hours later, and five suffered serious burns and concussions. After emergency treatment one of the injured men was taken to his boarding house to be cared for by his landlady. Lammot stopped in to see him soon afterward and was shocked and angered to find that he had been badly neglected by the landlady and her husband, who were heavy drinkers. He had the injured man moved to another home, engaged nurses to care for him, and visited him frequently during his convalescence.[6]

During the spring of 1864 a proposal Lammot had made back in 1856, to link the residences and mills on both sides of the creek, became a reality. The most direct means of getting across the creek was by a small, flat-bottomed boat propelled by an overhead rope and pulley. The crossing was at a narrow part of the stream just outside the entrance gate to the Upper Yard, and on the opposite shore it docked at the foot of a path that led uphill to the Louviers residences and the Louviers Woolen Mill. In stormy weather, or when the creek was frozen or running high and turbulent, the crossing was precarious and sometimes impossible. The alternative was to go by road about a mile up to the village of Rockland, cross the bridge at the Rockland Paper Mill, then turn down Rockland Road paralleling the east bank of the stream to Black Gates Road, the entrance to the Louviers establishments. Another choice was to go downstream through the Hagley powder yards to Henry Clay Village, cross the creek

through the double-lane covered bridge at the foot of Rising
Sun Lane, travel about a mile to the Rockland Road, then bear
left on Black Gates Road. These were the circuitous routes taken
by wagons and carriages carrying goods and persons to the homes
and mills on the opposite shore.

Though it is likely better ways to expedite the crossing had
been considered earlier, the first tangible suggestion had come
from Lammot in 1856. At a point a short distance below the
existing boat crossing he proposed constructing a suspension
bridge of 168 feet anchored to stone piers standing twenty-five
feet above the water level. He calculated the cost of chains and
suspension rods would total $1,480; the stone for the piers, planks
for decking, and all the labor could be supplied by the company.
For comparison he obtained from a local bridge builder an estimate of $6,000 as the cost for erecting a covered truss bridge at
the same location. By his calculations Lammot figured his proposed bridge could bear a maximum load of 5,000 pounds at its
middle.[7]

The bridge, however, was not built, possibly because the
Louviers Woolen Mill had closed down in 1856 and perhaps
Uncle Henry did not consider the greater convenience and time
saved sufficient to justify the expenditure. In 1859 the woolen
mill was leased to the firm of Green and Wilson, who converted
it into a keg mill, making metal kegs and tin canisters for packing
powder. The value of a bridge providing quick access between
keg mill and powder yards would seem to have been self evident,
but the roundabout way via the Rockland Road continued to
serve until 1864, when war demands necessitated the erection of
some temporary powdermaking facilities adjacent to the metal
keg mill. This made a bridge mandatory, and construction was
begun on a wooden bridge designed to carry both pedestrians
and carriages, wagons, and powder cars. By the end of April it
was far enough along to permit walking across, which pleased
Mrs. Henry du Pont, who was among the first to use it: "The
bridge is nearly finished, not yet passable for cars or carriages but
for foot passengers and we go over so pleasantly & nicely back-
ward and forward, the distance now seeming nothing. I went
over yesterday with your father to see your Uncle and Aunt."[8]

Powder Yard
Road

In 1856 I proposed building a wrought Iro
brandywine at the Woolen Mill. The fo
From Pier to pier - - - - - - -
From Powder Yard road to pier
From Woolen mill road to pier
2 Chains of 1½ inch Iron and suspension
to bear 5000lbs in middle of Span
Mr Quigley (bridgebuilder) proposed a c
put up at a cost of $5000 or at $10 p
piers — Both highths above the water

The delay of years between the proposal made in 1856 and
its fulfillment eight years later in 1864 when Uncle Henry finally
approved, illustrates their attitudes toward innovation. The
younger man was alert and ready to make changes, ready to break
with traditional practices, willing to risk the hazards and the costs
of innovations; his uncle, nineteen years his senior, cautious and
conservative, prone to hold on to what had proved satisfactory

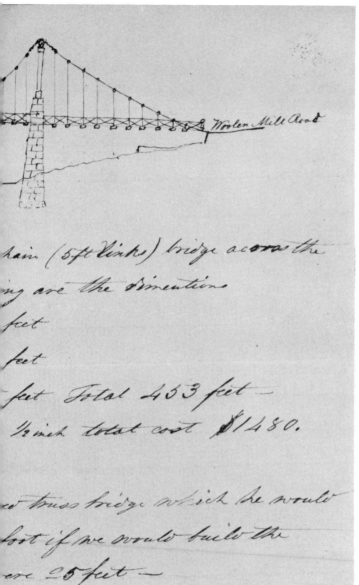

Worlen Mill Road

hain (5ft links) bridge across the

ng are the dimentions

feet

feet

feet Total 453 feet —

½ inch total cost $1480.

... truss bridge which he would

foot if we would build the

are 25 feet —

Lammot du Pont's design (1856) for a chain-link bridge that would give readier access to the mills and dwellings on opposite sides of the Brandywine. Construction was postponed until 1864, when a wooden plank bridge was erected.

over the years, to adopt new ideas only after protracted deliberation, and only when fully convinced they guaranteed success. Innovator and conservator probably counterbalanced each other in ways that prevented extreme swings in company operations and resulted in steady, consistent growth. But the balance was weighted toward Uncle Henry, for as senior partner his word was final. Lammot was the originator pushing for change, sometimes succeeding, sometimes put off, and sometimes assailed by misgivings that the family firm was jeopardizing its leadership by failing to keep pace with significant discoveries in the rapidly changing technology of explosives manufacture. Nitroglycerine and dynamite had been discovered by Alfred Nobel in Sweden in 1864.

Before dawn on Sunday morning July 10, 1864, the warning tocsin sounded throughout the Brandywine villages, and as the alarmed dwellers ran outside word spread that the Confederates were again staging their "annual invasion." A rebel cavalry force commanded by Maj. Harry W. Gilmore had swept into Maryland, looting, burning, cutting rail and telegraph lines, and derailing trains as far north as Hagerstown. If the raiders got to Elkton they could dash across country unhindered toward Wilmington. All through the church hour drums sounded, and from the pulpit of Christ Episcopal Church notice was read summoning the men of Company B of the Fifth Delaware Volunteers— Lammot's former command—to assemble immediately and march into Wilmington. But Lammot, helpless and bedfast by the recurrence of typhoid fever, was completely overcome at not being able to lead his men. His and other volunteer units were hastily despatched to the Gunpowder River in Maryland to repulse a crossing by the Confederates and to prevent destruction of the bridge over the river. Here a skirmish occurred, men on both sides were wounded and a few taken prisoner; but the Delawareans held, the bridge was damaged but not destroyed, and the invaders turned southward to try once more to take Washington. Company B was home within a week and ordered into temporary quarters at Camp Du Pont (formerly Camp Brandywine) on the Kennett Pike near the Buck Tavern until it was certain the rebel threat had ended. One can picture Lammot's cousins Alexis and Eugene, who had fought at Gunpowder River, gathered at his bedside telling their recumbent captain how the men of his old company had performed under fire.[9]

The intensity of the war in the summer months of 1864 led to conscription; volunteering and even the payment of bounties had left the ranks short of needed manpower. Quotas were again assigned each state and much closer scrutiny was given to requests for exemptions. Some Du Pont workmen talked of accepting the bounties and joining up before the draft caught up with them, a disturbing possibility that made Henry du Pont fear he would lose a large part of his work force. To insure against this, he went to Washington in the second week of August to again request exemption for his men. Approval did not come so readily this time, but exemption was granted provided that the powdermen were organized into a company of volunteer infantry solely for service in guarding the powder mills. Pledged to serve one to three years, and included in Delaware's draft quota, the men were to receive no bounties but they would be equipped and clothed by the government and would receive pay when ordered to active duty by the War Department.[10]

This arrangement kept the mills operating and at the same time provided them with a protective screen, and it obviously included exemption for Lammot. He was, strictly speaking, a powder workman, albeit one of the company's partners sharing responsibility for its continued operation. His health was so precarious from July into September that he could not have responded had he been drafted, nor could he have actively participated in the drills of the home guard company that was organized a week after exemption was granted. Incapacitated for military service for an indefinite time, he arranged to have a substitute serve in his stead by paying three hundred dollars to Philip Reynolds, a Delaware black man. Harry Belin in the company office and cousins Charles I. and Victor du Pont similarly procured substitutes from a rapidly shrinking pool of available able-bodied men.[11]

By the end of August, using a walking stick, Lammot was able to get out of the house to take short walks around the yard and garden and an occasional visit to the office. His stiff back made sitting down and getting up painful. He had lost weight and was very thin, yet his general health seemed good and his appetite had returned. It bothered him that Uncle Henry was saddled for so long a time with so many of his duties, and there is no indication they were shifted to brother Irénée or to younger cousin Eugene. These additional tasks thrust upon her husband also worried Aunt Louisa. She knew his great capacity for work, the orderly efficiency of his daily schedule that made use of every minute, but it allowed too little time for his family, and there was a limit to the burden, weighted further by his having to assume direct charge of all farm operations because the head farmer was also ill with a lingering fever.

Pouring out her concern in a letter to sister-in-law Sophie at Louviers and to her son, Louisa offers one of the very rare intimations that relations between branches of the family were becoming tinged with mistrust. She felt that Lammot and his mother were not altogether open and frank in telling her and her husband all they should know about Lammot's illness. A Philadelphia physician had been called into consultation by Dr. Negendank, Lammot's doctor. Uncle Henry had stopped in to see Lammot soon after the Philadelphia doctor's visit and he thought his nephew seemed pretty well, but there was a reserve evident when it came to discussing the doctor's opinion and recommendations. Such seeming reticence baffled Louisa: "If I had sickness I should not wish to conceal anything we were doing." She did not doubt the seriousness of Lammot's illness. "He has indeed had a hard time of it, poor fellow!" she informed her son, but she found his reluctance to talk about the state of his health a contradiction to his characteristic frank, open manner, and she dearly hoped he would recover quickly, for his own sake and for the relief it would bring her overworked husband.[12] It may have been Lammot's masculine pride, a refusal to recognize that he, a vigorous, strapping six-footer who had rarely been ill could be rendered almost a helpless invalid. But so it was, and to talk about his infirmity may have hurt his pride.

Aunt Sophie at Upper Louviers was a lady of boundless sympathy and generous heart to anyone in need of help. With other Wilmington and New Castle ladies touched by the wretched privations of the prisoners at Fort Delaware, she sent them books, newspapers, food packages, articles of clothing, and other incidentals not available from the prison commissary. She and her husband tried to get some prisoners released or paroled. Some were members of families such as the Manigaults whose friendship with the du Ponts dated back many years. Lammot's aid was enlisted and he wrote General Schoepf, commandant at the fort, sending him a list of the prisoners' names, soliciting his good offices in trying to obtain their release. His request was accompanied by a gift of fine quality cigars.

Schoepf's reply was disappointing. The War Department was presently forbidding any releases because recent experience had shown that the "many that professed to be Union men, upon being released, went right back to Rebeldom." For the cigars, the one luxury he permitted himself, he thanked Lammot and assured him he would enjoy them—damn what the doctors say! During his long illness Lammot received Schoepf's best wishes for a speedy recovery and an invitation to visit and have dinner at the fort, after which they could have a long talk over some of Lammot's Cuban perfectos.[13]

The fall months were spent catching up with matters he should know about. Charles Belin at Wapwallopen had a dossier on his operations for Lammot to review. There was danger of losing some workmen attracted to military service by bounties ranging from $300 to $500. Others, grumbling at the higher prices they had to pay for everything, were apt to leave and hunt for better-paying jobs elsewhere. It looked as if wages would have to go up to keep them. Poorly made kegs that leaked powder were a chronic problem, and he was getting complaints about short weight and the quality of powder. Competitors were cutting prices—should he do the same? Belin had experimented in making powder by adding small quantities of cement to the formula, with varying reactions from customers, some good, some bad. If Lammot was up to it he would like to see him soon to go over these and numerous other matters. In November, Lammot went up to Wapwallopen and spent a number of weeks with Belin, one consequence of which was his instruction to eliminate cement from the powder mixture.[14]

News of Union victories in the Shenandoah Valley, in Tennessee, and in Georgia with the capture of Atlanta and Savannah during the latter half of the year lifted northern morale and infused it with a determination to push on to a quick final victory. There were rallies, parades, prayer services, and torchlight processions in Wilmington and the upstream villages after the news first came by telegraph and was then enlarged upon in newspaper despatches. The local press noted with pride the battle at Cedar Creek, Virginia, in which Capt. Henry Algernon du Pont had commanded his artillery company with such deadly skill that captured rebel officers marveled at its accuracy, knowing "just where to throw shot to make them tell." As he read this Lammot must have been warmed by the praise bestowed upon his cousin, and by an added encomium paid the family's business: "The Du Ponts, it seems do not only know how to make the best powder in the world, but when made they know how to use it in defence of their country."[15]

The mood of optimism and the high spirits of Christmas preparations in the local villages were shattered by a terrible explosion on December 15. Ten men were killed when the upper press mill in Hagley Yard blew up again. Five adjacent mills were destroyed and a number of homes leveled or seriously damaged. Heavy beams were flung 300 feet and driven deep into the frozen ground. Aunt Joanna's (Mrs. Alexis I. du Pont's) house on a rise of land overlooking the press mill was nearly demolished and had to be abandoned, but no one in the family suffered injuries. Every pane of glass in nearby Christ Church was shattered. It was a Christmas without joy in the powder community.[16]

This accident was the third press mill to explode within two years, and a fourth occurred two months later, February 25, 1865, when the lower Hagley press mill blew up killing three men. One of the victims had recently bought a small farm out of his savings and was going to move onto it the next day. Production was curtailed by both presses being out of service for several months. It is conceivable this situation prompted Lammot to renew his interest in designing a safer, more efficient powder press. He had seen some improved presses in the European mills he had visited in 1858 and had his notes and sketches of them to refer to as he set about this challenging task. Considerable time must have been spent in his laboratory-workshop in the early months of 1865, certainly with some false starts, frustrations, and disappointments before he succeeded in constructing a workable horizontal press that could be operated either by hydraulic or steam power. This new press could be loaded more speedily with the soft "green" powder, and it eliminated the tedious manipulations necessary in the older vertical style screw press, which resembled the presses found in paper mills. His application for a patent was approved and Letters Patent No. 50,568 issued to him by the U.S. Patent Office on October 24, 1865. By an odd coincidence, on that same date an American patent, No. 50,617, was granted to Alfred Nobel of Sweden for developing an "Improved Substitute for Gunpowder"—nitroglycerine.

The new year was heralded with predictions of good times, prosperity, and reassurances that peace must not be far off. After the customary calling and giving of gifts on a snowy New Year's Day, a moonlight sleighing party for the younger du Ponts was organized by Lammot, his brother Fred home from Louisville for the holidays, and cousin Eugene. Cousin Ellen, one of the party, wrote her brother telling him what was planned: "There is a great sleighing party on foot for tonight. The gentlemen are going to get the sleighs and drivers from Wilmington & going to start at 5 in the evening. The moon rises at 7—and go up to West Chester or somewhere, get warm and get something to eat, dance if they can, and come home after midnight. That is the programme. Whether such an expedition could come off on the Brandywine nowadays remains to be proved." Ellen's doubts were groundless. Fourteen persons, brothers and sisters, cousins, in-laws, and a few close friends bundled into three large sleighs and glided merrily through the frosty moonlit night as far as Chester. Here they had supper, danced the night away, "and came home at unheard of Brandywine hours—perfectly enchanted," Ellen's mother informed her son Henry.[17] The party had a tonic effect upon Lammot. All traces of his lingering illness were gone, and his convalescence had ended, and he felt robust and invigorated.

In the new year mood of making resolutions, and catching up on things postponed by his illness, the next day he compiled a list of tasks that needed his attention and captioned his memorandum "Notes of Jobs on Hand." This enumeration of forty-four things he should do reflects a methodical, conscientious attitude toward his work, and a comprehensive grasp of matters, both of larger import and of the small, routinely essential details of everyday plant operation.

A railroad through the Brandywine valley to connect with

the Pennsylvania Railroad at Coatesville and then continue northward into the coal regions was then being advocated. Lammot saw this could benefit the valley's industries and the economy of Wilmington, and noted that his first task was to "discuss the Brandywine railroad and get partners to agree to use our influence to get it located so as to be useful to us." Should he fail to win their support, his next move was to try to obtain their approval to construct a horse-car railroad from the mills to the Du Pont Company wharf at Middleburgh on the Christina River. He viewed this as preferable to the existing wagon road that connected mills and shipping point. And within the yards he thought the narrow-gauge railroad connecting the mills should be extended further up into the Upper Yard.

In the mills themselves there were many jobs awaiting completion: (1) Finish installing a condenser in the lower coalhouse and put up vertical pipes with valve controls. (2) Raise the floor of the little coalhouse 18 inches to avoid having to step down into it. (3) Box the piping into this building to keep it from freezing. (4) Move the grate bars of the coal house furnaces into the center of each furnace. (5) Set up a vacuum boiler in which to soak timber to better preserve it. (6) Install a kettle in coalhouse in which to evaporate pyroligniate of soda. (7) Put a switch in the Upper Yard graining mill. (8) Get lock on the gunhouse fixed.

In the laboratory were some unfinished chemical experiments, and he had ideas for some new ones he wanted to try: (1) Continue experiments to determine the best way of making white acetate of soda from pyroligneous acid. (2) Try decomposing crude acetate of soda (when contaminated with tar) with oil of vitriol, economically. (3) Recrystallize crude acetate of soda to see if by second crystallization it can be bleached with chloride of lime. (4) Analyze sample of crude carbonate of soda from calcined acetate of soda to ascertain what percent of carbonate it contains. (5) Try the solubility of "gum damor [?]" in naphtha and ascertain its value for a varnish.

For Wapwallopen several things needed to be done: (1) Get barrels for storing naphtha ready to send up. (2) Assemble lumber for constructing glazing barrels. (3) Assemble materials for building new graining mill. (4) Pack and ship a box containing bolt cutters, covers, hydraulic piping, etc. (5) And, indicative of a new interest in coal mining, his last reminder to himself was to go to Scranton for a meeting of the coal company. The coal company is not named, but Du Pont's first investments were in the Mocanaqua Coal Company and the Mineral Spring Coal Company.[18]

Lammot's memorandum reveals more than the specific tasks that needed attention. There is no follow-up check-off to indicate which jobs got done, nor when, so we cannot judge his thoroughness or the speed at which he worked. Other sources, however, make clear that he was diligent in all that he undertook and that dilatory effort and procrastination were foreign to his nature. The memorandum is revealing for other reasons. The very act of sitting down and listing two-score tasks to undertake as the new year got under way shows initiative and purpose. The diversity of these jobs denotes familiarity and command of areas of plant operations that required the skills of engineer, mechanic, millwright, draftsman, architect, builder, carpenter, chemist, and manager. Not yet evident but as will become apparent in an analysis of a study he made in 1872, Lammot was groping toward a more logical, systematic sequence of steps in the powder process that would reduce wasted time and motion, save on labor, and ultimately reduce costs.

Of particular interest as a shadowy precursor influencing the future of Du Pont Company development was the increased attention Lammot was giving to the recovery of the by-products from powder manufacture. First, in the laboratory, and then by chemical engineering these could be transformed into intermediate products used in the manufacture of commodities that bore no resemblance to explosives. Long before Lammot's time the Du Pont Company had been selling flowers of sulphur, a by-product of the sublimation of sulphur, to apothecaries and pyroligneous acid collected in the distillation of wood into charcoal to chemical processors. Tar and creosote were other by-products of charcoal making. There had also been a limited market for common salt and Glauber salts, some of the residues left from refining saltpeter, but the bulk of the refinery residue—spoken of as "mud"—was used as a fertilizer on the company's farm lands. This "manure" also contained several other salts, sulphates of lime and magnesia, which Lammot's father in the 1840s had tried to recover economically but with small success. The nature of the work Lammot was assigning himself in the laboratory shows his desire to broaden the search for additional derivatives from the by-products of powdermaking for which there was a demand in the chemical, textile, and meat packing industries.

The transformation of the Du Pont Company from solely a maker of explosives to a diversified producer of chemicals and consumer products came about years after Lammot's death under the direction of his sons and nephews. But it was this shift to greater emphasis upon laboratory experiments with the by-products of powdermaking in the 1860s and 1870s that added impetus to diversification. In 1866 an addition was put on the charcoal house in the Upper Yard for the production of naphtha, and a new building named the "Acid Factory" was erected near the refinery.[19] Lammot's endeavors helped shape a spirit of imaginative enterprise among his successors who gave leadership to the family business. His younger contemporaries to whom he was mentor were to assert their belief that Lammot was the ablest of his generation and gifted with the most distinguished intelligence.

POSTWAR CHANGES

Shortly after 5 A.M. on April 10, 1865, a pounding on the door at Eleutherian Mills awakened Uncle Henry and his wife. It was Lammot calling out the happy news—the war was over! Lee and all his army had surrendered! This was amid the din of drumbeats, cannon firing, boat whistles, and the clangor of bells rolling up the valley from Wilmington. The cacaphony swelled as shouts, bells, guns, and drums in the creekside villages joined the clamor. "Everybody *here* is half crazy," wrote Aunt Joanna, "the men have holiday, and all the bells, including the Church bell, have never ceased ringing! It is a great day! How thankful we should be!" Aunt Louisa was grateful that her son Henry Algernon had come through the war unharmed, but, she confided to him, "I can't get into the spirit of these celebrations, much as I rejoice in this last bloodless victory, and I am thankful to be here in my quiet home. . . . I fear the bad effects of today on the men— two of them have already come reeling down the road—at this early hour."[20]

Lammot was named to a committee from Christiana Hundred to arrange a countywide victory celebration scheduled for April 17. His committee was busy making preparations when word of Lincoln's assassination was received on April 16 with shocked disbelief. Victory flags and bunting came down to be replaced with black mourning drapes as news of the tragedy spread throughout the North. Uncle Henry, who had become an admirer of Lincoln and had supported his reelection in 1864, was appalled at the president's murder. "I trust it was intended by the Almighty for some special purpose and that all will be well, but it is a fearful blow at Republican Institutions. . . . I believe that treason should be punished upon due conviction, if we calculate to avoid another Rebellion in the future," he told his son.[21]

The most illustrious military figure of the Brandywine community died soon after the war ended. Now on inactive duty, Rear Adm. Samuel Francis du Pont (Uncle Frank), had been suffering recurrent spells of choking caused by a stubborn throat ailment. In Philadelphia on Friday morning June 23 he had a fatal seizure and choked to death. His body was brought home to Upper Louviers where hundreds of saddened relatives, friends, and neighbors gathered to express condolences to Aunt Sophie. He was buried the following Sunday with impressive services at Christ Episcopal Church attended by high-ranking naval and army officers who came up on a special train from Washington, and buried in Sand Hole Cemetery, the family burial ground. The mourning period was but a few days gone when Lammot made an announcement that astonished every member of the family, including his closest confidante, his mother.

Lammot announced that he was engaged to be married! The news took everyone by surprise. No one was aware that he had paid special attention to any particular young woman, nor had anyone detected any marriageable female "setting her cap" for Lammot. He was thirty-four years old, looked upon as a confirmed bachelor with no romantic inclinations, and presumably happy to remain so. Brothers Irénée and Bidermann were married and already had young families; brother Fred (Alfred Victor) was still single and would stay a bachelor all his life. Of his three sisters the eldest, Victorine (Mrs. Peter Kemble), had been married since 1849 and now had teenage children; Sophie (Mary S.) the youngest, had married her cousin Charles I. du Pont, Jr., in 1862; and middle sister Polly (Emma Paulina) was unwed and would continue a spinster and companion to her mother the rest of her days.

It can only be conjectured whether Lammot was so wedded to his work and devoted to his widowed mother that he avoided romantic involvements, and this is a reasonable assumption. But, there had been occasions when he had showed interest in the opposite sex. When still in his young twenties, in 1854, he had made some joking allusions to looking for a pretty, rich young wife. Finding none in home territory, he had asked cousin Charles, partner in the Louisville paper mill, what the prospects were in that part of Kentucky, and had received this advice: "You enquire if there are any pretty and rich young ladies here. There may be, but as yet I have not had the pleasure of meeting them. I think the best thing you could do would be for you, after you have had the visit to France I hear is contemplated for you, is to return via Boston and bring Miss Bell Shurtleff with her $120,000 home with you." The only other reference to the Boston heiress was made by Lammot's mother when she informed her daughter Sophie that Miss Shurtleff was engaged to a Coolidge, "True, alas! No hopes for Lammot."[22]

There is an intimation of scandal in some "private news" Lammot passed on to Cousin Charles at this time. Biddy Dougherty, a powderman's widow, while on a drunken spree had charged that her daughter Biddy, a servant girl employed at Nemours, was "with child by one of Mr. Alfred's sons." The mother claimed her daughter had been dismissed by Mrs. Alfred du Pont "on account of us boys, and now she is in the family way. . . . Believe me there is not a word of truth in it," Lammot protested, "that is, as far as I am concerned." He asked his cousin to keep this confidential because no one else in the family except his brother Irénée knew anything about Mrs. Dougherty's allegation. A Mrs.

Bridget Dougherty, widow of Daniel Dougherty killed in the explosion of April 14, 1847, was then receiving a $100 annual pension from the company. She had a daughter named Betty to whom payments from the mother's pension account were sometimes made, but nothing more is heard of Mrs. Dougherty's accusation.[23]

A boating accident in September 1854 had literally thrown five young women into Lammot's arms. One was Charlotte Henderson, who was to marry brother Irénée four years later, and the others were relatives and friends of Charlotte's visiting on the Brandywine. Lammot took them all for an outing on the creek and while he was rowing close to a dam the boat capsized throwing all of them into the water. Cool-headed and a good swimmer, he got them all to shore, frightened and soaking wet but otherwise unharmed. This episode, of course, got into the network of family correspondence and cousin Charles, ever a willing assistant to Cupid, had congratulated Lammot on the exploit. He reminded him that according to the rules of romance, when a young gentleman rescues a young lady from drowning he is bound to fall in love with her. In this perplexing situation Lammot should fall in love with five young women. What a dilemma! "I suppose," Charles observed, "the result will be that you will not fall in love with any of them."[24]

But apparently he did; not right away, for the years 1855 through 1858 had been eventful ones—the Crimean War need for powder, the pace of production in the refinery and mills, the deaths of his father and Uncle Alexis, his trip to Europe, and his work developing Mammoth powder—allowed little time for romance. In the summer of 1859 one of the young women he had rescued, Gertrude Shepard, was again visiting her cousin Charlotte, now Irénée's bride of less than a year, and Lammot's perceptive young cousin Ellen thought he had at last (at age twenty-eight) fallen in love: "I think he has lost his heart. . . . I think he greatly admires Gerty and loves her. . . . I have been on the *qui vive* and think that the affair is far advanced. I do not think it will be anything this time but I hope it may at some future time." Nothing more is heard of this budding romance until Christmas season of that year when Ellen spoke of "Gerty"

as "such a dear little thing. I hope and trust Lammot's admiration will not expire. I think it is quite lively from what I saw of
it last Thursday night." Expire it apparently did, for no further
comment appeared to suggest that Lammot had become Miss
Shepard's suitor.

A letter from Uncle Henry to Lammot in London in January 1862 winding up the saltpeter purchase must have piqued
his curiosity: "A young lady who has been on a visit to the Brandywine has said that it is an earthly Paradise & Mr. Lammot du
Pont a living angel. I hope you will provide yourself with a fine
pair of wings before you return."[25] This was a rare flash of levity
from his usually humorless uncle. Could he have been speaking
of Miss Shepard, breathing warmth into a cooled-off romance by
ranking Lammot among the seraphim? When Lammot made
known in 1865 whom he was going to marry he declared that
he had been in love with his "intended" for four years, proof that
whatever affinity there may have been for Gertrude Shepard had
ended years earlier.

It was the week after Uncle Frank's funeral that he informed
his mother, then Uncle Henry and Aunt Louisa, followed by the
other Brandywine relatives, that he was in love with a neighborhood girl who had accepted his offer of marriage. That the announcement met with qualified approval, mingled with some
misgivings, is evident in the responses of several family members.
First his mother, from whom her second son concealed very little:
"Lammot is engaged to be married! Now, guess, and guess again.
No one had the least idea—not a single individual, and the lady,
I think was as much surprised as anyone. Even sharp sighted
Polly [sister Paulina] had no notion of it. Mary Belin!! I have no
objection but health. She is very delicate & certainly will go into
a consumption. Has had severe hemorrhages & never without a
cough."[26]

Uncle Henry and Aunt Louisa were given the news on a
Sunday afternoon as they departed with Lammot from Upper
Louviers, where they had gone together to pay Aunt Sophie a
sympathy visit. Uncle Henry *"had not the slightest* idea" that his
nephew had been carrying on a courtship right under his nose.
When they recovered their poise, uncle and aunt congratulated

Lammot, assuring him of their best wishes and interest in all that related to him. "He seemed quite charmed with his fate," observed his aunt. "She is a nice, sweet tempered girl." But Uncle Henry may have been annoyed that his nephew had been so secretive, and Aunt Louisa felt it would have been more appropriate if he had delayed the announcement, allowing the family time to "feel less absorbed in the great sorrow [the death of Uncle Frank] which now fills our hearts and seems to leave room for no other thoughts."[27]

Their daughter Lina broke the news to her brother Henry Algernon exclaiming that she was "petrified" by it, just as everyone else was taken unawares. "Few thought he would ever marry, still less the lady he has chosen!. . . Well, the lady is *Mary Belin*!!! He says he has been four years in love—mighty slow affair it has been indeed. There is certainly nothing very new or jubilant in the match, but Mary is a very amiable good girl and except her health there is no great objection to be made." Then, with reference to the du Pont proclivity for consanguinary marriages and marriages within the close-knit circle of friends, she observed that "it is like the squirrel in a cage—we go round and round but never out of the circle. Yet Lammot seems to be very happy and well pleased, and so might all his friends be also."

Aunt Eleuthera was happy for Lammot, offering her best wishes after giving up guessing, at his insistence, who his fiancée might be. But she too was troubled by his fiancée's health: "Mary Belin is so delicate, it makes me tremble to look at their future, but sometimes these delicate people live a great many years after the strong and the healthy."[28]

Who was Mary Belin, Lammot's betrothed, whose precarious health created doubts that theirs could be a lasting marriage? Mary was born into a family from which came three generations of head bookkeepers for the Du Pont Company. Her grandfather, Augustus Belin, whose family had fled the Negro uprisings in San Domingo in the 1780s, held this position from 1823 to 1844. He was succeeded by his son Henry Hedrick Belin, Mary's father, a graduate of West Point Military Academy in topographical engineering, who filled the position until 1865. His older brother was Charles A. Belin, who had been made super-

intendent of the Wapwallopen mills in 1859. Mary was the second of three children born to Henry H. Belin and his wife Isabella,
née d'Andelot. Their first child, Louisa, born in 1836, had died
at the age of twenty-three. Mary had been born in 1839, and a
brother, named Henry Belin, Jr., called Harry by family and
friends, was born in 1843. Brother Harry had graduated from
Yale in 1863 and began a clerkship in the company office assisting his father. He became a friend of Lammot's, a member of the
Home Guard Company, and he took over his father's position in
1866. These business ties were to strengthen into ties of kinship
when Harry married a relative of Lammot's, Margaretta Elizabeth Lammot, and further strengthened now that his sister was
about to marry Lammot.

The Belin home was a roomy frame house located on Smith's
Lane, sometimes called Hagley Yard Road, which began at the
back of Mrs. T. M. (Eleuthera du Pont) Smith's property near
Christ Episcopal Church and wound downhill past Free Park, a
cluster of workmen's homes, into the Hagley Yard, terminating
at the machine shop. Directly across the way from the Belin home
was a small stone building that housed the Brandywine Manufacturers Sunday School, which Mary may have attended as a
child and where as a young woman she assisted Lammot's aunts,
Victorine, Sophie, and Eleuthera, who had been its pillars since
its establishment in 1816. The Sunday School building was the
place of worship for the parishoners of Christ Episcopal Church
from the congregation's organization in 1851 until a new edifice
was erected in 1856 on higher ground at the head of Smith's
Lane. Lammot is said to have contributed to the building fund
with the understanding that windows would be put in the church
spire so that he might climb up and view the countryside when
he was so inclined.[29]

Mary's father was one of the church's organizers, a vestry-
man and also church treasurer, a devotion shared by his wife
Isabella until her death in 1863. Mary taught Sunday School,
played the piano and organ, sang, and directed the church choir.
Among her friends in these and other activities, such as musicales
to raise money for wartime relief, selling tickets for the Sanitary
Fair in Philadelphia, helping at church picnics and suppers, and
going on sleighing parties, were the younger members of the

Brinckle, Osborne, Gilpin, Brindley, and du Pont families. After her mother's death in 1863 she took charge of the household, which included caring for her sickly grandmother, Mrs. Henry Victor d'Andelot.

This proved too much for her and her own health became impaired, a condition noted by her nearest du Pont neighbors, Mrs. Alexis I. (Joanna) du Pont and Mrs. Thomas M. Smith. The former told her daughter, "Mary Belin has had a spitting of blood and could not play the organ." And Mrs. Smith expressed concern because "Mary Belin is too delicate to bear the fatigues of nursing, having had several hemorrhages. Tho' her health is better now than it has been for a long time, still, she has some cough." Her health improved after she was relieved of the care of her grandmother by an aunt who took the elderly lady to live with her. Mary's place in the social milieu of the powder mill community was deftly fixed by Mrs. Henry du Pont soon after Mary and Lammot returned from their honeymoon: "It seems so natural to see Mary Belin everywhere that one does not think of her as his wife."[30]

If Lammot's assertion that he had fallen in love with Mary four years before their marriage is correct, she seems to have been oblivious to it for some time. His first awareness of her in a social way may have occurred in the summer of 1862, when he sent her a formally worded invitation, written while at work in the refinery: "Miss Belin: The pleasure of your company is respectfully requested at Nemours, at 5 minutes of 8 o'clock in the evening, to meet a few friends at a bachelor's soirée. Your bachelor friend, L. du Pont."[31] The invitation was written on July 24, and as no other date was mentioned, presumably the party was to be the same evening, rather short notice for a young lady to prepare herself for an evening in a du Pont household. It may have been a last-minute invitation, forgotten until the eleventh hour, for Lammot was woefully oblivious to social engagements, much to the chagrin of his mother and, later, to the embarrassment of Mary. Signing "Your bachelor friend" suggests that earlier there may have been some lighthearted banter between them about his status as a very eligible bachelor at the venerable age of thirty-one.

Mary's musical talents had her participating in local concerts to raise money for the Sanitary Fair, the funds going to aid soldiers and their families. Tickets for adults cost a dollar, and a half-ticket for children fifty cents. Responding to Mary's solicitation to support the cause, Lammot jestingly replied he would buy a children's half-ticket for fifty cents "as I think that amount would fully represent my musical talent. . . . Enclosed please find 50 cts." The half ticket was sent and it has survived among his papers, accompanied by a thank-you note from Mary.[32] At Nemours, during the years that followed their marriage, music was very much a part of family life with Mary playing and singing, and the children joining in with their voices and instruments.

Few letters written by Mary and Lammot during their courtship have survived; those of an intimate nature were written soon after the announcement of their engagement at the beginning of July 1865. In one note Mary scolded him for dashing off and not staying for tea with her and some visiting relatives; "I am right mad with you and if I had you here would give you a good tickling for punishment." She asked that he stop in to see her early the next day "on *business*; remember I am not hoaxing you. I really have something to say to you. Our friends will hear, rain or shine. P.S. Is this note *too* affectionate?"[33]

Not long after this he took her with him to Wapwallopen to visit her uncle and aunt, the Charles Belins. She remained with them after he returned to Wilmington, a doleful separation for Lammot, according to his cousin Lina: "Lammot took his beloved to Wapwallopen and has returned without her looking very sad, which had caused much amusement."[34] From Wapwallopen Mary wrote him a warm, loving letter, but one that also reflected the latent worry of all women who had loved ones working in the powder business. A recent explosion at Wapwallopen had badly injured a number of workmen, some of whom it was feared would die. This tragedy preoccupied everyone in the Belin household: "Uncle has talked so much about the danger of powdermaking, and the risk that you run that he has made me quite nervous about you, and I shall be afraid to let you come up here anymore. My only hope is that even if you do not care for yourself, for my sake you will not expose yourself needlessly."[35]

Lammot's brothers in Louisville, Fred and Bidermann, were

pleased to learn of his engagement to Mary, whom they knew and liked. Bidermann, happily wed for four years, praised Mary as a home woman, cheerful, affectionate, and domestic, qualities that made a man truly happy. He chided Lammot for taking so long to pop the question; once married he would berate himself as a fool for not having proposed to Mary sooner. With an admiration rarely evident when brother speaks of brother, Bidermann instructed Lammot to "tell her henceforth her life is mutually entwined with the noblest man I ever met." Brother Fred extended his best wishes, concluding, "So you were determined not to be the last; one by one you have all *dropped off* but Polly and myself. Until we meet, accept of all the joy and happiness (one can send in a letter) from the last old Bach."[36]

Mary is nowhere spoken of as the daughter of a company employee, implying she was not of Lammot's economic and cultural class, therefore marrying above herself. The Belins had been a Brandywine family for over forty years, the men holding responsible positions in the company's administration, trusted by E. I. du Pont, the founder, and by his sons, first Alfred Victor, and now Henry du Pont. Time, proximity, and shared experiences had fashioned a friendship between the two families that had nearly obliterated any social distinctions. If any of Lammot's kinfolk had a snobbish, superior attitude toward Mary, no traces of it are to be found in the voluminous flow of letters that passed between them.

In none of the correspondence is mention made that Mary had Jewish forebears. Her maternal grandmother, Isabella d'Andelot, whom she had nursed in 1863–64, was the daughter of Moses Homberg, a prominent Jewish merchant in Philadelphia. Isabella had married Henry Victor d'Andelot, a French sea captain. Their daughter, another Isabella (1813–63), had married Henry Hedrick Belin (1804–91), and Mary was the second of their three children. Sometime in the intervening years adherence to the Jewish faith had yielded to Episcopalianism, an apostasy not uncommon in Philadelphia's Jewish and Quaker families as they became affluent and gained social status. By Mary's time it would appear there was little awareness that she was part Jewish. In the surviving Belin family papers there are no allusions to it, and a similar absence in du Pont papers suggests there was no consciousness of her Jewish background. If it was known, it in no way prejudiced their liking and acceptance of Mary as a lovely, good-natured woman who would make Lammot an excellent wife.

They were married at 11 A.M. on Tuesday, October 3, 1865, in Christ Episcopal Church by the Reverend Mr. Leighton Coleman, rector of St. John's Episcopal Church in Brandywine Village. Coleman, later Protestant Episcopal bishop of Delaware, was cousin-in-law to Lammot, the husband of Frances E. (Fanny) du Pont, daughter of his Uncle Alexis and Aunt Joanna. The church was beautifully decorated with late summer flowers by Fanny aided by another cousin, Eleuthera, and the Brinckle sisters, daughters of the rector of Christ Church and friends of Mary's. Lucy Osborn, another friend, played the organ. In a brief service the Reverend Mr. Coleman read the marriage sacrament exceedingly well; it was impressive and solemn, but not sad. Ranged before the altar with bride and groom were their five bridesmaids and five groomsmen, an attractive wedding party, said Aunt Eleuthera, "and Mary Belin really pretty, which is remarkable because I have never before seen her appear so well." Eleuthera's compliment was echoed by Aunt Louisa. "The bride looked really pretty—better than she ever looked in her life." All the relatives were there except Aunt Sophie, who remained cloistered at Upper Louviers in mourning for her husband.[37]

After fifteen minutes in the narthex receiving the congratulations of their guests, the newlyweds and the bridal party drove into Wilmington to catch the noon train to New York. From there they journeyed north to Albany and then on to Niagara Falls. Taking the entire bridal party with them on their honeymoon was Mary's and Lammot's way of making up for the customary round of prenuptial parties and dinners that had been foregone out of respect for Uncle Frank's death. Mary's bridesmaids were a cousin, Elizabeth Mathieu of Philadelphia; a New Castle friend, Annie Driver; and three cousins of Lammot's, Amelia (Amy), Ellen, and Irene du Pont. The groomsmen were Lammot's brother Fred, his cousin Eugene, Mary's brother Harry, and two cousins on the Lammot side of the family, William Lammot and Edgar Hounsfield. To add to their sightseeing pleasure the bridal couple presented each of the bridesmaids with a pair

The marriage certificate of Lammot du Pont and Mary Belin. They were married on October 3, 1865, in Christ Episcopal Church, Christiana Hundred, New Castle County, Delaware. The ceremony was performed by Lammot's cousin-in-law the Reverend Mr. Leighton Coleman.

Husbands, love your wives, even as Christ also loved the Church.

In the name of the Father, and of the Son, and of the Holy Ghost. Amen.

Being brings together of the grace of life.

This is to Certify, that

Lammot du Pont

And

Mary Belin

Were joined together in Holy Matrimony, on the *third* day of *October* in the year of our Lord one thousand eight hundred and *sixty-five* according to the rites and usages of the Protestant Episcopal Church.

The record whereof is made in the "Register of Marriages" at *Christ Church Christiana Hundred* in the *Diocese of Delaware*

Witnesses:

Leighton Coleman
Rector of *St. John's Church*
Brandywine Village

Wherefore they are no more twain, but one flesh; what therefore God hath joined together let not man put asunder.

Wives, submit yourselves unto your own husbands, as it is fit in the Lord.

of binoculars; what gifts were made to the groomsmen is not known. Lammot took care of all travel and hotel accommodations as host of the wedding party.

After a few days at Niagara they went to Montreal and then on to Quebec, where they toured the old city and the Citadel. Turning homeward, favored by moonlit nights, they went by train to Portland, Maine, thence to Boston and New York, arriving in Wilmington on October 24, ending a three-week honeymoon trip enjoyed by all. Apart from the bride and groom, the two for whom the trip was especially blissful were Lammot's cousins, Eugene and Amy, who immediately upon their return announced their own engagement. "Now," wrote Cousin Ellen, "the last fish on the shore is safely hooked up & there will be an end to the marrying in the family."[38]

Lammot and Mary made their home with his mother and sister at Nemours. The house had been enlarged since its construction when his parents married in 1824 to accommodate their family as it had increased over the years. Since his father's death in 1856 and Irénée's marriage in 1858, Lammot had been the male head of the household, so it was natural for him and Mary to make it their home rather than establish a place of their own. It was to be their home for sixteen years, until late in 1881 when they moved to Philadelphia. At Nemours were born nine of their eleven children, five boys and four girls. In 1868, following the birth of their second child, Lammot's mother and sister moved to a property called Green Hill, a few miles away on the Kennett Pike. They changed its name to Goodstay, anglicizing Bon Séjour, the home at Bergen Point (Bayonne), New Jersey, where the du Pont family had lived for two years after first arriving in this country in 1800.

When they set up housekeeping in October 1865, Mary was twenty-six and Lammot thirty-four years of age. His salary— "yearly allowance"—had been raised from $3,000 to $4,000 in 1863; Uncle Henry apparently saw no reason why marriage should alter this, so it remained at $4,000 until 1871 when, by then a father of three, Lammot was given a thousand-dollar increase. His financial interest in the firm as a junior partner amounted to five shares valued at $20,000 each for a total of $100,000. This

The du Pont wedding party at Niagara Falls, early October 1865. Lammot and Mary are in the center, she in profile.

represented slightly less than one-sixth (16.13 percent) of the
company's capital of $620,000; hence he received a proportion-
ate share of the annual earnings. Brother Irénée held an equal
interest; Cousin Eugene had one share, or 3.22 percent; and Uncle
Henry's twenty shares—$400,000—represented 64.52 percent
ownership of the firm. Some of these shares he held as trustee
for his sisters, silent partners in the company, and as administrator of the estate of his younger brother Alexis. Lammot's income
in 1865 was comfortable to ample for its time. In the next ten
years it was to be augmented by earnings from investments in
outside enterprises and by the rapid growth of the family business.[39]

Chapter VII

New Ventures

L AMMOT'S FREQUENT TRIPS into the anthracite region, his conversations with company agents and mine operators, and, more impressively, the mounting demand for powder to mine the abundant "black diamonds," convinced him there was money to be made in coal mining. In a rapidly industrializing America dependent upon steam power, coal was replacing wood as the common fuel, and anthracite mining was entering a boom period that saw its production increase by ten million tons between 1870 and 1879.[1] Discussions with Uncle Henry and partners Irénée and Eugene put his proposal under careful scrutiny during the latter part of 1865. The profits of the war years provided a cushion of risk capital, and the senior partner's hesitancy about investing surplus company funds in any industry other than explosives was dispelled by November of that year.

THE MOCANAQUA COAL COMPANY

The first step was modest and cautious, not a heavy commitment of funds to a full-scale, major mining operation. Lammot made an agreement with the Shickshinny Coal and Iron Company allowing the Du Pont Company to take out 30,000 tons of coal during the first year at twelve cents a ton from its Mocanaqua mines. The mines were located seventeen miles south of Wilkes-Barre on the east side of the Susquehanna River and about seven miles upstream from the Du Pont mill at Wapwallopen. An assessment of five cents a ton was added for the use of mining equipment and the locomotives, track, and cars that carried the coal to shipping points on both railroad and canal. Output could be increased 10,000 tons annually until the yearly output totaled 100,000 tons, at which time the lease would be renegotiated.[2]

For reasons not entirely clear, but possibly because of a lawsuit brought by a disgruntled shareholder in the Shickshinny Coal and Iron Company, who complained that the lease was not in the best interest of its shareholders, actual mining operations did not commence for another year. In November 1866 the Mocanaqua Coal Company was organized with a capital fund of $70,000 furnished by the Du Pont Company, and Lammot was made its president. Two Philadelphians, Charles Gibbons, an attorney, and George Helmuth, a merchandise broker, subscribed additional capital and were made directors, but their association with the company was short lived. The superintendent in charge of operations at Mocanaqua was Andrew J. Cohen, a Marylander whose fitness for the position very early came into question, though he remained until 1873. The secretary-treasurer was George L. Breck, son of William Breck, a cousin-in-law of Lammot's and the powder company's agent at Wilkes-Barre. In addition to keeping the coal company's books the younger Breck, aided by an advance of $7,000 from the powder company, established a company store to supply groceries, dry goods, and miners' supplies to workmen and their families, a number of whom lived in the nearby village of Hartville.[3]

Coal sales for 1867 amounted to a modest 1,723 tons for $3,142, the four grades produced ranging in price from $1.15 to $2.50 a ton. A considerable part of the year was needed to get the pits ready and to accumulate a supply in storage bins. Some of the coal first mined was sent gratis to the Wapwallopen mill for trial in the powder company's refinery and dry house furnaces, but Superintendent Belin did not think much of it: "It is decidedly an economical coal for I believe a ton would last a year, but the man who has to try to make it burn will stand a good chance of losing his soul by hard swearing. I am not anxious to receive any more until Mr. Cohen penetrates a little deeper in the bowels of the earth and finds a more combustible article."

Dealers in Lancaster and Erie, Havre de Grace, and Wilmington were the first to handle Mocanaqua coal. In Wilmington, Mocanaqua coal was sold by the firm of Foxwell and Gallagher. Lammot was president of this firm; C. Layton Foxwell, agent; and Charles H. Gallagher its salesman. Its letterheads featured "The Mocanaqua Coal Company's Free Burning Lehigh" above the names of three other brands it sold. These and other outlets opened in 1868 account for sales that year amounting to $31,121. Encouraged by this promising upswing, a decision was made to void the leasing agreement and to purchase the mine property outright. Initial purchase outlay and additional expenses incurred in buying more equipment raised the powder company's investment in the mining venture to $155,500 by the close of 1868.[4]

Until the summer of 1868 none of the du Pont partners except Lammot had spent any time at Mocanaqua to observe its operations. The coal venture had been undertaken at his instigation, and it was recognized that he had wide authority over it, so he was virtually left alone to direct it and turn a profit. But now that Du Pont was committed to mining as a secondary venture with a sizable financial stake in Mocanaqua, it seemed advisable that other members of the powder firm should become better informed about it. This may have been the reason brother Irénée visited the mine late in August 1868. The voluble and sometimes excitable Superintendent Cohen showed him around the two thousand-acre property, emphasizing the potential of the mines, which "may pay as well some day as capital invested in gold bound securities at 10%, if not better." To attain this they would have to be enlarged and be well managed, and Cohen was not hesitant in asserting that he was the man who could do it. He was confident Irénée would make a favorable report to his uncle, but he knew the decision would be Uncle Henry's whether more powder money would go into further development of the mines. Cohen urged a visit by the senior partner: "I really think he owes it to me, if not to himself, to see for himself what proportions the 'Baby Moc' has assumed." Uncle Henry was not to be hurried, however; two more years were to pass before he set foot on the Mocanaqua property.[5]

Several conditions in the mining industry began to dampen Cohen's optimism and to erode Lammot's confidence in the Mocanaqua investment. The high prices coal had brought during the war years had dropped drastically in the glutted postwar market, dragging miners' wages down with them. Throughout the coal fields layoffs and strikes occurred, often accompanied by violence. Those who remained at work voiced grievances about pay cuts when their working day was shortened, about hazards in the mines, overcharges on powder and oil they had to buy from the mineowners, and about their "enslavement" to the company store. In the spring of 1868 a number of miners in the Schuylkill district organized the Workingmen's Benevolent Association, progenitor of the United Mine Workers, for the purpose of bettering their lot by united action. Organizers were sent into other areas to talk to miners there about the advantages of unionization.

Companies such as Mocanaqua had to send their coal to market on canal and railroad lines owned by other competing coal companies, usually larger, more powerful corporations. When competition for business sharpened, the latter could squeeze their smaller rivals by raising freight and toll rates, by declaring all their cars and boats were in use, or by claiming breakdowns in

A canal boat manifest, 1869, for shipment of ninety-two tons of No. 2 coal to W. and R. H. Gause, coal and lumber merchants in Wilmington, Delaware.

the system. In the Wyoming–Wilkes-Barre basin, where Mocanaqua was located, transportation facilities were controlled by the Pennsylvania Canal Company, the Susquehanna Canal Company, the Delaware, Lackawanna and Western Railroad, the Northern Central Railroad, and the Reading Railroad, all major coal producers as well as public carriers.

Lammot was first drawn into labor problems at Mocanaqua by a letter he received in December 1868 from a group of miners who signed themselves "The Welsh." They informed him that they had left jobs elsewhere to work at Mocanaqua because Superintendent Cohen had guaranteed them work all through the winter, so they had come bringing their families with them. But they had been at work only a short time when the breaker was shut down, putting an end to operations. When questioned about starting up again, he swore at the men, repeatedly telling them to "Go to Hell!" In restrained but unmistakably direct language they told Lammot that Cohen was not a fit person to supervise a coal mine, and he was a heavy drinker. Cursing them as "Damn Rascals!" he had cut off their credit at the company store and had left for Philadelphia a fortnight before Christmas without paying them their wages. They had been given no indication when work would resume. Politely, they asked Lammot to look into the matter, do what he could to ease their plight, and to take steps to operate the colliery more efficiently.[6]

Lammot's response is not known. There had been few serious disputes in the powder mills to give him experience in handling labor problems. Those that did occur were dealt with by one of the yard superintendents or by Uncle Henry. This was done in firm, positive manner, with the individual workman concerned soon being made aware where authority lay. Yet oral tradition has it that beneath Uncle Henry's arbitrary, gruff manner there was consideration and understanding that had the final outcome of a confrontation less harsh than first perceived. Sometimes it was a transfer to another job; if drunkenness caused the problem the workman was "dried out" by being assigned work on one of the farms, or by assisting masons laying up stone walls around the borders of the company's extensive holdings. But any move to unionize the powder workmen met prompt and steady resistance. This policy was continued by Eugene du Pont, Uncle Henry's successor, and by Lammot's sons and nephews when they took over direction of the company in the early 1900s. In the 1950s a retired powderman recalled that in these years two workmen surreptitiously persuaded others to join them in striking the mills. After two weeks the strike was over and its leaders went to Lammot du Pont II confessing their roles in the affair. The younger Lammot angrily responded, "You're going to do more than confess; you'll never work for Du Pont again!" And, according to the memorialist, they never did.[7]

"The Welsh" at Mocanaqua, however, had not struck; they wanted to work but had been locked out by the superintendent. In Philadelphia for the Christmas holidays, Cohen may well have visited Lammot at Nemours at which time the complaint of the miners probably would have been discussed, but how it was resolved is not known. Cohen's seemingly capricious action may have been a calculated move provoked by Mocanaqua's storage bins being full of coal for which there was no demand. "Coal is a *dead* letter," he informed Lammot in early January 1869. "Damn the stuff! You can't give it away." Overtures had been made to him by other colliery owners to join in a "suspension," to hold back coal from the market and thus create a shortage, a collusion that would presumably benefit all of them in time. But Cohen had little faith in the durability of such agreements—"You know my skepticism with regard to men *generally*." He preferred to act alone rather than make promises he knew he would not keep if it was to his advantage to break them. He was aware that some attempts at controlling the market had earlier been made in the powder business, and they too had failed.[8]

By midyear 1869 the coal trade began to pick up. Cohen reported over 7,000 tons shipped in July, even though the Fourth of July holiday had been turned into a four-day drunken celebration by the miners. The edict of a union leader that all the Mocanaqua miners had to belong to the union, making it a closed shop, had been defied by Cohen and he believed his workmen supported him. "There are," he wrote Lammot, "hundreds of miners that hate union as much as either you or I. . . . This will be the haven for a while at least of all opposed to it." He introduced the "breadbasket" or sliding scale wage schedule by which the miners' wages were tied to the price of coal on a monthly basis, an arrangement that for the time being satisfied the miners. Their average earnings for a sixty-hour work week then ranged from fifteen to eighteen dollars.[9]

The revival of the coal business, accompanied by the improved relations between operators and miners, should have encouraged Lammot to expand Mocanaqua and aggressively seek a larger share of the market. Offsetting these brighter developments, however, was the transportation squeeze put on by the rail and canal companies. As common carriers their charters from the state forbade discrimination, but regulation was lax, so they raised freight rates to levels where the mines dependent upon them could no longer operate at a profit. Rates kept going up as business improved during the year, but by September they had become so extortionate that Lammot declared he was totally disgusted with the coal business: "As we cannot fight either the Reading R. R. or the Delaware, Lackawanna and Western R. R., we have determined to sell out." This was in a letter offering the Mocanaqua mines to the Pennsylvania Canal Company for $860,000. Included were a mansion house, a thirty-room hotel, forty workmen's homes, and Paddie's Run Bridge, a toll bridge across the Susquehanna River linking Mocanaqua with Shickshinny. With some improvements, Lammot predicted the mines could produce 16,000 tons a month, and he prophesied the land would be worth $1,000 an acre within five years. He was ready to sell at a loss because of transportation difficulties, and he wanted to get out of the coal business because it was an embarrassment to compete with rival coal companies to which the Du Pont Company was at the same time selling black powder. The Du Pont Company henceforth would devote all its time and assets to powder manufacture. The offer was declined by the canal company; it already had its own mines, the Susquehanna Coal Company, and it needed its funds to keep this and its canal operations financially sound.[10]

During the next three years Lammot offered the coal property to several likely prospects: to Moses Taylor, long a financier-investor in coal, iron, and railroad companies; to an iron manufacturer, Robert Woolley of Danville, Pennsylvania; to Lewis Landmesser, a speculator in coal lands; and to Franklin B. Gowen, president of the Philadelphia and Reading Railroad Company, parent of the Philadelphia and Reading Coal and Iron Company. With each offer the price dropped and the terms were made more palatable, but there were no takers.[11]

Operations continued at the mines during the time they were up for sale. Tonnage shipped in 1870 amounted to 25,891 tons, and the following year this doubled to 53,603 tons. Daily production in February 1871 reached 200 cars of coal, all of which led to more test borings in search of untapped seams. The explorations were moderately successful, and the results of the various strata readings were forwarded to Lammot by George L. Breck, secretary-treasurer and company storekeeper.[12]

Toward the end of 1872 there was a flurry of excitement when it was reported that traces of silver had been found in the mines. Whether this was a "salting"—the placing of some silver-like material as bait to induce Lammot to invest more heavily in greater development of the mine—can only be guessed. Uncle Charles Belin at Wapwallopen was outrightly skeptical, but he sent Lammot a microscopic specimen of the "silver ore" which had been given to him by someone who firmly believed there were "rich mines of silver at Mocanaqua." Tongue in cheek, he asked that "when the grand development is made of the vast gold and silver treasures, you will not forget your needy uncle." Possibly Lammot had the specimen analyzed and found it worthless, for in a reply to a letter from him his uncle-in-law concluded, "It is very evident your faith is not strong [in silver]. . . . I am afraid you are wedded to paper money."[13] Belin's comment could also have been alluding to the current controversy over demonetizing silver and putting the nation on the gold standard, which occurred early the following year.

In the months shortly before the decision was made to get out of the coal business, March 1873, Lammot struck back at one of the railroad companies whose tactics had crippled the Mocanaqua mines. He took the Northern Central Railroad to court, suing it for damages, in the name of his friend and employee, Charles H. Gallagher. He charged it with discrimination for not supplying transportation facilities for hauling the Mocanaqua coal on the same terms given to other producers, a violation of its state charter. For the two years 1870 and 1871 he calculated Mocanaqua had suffered losses amounting to $123,096. Lammot won the case, bringing this word from Gallagher: "I desire to offer you my congratulations upon the happy termination of your suit against the monopoly, and trust you may now find the coal business more remunerative."[14] The decision certainly gave Lammot some satisfaction even if the damages awarded were minor, yet it was more a moral than deterrent victory for it did not prevent shutting down Mocanaqua.

If the coal haulers had not forced Lammot to go out of business, it is likely Mocanaqua would have succumbed during the severe depression with its attendant labor strife that began in 1873. This was one of the nation's worst depressions, bringing on numerous factory closings and massive unemployment. It was signaled by the failure of the banking house of Jay Cooke and Company in September 1873, and, in domino effect, every segment of the country's economy suffered during the remaining years of the decade. Using the powder business as a barometer to indicate conditions in the basic extractive and construction industries that depended upon explosives, the Du Pont Company sales declined 8 percent in 1873, 3 percent in 1874, and then plummeted another 18 percent in 1875.[15] By 1877–78 it was estimated three million persons were unemployed and that only one-fifth of the nation's labor force worked regularly. Wages were cut 20 to 60 percent, and labor's drive for an eight-hour day was forgotten in the scramble for a diminishing number of jobs that demanded ten hours a day.

During the mid-seventies while efforts were continued to sell or lease it, Mocanaqua remained inactive. Off and on prospective purchasers and lessees were taken onto the property by George L. Breck, who had custody of it, and on occasion by Lammot. A former employee at Mocanaqua, David Richards, who had quit after a dispute with Superintendent Cohen and was now a mine superintendent for the Lehigh and Wilkes-Barre Coal Company, inquired about working it on a contract basis. He and two associates, experienced coal contractors, would put up adequate security if an agreement could be worked out. The mine could be made to pay if managed "in the proper way"—an

indirect criticism of Cohen's management—Richards assured
Lammot. No reply from Lammot has been found, but in other
correspondence it is made clear he preferred to sell rather than
lease the mine.[16]

In early 1876 the coal mining industry began to recuperate.
After months of negotiation, Charles Parrish, president of the
Lehigh and Wilkes-Barre Coal Company, agreed to lease Mocanaqua. The contract stipulated an annual rental of $57,000, with
the option to purchase the property at the end of a year for
$182,500, subject to a bonded debt of $100,000, payment to be
made over a period of five years. The lease appears to have been
renewed annually until 1881, when Parrish bought Mocanaqua
for $285,000. The price at which it sold equaled the figure ap-
pearing in the Du Pont Company ledger showing the amount
that had been invested in the mining property since its acquisition in 1866.[17]

It can be argued that the $285,000 Du Pont sank into Mo-
canaqua could have earned a profit for the company if invested
more wisely elsewhere, so it is incorrect to conclude that the
company got out of the coal business with no loss. It can also be
speculated that the venture might have been more successful if
Lammot had been its resident manager rather than entrusting it
to Cohen and Breck, whose activities he directed at a distance
from the Brandywine. An offsetting factor was his own inexpe-
rience in the coal industry, and though a quick learner, the intri-
cacies of the business, the labor unrest, the damage suffered at
the hands of the railroad and canal companies, and the depressed
business conditions of the 1870s, all militated against the success
of a newcomer striking it rich in a promising bonanza that had
temporarily gone into decline. The Du Pont partners may have
chalked it up to experience, an unfortunate gamble, and they no
doubt closed the books on Mocanaqua thankful that their losses
had not been greater.

THE WILMINGTON AND NORTHERN RAILROAD

Closer to home, from the lower Brandywine valley extending
northward to Birdsboro in Berks County, Pennsylvania, a railroad company organized in 1866 had begun limited operation

as far as Birdsboro in January 1870. This was the Wilmington and Reading Railroad, the culmination of an ambitious plan first projected in the 1840s to stimulate trade and industrial development throughout the valley and to promote Wilmington's growth as a port city. Offering both freight and passenger service over its seventy-one miles of track between Wilmington and Reading by June 1871, it served twenty-five towns and villages, the largest of which were Coatesville and Birdsboro. At Coatesville it connected with the main line of the Pennsylvania Railroad, and at Birdsboro with the Philadelphia and Reading Railroad, over whose tracks it ran for eight miles into Reading.

In these and other communities along its route were fifty-eight manufacturing establishments—furnaces, foundries, rolling mills, cotton and woolen factories, paper mills, grist and flour mills, and the powder mills. Delaware legislation forbade railroads coming within a half mile of powder mills, a safety measure against sparks belched from locomotive smokestacks. Within easy reach of the Wilmington and Reading Railroad were iron ore mines, limestone and serpentine stone quarries, woodlands that yielded timber, and the fertile fields and dairy farms of Chester and Berks counties. The products of these establishments and the supplies they needed could be carried by the new railroad at lower rates and with better service than those offered by existing transportation systems. So proclaimed the company's prospectus of 1869 that had accompanied its offer to the public of $1,250,000 in first-mortgage bonds on which it promised to pay an interest rate of 7 percent. Shares of stock at fifty dollars a share had already been issued to the amount of $800,000.

Special emphasis was placed upon the future of the railroad as a coal carrier. In 1868 the industries and homes in the towns and villages within the valley had consumed over 247,000 tons of anthracite and 54,000 tons of bituminous coal. Wilmington was increasing in population, pushing out its boundaries, erecting more homes, and experiencing remarkable industrial growth. Located principally on the banks of the Christiana and Delaware rivers were the shipbuilding, railroad car building, and car wheel factories; carriage factories, tanneries, fertilizer plants, and machine shops, all consuming coal in the steam plants that powered their machinery.

The Wilmington and Reading Railroad, by its geographical routing and the connections it anticipated making with a number of canals and railroads in the Pennsylvania mining areas, was pictured as a great avenue down which immense amounts of coal would move to Wilmington to make it a busy depot from which coal would be shipped to cities up and down the eastern seaboard. Two steamship companies had recently obtained charters from the state of Delaware and would soon be engaged in this trade. These carriers would get coal to New York and Boston two or three days sooner and at lower cost than by present means. At Wilmington coal would also be transshipped onto the Delaware Railroad, which ran south through the Delmarva Peninsula, with connections into Maryland and Virginia. And there was an assured return traffic of agricultural products, particularly peaches, Delaware's major fruit crop, shipped to northern Delaware and eastern Pennsylvania. Other important connections that would stimulate the Wilmington and Reading's trade were those with the Philadelphia, Wilmington, and Baltimore Railroad in Wilmington (the Atlantic corridor of the Pennsylvania Railroad), and with the Baltimore Central Railroad at Chadds Ford, which connected Philadelphia with Port Deposit, Maryland, on the Susquehanna River.

Coal carried by the Wilmington and Reading Railroad, it was estimated, would earn $198,428 annually. This approximated 40 percent of the company's projected total earnings from all freight and passenger traffic, which were set at $496,419. Operating costs would absorb about 60 percent of this figure, leaving a net revenue of $198,567, just about what the coal trade would earn. This profit would permit the payment of the 7 percent interest on the first-mortgage bonds, plus an appropriate sum to go into a sinking fund, and sufficient left over to declare a 10 percent stock dividend.[18]

The promoters of the valley railroad were manufacturers, merchants, and professional men from Reading, Birdsboro, Coatesville, and Wilmington. The first president was Hugh E. Steele, in the iron business at Laurel Run, Pennsylvania. Directors of the company were Hiester Clymer of Reading; George and Edward Brooke, who had iron works at Birdsboro; C. E.

and J. L. Pennock of Coatesville, machine builders; and Dr. Charles Huston, head of Lukens Steel Company, also at Coatesville. From Wilmington were Charles Warner, in coal handling, building supplies, and shipping; Edward Betts and Evan C. Stotsenburg, foundrymen and toolmakers; Joseph Tatnall, banker and grain miller; and Irénée and Victor du Pont, Lammot's brother and cousin. William H. Hilles, a foundryman in Wilmington was secretary of the company.

The potential value of the railroad was apparent to the Du Pont Company. A siding was put in from the Upper Powder Yard to Du Pont Station (present Montchanin) from which it shipped powder northward to Reading and from there to agents in the coal communities not supplied by the Wapwallopen Mills. Raw materials, kegs, and machinery, which were usually sent from the home mills, went up to Wapwallopen via this route. Shipments of powder to be sent west, which heretofore had been taken by wagon to Coatesville to be put on Pennsylvania Railroad cars, could now get to that junction more quickly and safely on the Wilmington and Reading. In the opposite direction coal for the Brandywine powder mills began arriving from the Mocanaqua mines soon after the opening of the railroad in January 1870.

The passenger and telegraph service the new railroad offered were great conveniences and timesavers to Lammot on his frequent trips into Pennsylvania. It facilitated his visits to a number of the other powder mills located in the coal fields that were Du Pont competitors. With their owners he negotiated agreements on prices, production quotas, division of markets, and, in some instances, part ownership or outright acquisition. This is the story of expansion, consolidation, and the formation of the powder trust, the Gunpowder Trade Association, discussed in a subsequent chapter.

The Du Pont Company's financial stake in the railroad began with the purchase of 1,360 shares of stock worth $68,000 at the time of its organization. By 1876 this investment, added to those of individual members of the family, had increased to $370,400, making them the largest single bloc of owners of the railroad.[19] The value of this investment, however, began declining by the mid-seventies, made starkly real by the failure to pay the semiannual interest on the mortgage bonds when it fell due in April and October 1875. Carloadings had fallen off as industries up and down the valley suffered from the general business slump that followed the Panic of 1873. Hard times hurt the coal business, made more virulent by the violence that occurred at the mines. The optimistic, confident belief that the Wilmington and Reading Railroad would become a major coal carrier turning Wilmington into a bustling entrepôt for its export faded into disillusionment as the depression grew worse. The railroad's gross receipts of $251,496 in 1873 dropped to $193,825 in 1874, and the net earnings for that year amounted to only $7,807, a trifle more than 4 percent of its gross earnings.[20]

This effort to penetrate the coal fields, to divert trade from Philadelphia to Wilmington, and to compete with the area's major coal carrier, the feisty Philadelphia and Reading Railroad, was a challenge its aggressive president, Franklin B. Gowen, could not brook. To Gowen the Wilmington and Reading Railroad was an interloper that had to be eliminated. Late in 1872 he canceled the agreement that had allowed it to run its cars over the eight-mile stretch of Reading Railroad track between Birdsboro and Reading, thus cutting off access to its northern terminal. The Wilmington and Reading responded by putting down its own track between these two points, almost parallel to the Philadelphia and Reading, a move that provoked violence between employees of the two lines and at a cost which the Wilmington and Reading in its weakened financial condition could hardly sustain.[21]

A second tactic to thwart Gowen's intent to shut it out of the coal trade was undertaken by the Wilmington and Reading in 1874 when it made connections with the newly built Berks County Railroad. This line extended forty-four miles in a northeasterly direction from High Junction near Reading to the town of Slatington on the Lehigh River. It ran through farming country and areas containing limestone deposits and slate quarries, resources important to the cement and construction industries. Coal was to be its principal freight, however, for at Slatington the Berks County Railroad took coal brought down from the

Lehigh coal fields on the Lehigh Valley Railroad and carried it to its junction with the Wilmington and Reading at High Junction, where it came down the valley to Wilmington. Freight rates on the Lehigh Valley Railroad were then lower than the Reading's, so the Lehigh coal producers gave it their business. But only for a short time. Again the powerful Gowen was the nemesis who balked this freight connection needed so badly to bolster the faltering Wilmington and Reading.

Inexplicably, the low rates charged by the Lehigh Valley Railroad suddenly shot upward, so much higher than the Reading's that the coal companies in the Lehigh region quickly switched over to Gowen's Philadelphia and Reading. It was suspected that Gowen had threatened Asa Packer, president of the Lehigh Valley Railroad, with cutting off his line's access to Philadelphia by denying the Lehigh Valley Railroad use of the Reading's tracks over which it came into the city, unless Packer helped crush the upstart competitor.[22] The Lehigh Valley Railroad was forced to capitulate, thereby ending the brief prosperity of the Berks County Railroad, pushing both it and the Wilmington and Reading closer to bankruptcy.

Henry du Pont and his partners were fully aware of the Wilmington and Reading's condition and the jeopardy in which this placed their sizable investment. From time to time loans had been made to it by the Du Pont Company to meet current operating expenses. The directorships held by Irénée and cousin Victor were the Du Pont Company's direct ties to the railroad's administration, but their participation in its affairs appears to have been occasional and desultory. In September 1874 it was noted that Irénée was too busy in the powder mills to attend with any regularity the directors' meeting held at company headquarters in Coatesville. Victor's involvement seems to have been limited to legal counsel on such matters as the acquisition of property, easements, damages, and contracts. The closest tie between the railroad's management and the Du Pont Company was Robert Frazer, the Wilmington and Reading's president. Frazer, a Philadelphia friend of Lammot's, was a nephew of Professor John F. Frazer, Lammot's instructor in chemistry and mechanics at the University of Pennsylvania.

In 1875 and again in 1876 the continuing poor state of the economy forced the railroad to default on paying the interest due the first-mortgage bondholders. A group of these, including Lammot, petitioned the district U.S. Circuit Court to have it declared bankrupt and its assets sold at public sale, their plan being to purchase its assets and reorganize the line. A Committee of Purchasers, led by Lammot, was empowered to act as attorneys-in-fact with authority to make the purchase on behalf of the first-mortgage bondholders. Failure to act quickly could result in the assets being acquired by other creditors or by another railroad company, the most likely one being the rival Philadelphia and Reading Railroad. This company owned or indirectly controlled a bloc of the Wilmington and Reading's first-mortgage bonds and a number of its second-mortgage bonds. If it got control of 51 percent of the outstanding first-mortgage bonds it could take over the railroad.[23] This the Committee of Purchasers was determined to prevent.

Through correspondence, personal solicitation, newspaper advertisements, and hired agents, it invited owners of Wilmington and Reading bonds to pool them in its custody for deposit with the Fidelity Insurance Trust and Safe Deposit Company in Philadelphia, its trust agent. The objective was to obtain at least $560,151 worth of the bonds, slightly more than half of the value of the total bonds outstanding, which amounted to $1,120,300.[24]

The Philadelphia and Reading had, of course, created its own pool for the same purpose, and throughout 1876 there was keen solicitation of large and small bondholders by each group to have them join their respective pools. While this struggle was going on, the U.S. Circuit Court formally declared the Wilmington and Reading bankrupt and ordered it sold to the highest bidder. This decision spurred on both factions to secure the majority of bonds needed, and Lammot's papers clearly show that he and the Philadelphia counsel for the Committee of Purchasers, Lewis Waln Smith, were most active in locating and persuading bondholders to join their pool. Their efforts were successful, for by mid-September they controlled $1,053,700 worth of bonds, far in excess of the 51 percent needed.[25]

The defeated Philadelphia and Reading Railroad then made overtures to merge its pool of bonds with those of the Committee of Purchasers, thus creating a joint interest in acquiring the bankrupt line. When the proposal was rejected, it appealed to the courts and a judge ordered a temporary stay of the sale, a stratagem that could mean years of costly delay to Lammot's group. They immediately responded by appealing to the U.S. Supreme Court to have the stay order vacated. The court did so quite expeditiously and ordered the sale to proceed forthwith. On December 4, 1876, the Wilmington and Reading's assets were sold to the Committee of Purchasers for $100,000.[26]

The $100,000 purchase money was raised by the Committee of Purchasers from a number of banks, a first mortgage on the railroad property being given as collateral. To pay off the loan, all those who had pooled their bonds were assessed $6 for every $100 bond pooled and were asked to make prompt payment. With Lammot presiding, the new company, taking the name Wilmington and Northern Railroad, was organized in attorney Smith's office on March 8, 1877. Its capital was $1,500,000, divided into shares valued at $50 each. The holders of the old Wilmington and Reading bonds were thus converted from creditors to shareholders by receiving two shares for every $100 bond formerly held. Lammot and the other members of the Committee of Purchasers became directors of the company, and Robert Frazer, president of the old Wilmington and Reading Railroad, was named president of the new Wilmington and Northern Railroad.[27]

Almost immediately another controversy erupted with the Philadelphia and Reading Railroad, pitting Lammot once more against Gowen. Both wanted to gain control of the Berks County Railroad, the feeder line running between Slatington in Lehigh County and Reading. Its principal freight was coal, but it also carried limestone, slate, and agricultural products. The large coal tonnage it carried for transfer to the Wilmington and Northern at Reading was essential for the latter's survival. But by June 1877 this was jeopardized when the Berks County Railroad was faced with bankruptcy for having failed to pay the interest on its first-mortage bonds for the past three years.

Repeated again was the creation of two bond pools, one directed by Lammot for the Wilmington and Northern Railroad, the other by a Reading banker named Moses Graeff, acting for Gowen's Philadelphia and Reading Railroad. Each sought out the bondholders, located mainly in towns and villages, and on scattered farms throughout Berks and Lehigh counties, persuading them to commit their holdings to the respective pools. The Du Pont Company and members of the family together owned $118,000 worth of bonds, making it the largest bond creditor. This time the Philadelphia and Reading offered a more enticing and safer investment to those it solicited, promising to exchange its own debenture bonds at a ratio of 60 percent for the Berks County Railroad bonds placed in its pool. Lammot's offer of shares of stock in the new company rather than bonds did not appeal to the majority of the cautious and conservative Pennsylvania-Germans who held the bonds of the now bankrupt feeder railroad.[28]

When Lammot learned that the rival pool had acquired $800,000 worth of bonds, more than the 51 percent needed, he hit upon another way to outsmart the Philadelphia and Reading Railroad. He would build a competing line roughly paralleling the existing route, with the same terminals, and serving the same communities as the Berks County Railroad. A surveyor was engaged to study possible routes, survey the most feasible one, and make an estimate of costs. He was pledged to secrecy, for Lammot wanted no one to know what was afoot. A partial survey and report were made in late summer 1878; a range of hills that would need to be tunneled had stopped the surveyor, but he was optimistic about the contemplated route and calculated the cost would be $1,000 to $5,000 for each mile of track laid down.[29]

It is uncertain whether Lammot really planned to construct a rival rail line. The costs, securing a charter, the time needed for construction, the obstructions of the Philadelphia and Reading would put in his way, and other pressing Du Pont Company matters that demanded his attention, all suggest that this was a feint to force Gowen to offer some kind of compromise. Despite the secrecy surrounding his preliminary moves, Lammot assumed that word of his planned rival route would leak out, and if Gowen regarded it as a real threat he might consider it advisable to head it off by proposing that the rival pools merge and work out a mutually satisfactory sharing of ownership in the Berks County Railroad.

Beginning in January 1879, in an exchange of letters and in personal visits, Lammot and Gowen dickered and tested each other in negotiating an agreement both could accept. When a stalemate occurred after several months of talk, Lammot offered to buy all the bonds in the Philadelphia and Reading Railroad pool if it would drop its attempts to obtain the bankrupt line. Gowen's reply was blunt—Lammot should stick to powdermaking and stay out of railroading: "You must remember that we are in the railroad business and you are in the manufacturing business, and we think that where we conflict with each other you ought to give the railroad over to us and let us protect your manufacturing industries."[30]

Lammot was not deterred. He realized that the future of the Wilmington and Northern Railroad depended upon the uninterrupted flow of coal brought to it by the Berks County line, so compromise was preferable to a continued standoff. Through Philadelphia connections he had heard rumors that the Philadelphia and Reading was in financial difficulties, hence might be more amenable to new proposals. Accordingly he submitted another agreement which, with a few modifications, was accepted by Gowen and became effective in November 1879. This called for Lammot's bond pool to transfer its bonds into the Philadelphia and Reading's pool at an exchange rate of $60 for every $100 bond, compensation to be made with the first-mortgage bonds of the new railroad the Philadelphia and Reading would organize to replace the Berks County Railroad. The Wilmington and Northern would get half of all coal destined for Delaware and Maryland's Eastern Shore transshipped from Reading. Other products, such as lumber and pig iron originating north of Birdsboro that had been carried south by the Philadelphia and Reading to Delaware and points south, would be transferred to Wilmington and Northern cars. Seasonal products such as peaches and oysters originating in Maryland and Delaware would be carried north by the Wilmington and Northern to Birdsboro and then transferred to the Philadelphia and Reading to carry them to other points in Pennsylvania and New York State. Both railroads agreed to a uniform schedule of freight rates, and the Wilmington and Northern pledged it would try to keep competing railroads out of Birdsboro and Reading.[31] The line born out of this agreement was named the Schuylkill and Lehigh Railroad.

Lammot acknowledged to a confidant that his pride had suffered by having to accept less than he had hoped for, but Gowen would yield nothing more and this was in the best interests of his bondholders. He noted that he had tried to prolong negotiations, counting on the weakened financial condition of the Philadelphia and Reading to give him an advantage in pushing for more favorable terms. But time was not in his favor. "Having satisfied myself that the day of putting the Philadelphia and Reading into the hands of receivers was not as close as we expected, I tried what terms I could with Mr. Gowen."[32] A year later, May 1880, the Philadelphia and Reading Railroad was declared bankrupt and went into receivership.

The agreement worked out by Lammot was formally signed, not by him, but by Col. Henry Algernon du Pont, his cousin, who had succeeded Robert Frazer as president of the Wilmington and Northern. He had had no active role in any of the railroad negotiations carried on by Lammot to make the Wilmington and Northern a profitable line, thus protecting the Du Pont investment in it. The colonel, unable to shed an imperious air of command fostered by nearly twenty years of service in the army, did not have the temperament needed to work in harmony with the directors of the railroad. Very early Lammot had to act as conciliator and trouble-shooter, as he mentions in a letter to his uncle at Wapwallopen: "I go tomorrow to elect him a new board that he can work smoothly with."[33]

For the next twenty years the Wilmington and Northern provided freight and limited passenger service through the Brandywine region as far north as Reading. Its operations continued modest in size; some short extensions were built and new connections were made, but its earnings were modest. It remained solvent and independent until 1898, when Colonel du Pont leased it to its erstwhile rival, the Philadelphia and Reading Railroad,

Henry Algernon du Pont (1838–1926), Civil War colonel, gentleman farmer, railroad president, and U.S. senator from Delaware.

on a 999-year lease; the colonel had been made a director of the Philadelphia and Reading in 1897. Today the Wilmington and Northern, dubbed the "Weak and Nervous" by a local wag, operates an occasional freight train over limited distances of the track.

WYOMING: SULPHUR BEDS AND SODA LAKES

The mining frontier that had begun with the discovery of gold in California in the 1840s had extended eastward into Nevada, Colorado, Utah, and the Wyoming Territory during the 1860s and 1870s. Along with gold, silver, copper, and lead, deposits of coal, sulphur, and soda were being found in these regions and in Idaho and Montana. A vast territory embracing the slopes and valleys of the Sierra, Wasatch, and Rocky Mountain ranges drew thousands of prospectors and fortune hunters. Speeding up entry into these once remote areas was the new transcontinental railroad that linked east and west when the Union Pacific and Central Pacific railroads connected at Promontory Point, Utah, in May 1869.[34]

Lammot's introduction to the mineral riches of this region came about when he was introduced to a Dr. George B. Graeff, a Baltimore physician who had given up his practice and had gone west convinced that his fortune could be made more speedily on the beckoning mineral frontier. For five years he had prospected through Utah, Nevada, Colorado, Arizona, and Wyoming Territory, first lured on by silver, but he had soon realized there might be richer returns in finds of other metals and minerals: copper, carbonate of soda, sulphate of soda, nitrate of soda, chloride ammonia, muriate of ammonia, and sulphur. Armed with a smattering of knowledge of geology, mineralogy, and chemistry, Graeff was usually accompanied by two hunter-prospectors named Boney Earnest and Tom Sun. His eastern correspondent was an Edward Reilly of New Haven, a man with interests in the Pennsylvania anthracite mines, who brought Graeff and Lammot together in 1875.

The advantages of having domestic sources of sulphur and saltpeter rather than having to rely upon imports from foreign sources were obvious to the Du Pont Company and all other powder manufacturers. They and chemical manufacturers would be the most likely customers of those discovering and developing deposits of sulphur and carbonate of soda. The latter could be treated with nitric acid to form sodium nitrate, and from sulphur ore could be made pure sulphur for black powder and sulphuric acid, which was widely used in dyeing, bleaching, tanning, glass-making, soapmaking, drugs, and fertilizers.

Flushed with optimism but short in capital, Graeff sought Lammot's backing to develop a sulphur deposit he had discovered near the town of Hilliard in the southwestern corner of Wyoming Territory. As a personal investment with no company involvement, Lammot furnished funds to Reilly to travel to Wyoming to buy the supplies and equipment needed and make a thorough assessment of the mine. Samples of the ore he sent back were analyzed by several testing laboratories at Lammot's request, but the results were not promising, the yield of quality sulphur from the ore being only about 50 percent.[35] Further digging on the site by Graeff's men and Reilly indicated that the deposit was a shallow one and the sulphur lower down of poorer quality. Disappointed but willing to gamble a little further, Lammot engaged Irving A. Stearns, a mining engineer he had employed at the Mocanaqua mines, to go to Wyoming to examine the mine and give his opinion of its possible worth.

While in the west Stearns was shown other sulphur deposits and some soda lakes by Graeff and Reilly. The lakes were located in the Natrona Mining District in Carbon County, between Rawlins and Fort Casper. They covered a total area of about fifteen miles and had no visible outlets. The Mormons traveling the Emigrant Road to Utah in the 1840s had examined them and recognized their value. After making their settlement at Salt Lake they had sent work crews with wagons back to the lakes to dig and haul the soda to Salt Lake City, where it was refined for use in a variety of commodities. According to Graeff a new three-inch crust of soda formed on the surface of the lakes each year, and at minimal effort and little expense he speculated millions of tons could be dug out! Impressed by this possibility, Stearns reported to Lammot that mining the lakes might be a more profitable undertaking than working the sulphur mine. Lammot analyzed the samples of soda sent to him and found they yielded 47.61 percent sodium carbonate, which, when calcined, yielded 61.17 percent soda ash, a basic ingredient of glass, soap, and paper. As a check on his own analysis he had the respected Philadelphia firm of laboratory chemists Booth and Garrett make another analysis, and its results showed a yield of 52.23 percent soda ash.[36]

Convinced he was on to something promising, Lammot, in partnership with Stearns and a dealer in Pennsylvania coal lands named Thomas D. Conyngham, organized the Wyoming Soda Company and bought Graeff's claims to the five soda lakes in September 1875. The lakes were given the names New York, Philadelphia, Wilmington, Wilkes-Barre, and Omaha. Ownership of the company was divided with Lammot holding a 40 percent interest, Stearns and Conyngham 20 percent each, and Reilly and Graeff 10 percent each.[37]

Lammot's knowledge of the soda lakes had all come second-

A "soda lake" near Laramie, Wyoming. These lakes were foreseen as sources of sodium nitrate and sodium carbonate for the manufacture of black powder, glass, soap, and paper.

hand from Graeff, Reilly, and Stearns. His numerous other responsibilities had not permitted him to make a trip west, but in
the spring of 1876 he decided he would go. It was a most unpro-
pitious time, for the Sioux Indians and their Cheyenne and Arap-
ahoe allies had taken to the war path and were harassing mining
camps and settlers in the Black Hills of South Dakota seeking
gold on lands which a treaty of 1868 had reserved for the Sioux.
The Indian chiefs Sitting Bull and Crazy Horse and their war-
riors were being hunted by U.S. Army troops commanded by
Generals George A. Custer and George Crook. Lammot learned
of this from Dr. Graeff, who had sought the security of Omaha
from where he wrote cautioning Lammot to postpone his journey: "The Indians are swarming over the whole country, and the
miners in the Black Hills are suffering every day. I had yesterday
an interview with Gen'l. Crook. He is now preparing for another
expedition against them. He will attack Sitting Bull in his fast-
nesses and will continue it until the Sioux tribes are driven to
agree to go to the agencies on the Missouri River—and stay there.
Until this is done we will have no safety."[38]

Lammot waited two months and then wrote to the commanding officer of Fort Fred Steele, the army post nearest the
soda lakes, inquiring if it was now safe to travel in that region.
His letter was dated June 27, 1876, the day after Sitting Bull and
his followers killed General Custer and 264 of his men at the
Battle of the Little Big Horn. Again Lammot was told to stay
away. The commander of the fort informed him that though there
were no Indians near the soda lakes at the moment, the Sweet-
water River valley near the lakes was one of their favorite haunts
and they might suddenly arrive, for they traveled swiftly and could
appear when least expected.[39]

The contemplated trip to the "wild west" met with some
opposition from Lammot's family. He and Mary were now the
parents of five children, all less than eight years of age: Louisa
and Sophie and three boys, Pierre, Henry, and William. Mary
was again pregnant and in December 1876 gave birth to their
fourth son, whom they named Irénée. Mary's brother, Henry
Belin, Jr., expressed the concern of family members: "I hope you
will not think of going out there this fall for it certainly will not

be safe, even if the Indians are whipped in the coming fight. There will still be wandering bands of them about only too glad to have a chance at any white man they may meet."[40]

After hearing from Graeff that Wyoming was now safe, early in October Lammot secured train reservations for himself and Irving A. Stearns from Philadelphia to Rawlins. Some denizens of the City of Brotherly Love proved less than fraternal, for shortly before departure time as Lammot passed through a knot of people at Broad and Walnut streets he was jostled and someone deftly picked his pocket. To Mary in a letter written enroute, he exclaimed, "What do you think, for the first time in my life I have had my *pocket picked*!" Gone with $645 in cash were his keys, baggage claim checks, and some notes. (Elsewhere Lammot noted that during the 1870s he traveled an average of 10,000 miles a year). Not wishing to cancel the trip, he made some quick calls on friends in the city and borrowed over $600. It was a disquieting way to set off; he upbraided himself for allowing his pocket to be picked, but assured Mary he would manage all right.[41]

Upon arrival at Rawlins he engaged wagons and horses, bought tools and provisions and 3,300 rounds of ammunition for ten rifles and a shotgun. Ten men made up the party. Besides himself and Stearns were Graeff and his two men, Boney Earnest and Tom Sun, and five others, "so you can see we were well prepared for any trouble," he wrote Mary. On the way to the lakes the hunters provided the excitement of some promised big-game hunting which Lammot recounted to his wife: "What would you say of your old Hub. [he was forty-five years old] mounting a mustang horse and chasing elk? I thought I had better sense, but alas, not so. We sighted a herd of 14 at ten o'clock of the morning of our arrival and Thos. Sun and self mounted the two spare horses with our rifles and put after them and ran 17 miles, at the end of which time I think the elk had gained, say, 2 miles on us. How I felt the next morning, you can judge, but fortunately I had on my red flannel shirt so no one knew the skin was off my *unmentionable*. Since then I have felt very much like a ramrod." One gets the impression that for the next few days Lammot ate standing up. Their meals would have provided a variety of meat, for they bagged one elk, four antelopes, two blacktail deer, plus some rabbits and sage hens. But not an Indian had been seen. The serious business of the trip had been attended to, however; he would be bringing home many samples from the soda lakes to be analyzed.[42]

At Graeff's urging the trip was extended a number of weeks so that he could show Lammot other metal and mineral deposits, including more soda lakes, in Wyoming and in Utah and Idaho. All that was needed, proclaimed the physician-prospector, was capital: "The wealth of these hills in precious metals," he said, "now looks greater than California ever proved itself," clearly with the hope that it would be du Pont capital that would finance their exploitation. Graeff enjoyed Lammot's and Stearns's company, for they were intelligent and interested listeners and observers with inquiring minds who provided the intellectual stimulation he lacked on his long trips with Earnest and Sun. Letters from Graeff following Lammot's return home expressed gratitude for his kindness and liberal generosity; "I will not ever forget it, and I am glad that I met you." He also conveyed the thanks of Earnest and Sun for the binoculars Lammot had sent each of them in appreciation for the good hunting they had provided.[43]

Development of the soda lakes remained dormant for the next few years as Lammot was kept extremely busy with powder mill matters. As most caustic soda used in this country was imported from Britain, some of its major producers were solicited by Stearns about purchasing the lakes, but with no success. The caustic soda business was in about the same condition as the American anthracite industry—virtually dead, in Stearns's opinion. He encountered similar refusals from chemical concerns in London, Liverpool and Newcastle-on-Tyne; they were not prepared to risk any capital in dubious foreign investments, certainly not in the wild west of Wyoming Territory.[44]

The Wyoming Soda Company remained a paper organization. Between 1875 and 1881 Lammot calculated he had spent $29,475 on the venture, but at the beginning of 1884, in an inventory of his assets, he put a value of $50,000 on the soda lakes. After his death the executors of his estate, combining some coal and limestone holdings he had acquired, in 1899 pooled his

Wyoming properties and organized the Natrona Alkali Company. This was headed by his son Pierre, aided by his uncle Henry Belin, Jr., and Stearns, his father's associate, and capitalized at $500,000 for the proclaimed purpose of developing lands in Wyoming containing deposits of soda, coal, iron, petroleum, and other minerals, as well as timber and farming land. Its headquarters was in Wilkes-Barre, with a lawyer in Cheyenne acting as its resident agent. Annual meetings alternated between these cities for many years; the directors considered offers to lease or purchase its properties, and it regularly paid its taxes, but no funds were spent to exploit the resources it controlled. Periodically analyses were made of the soda in the lakes, but they consistently showed too low a percentage of sodium carbonate to warrant the cost of extraction. Ownership was retained by Lammot's heirs until 1977, when his grandchildren sold the Wyoming properties for the sum of $67,000.[45]

In retrospect it is evident that the coal mining, the railroad, and the soda lakes investments were failures. There are hints that other members of the firm thought that Lammot was too ready to take risks with his own and company funds, but his proven achievements and his stature in the family business may have stilled their doubts about the wisdom of getting into these other enterprises. The post–Civil War years witnessed the organization of many large companies and huge fortunes accumulated in coal mining and railroading. The mineral riches of the montane west were luring another generation of prospectors and capitalized companies to seek the minerals, metals, and other raw materials needed by a diversified, expanding industrial society being created out of a plenitude of inventions, innovations, and striking advances in engineering technology and chemistry. Infected by the optimism created by this surge in so many areas of the nation's development, men of Lammot's innovative and venturesome temperament, impelled by a desire to accumulate wealth for themselves and family, became the promoters and investors in the promising new enterprises.

The reasons for the scant success in some, and the outright failure of other, of the ancillary ventures of Lammot have been already set forth with some specificity—and some speculation—

but the most obvious reason was his overextending himself and taking on too much work in businesses in which he had no experience and scant preparation. And, it needs to be remembered, this was being done after the initial bloom of postwar prosperity was beginning to fade.

In some instances he may have been a gullible victim of misrepresentation, and those on whom he relied for guidance and advice, with the possible exception of the mining engineer Irving Stearns, may not have served him well enough. He could not give adequate time and attention to these other undertakings because he still had the responsibility of supervising all Du Pont operations outside of Delaware. He continued to be the "life of the business" during the years when the family firm was becoming the leading company of its kind in the country.

Chapter VIII

Upgrading Operations and Technological Triumphs

COAL MINING, RAILROADS, and western mineral deposits consumed much of Lammot's time and attention, and they seasoned him in enterprises that provided him with broader, more varied experiences in the business world. They were, however, all subordinated to the family business. His days were spent in the laboratory or machine shop; in the mills; on the cannon-testing range with government ordnance officers; traveling to other powder plants and calling on company agents. Meetings took place in the office with Uncle Henry, brother Irénée, cousins Eugene, and Francis Gurney du Pont, a younger brother of Eugene's. Francis, called Frank by all the family, graduated from the University of Pennsylvania in 1870 and began working in the powder yards the following year. Early in his career he displayed an aptitude for mechanics and chemistry, talents encouraged by Lammot, who became his mentor in all things relating to powdermaking.

A matter that engaged the attention of the partners was the general condition of the powder industry and Du Pont's place in it as revealed in the census returns of 1870. When the reports became available Lammot abstracted all the information pertinent to the explosives industry from *The Statistics of the Wealth and Industry of the United States*, volume three of the *Ninth Census Report*. The summary and comparative figures were given in the aggregate for all powder firms within each state, but as Du Pont was the only powder company in Delaware the statistics for the state pertained to it alone.

Its preeminence in the industry became apparent in a number of the categories covered by the census. Its capital investment of $1,400,000 was nearly twice the amount ($752,900) invested in all fifteen Pennsylvania powder mills, and $350,000 more than that of the five New York state mills. Du Pont employed 318 workers, more than a third of all 893 workers in the entire industry, and nearly double the 184 workers reported in the Pennsylvania mills. The total wages paid annually by Du Pont amounted to $180,000, more than twice the $77,045 paid to all Pennsylvania powdermen, and $60,000 more than the $120,000 paid by the two mills in Connecticut. Forty waterwheels (including turbines) and three steam engines provided power to the Du Pont mills; the next state with most prime movers was Connecticut, which had thirty-three waterwheels and four steam engines.

These figures confirmed the partners' understanding of where Du Pont ranked in the industry, and it was satisfying to know that it was maintaining its established role of leadership. Yet there were some disquieting conclusions to be drawn from other groups of census statistics. The total value of its annual output of powder was only third with a total product value of $737,800, outranked by Pennsylvania's $873,000 and Connecticut's $761,000. This could be explained if it was known whether the mills in these states turned out a significantly larger proportion of sporting and hunting powder than blasting powder, for these powders sold at considerably higher prices than blasting powder. Breaking down these totals to ascertain the value of powder produced by each workman revealed that Du Pont workers were the least productive in the industry. Each man produced an average of $2,320 worth of powder annually, a very poor performance when compared to the California powderman's average of $7,020. In all other states individual productivity was well above that of the Brandywine powdermen; even Pennsylvania's workmen, next lowest in individual productivity to Du Pont's, turned out an annual average of $4,740 worth of powder, better than twice the Du Pont output. There was a very rough correlation between the wages paid to workmen and their individual productivity; California workmen received an average annual wage of $858, Du Pont workmen an average of $566, and Pennsylvania workmen $419, the lowest wage in all the states.

Equally disturbing was another census disclosure. In a column that showed the value of powder produced for each dollar of capital invested the Du Pont Company had the lowest return, a mere 52¢; this was about half of California's return of $1.02, and well below Connecticut's $1.20. A similar shocking figure appeared in another category showing the percentage of gross profits earned on the amount of invested capital. Du Pont had a 22 percent return compared to California's 61 percent and Ohio's 59 percent. Again Du Pont ranked at the bottom. Even when making allowances for probable errors and incomplete data upon which these conclusions were based, it was clearly evident that the family business was not operating efficiently and changes were necessary![1]

Where to start to look for the causes of what seemed the key deficiency—the low output of the individual workman in the Brandywine mills? Were 318 too many workmen on the payroll when measured against total production? Were the pruning of surplus help and tightening up of the work habits of those retained the first necessary steps? Young Frank du Pont, now on the job about a year, submitted his suggestions to Lammot for the "Reorganization of Hagley Yard." In these he characterized the workmen as "a set of lazy rascals who think themselves hard worked to do ¼ hour's work out of every hour," and they were paid twice what they were worth![2] It is doubtful if Lammot fully shared his cousin's harsh and immature judgment, for he knew most of the workmen personally, and the younger man did not. He believed the real cause for the low output was a now obsolete system of production that wasted time, effort, and money.

For seven decades the mills in the Du Pont powder yards had been built, rebuilt after explosions and fires, modified, and sometimes converted to a different use. Each step in the process of making powder took place in a different mill, and each mill, for safety reasons, was located a distance from its neighbor. Mills with power-driven machinery had to be located between the raceway and the creek to receive the water that turned the wheel or turbine that drove the mill machinery. Mills where all work was performed manually could be placed at any suitable location. Some of the older mills of both types had been changed over to powdermaking from such earlier uses as a sawmill, a slitting mill, a gristmill, a carpenter shop, and a cotton spinning mill, all of which had been on the property when acquired by Du Pont. Locating a new mill was determined by its power needs, and with an eye to its vulnerability if a neighboring mill exploded or caught fire. Trees were allowed to grow between mills and others were purposely planted to serve as barriers against hurtling stones and shattered machinery. Paths and roads, some carrying a narrow-gauge track on which flatcars and boxcars could be pushed or pulled by horses, mules, or men, linked the mills together. Safety, proximity to waterpower, the use of already existing structures, and the pervading influence of habit and custom had established the flow pattern in the Du Pont yards; it was one of meandering and uncoordinated movements and frequent backtracking wasteful of time and energy as men and materials moved from one building to another. The loss in time, the duplication of human effort needed to shift materials so often, and the frequent delays when a mill was not ready to receive materials, all these factors convinced Lammot that here could be a major reason for the high cost and low productivity of the plant.

Along with other expanding companies in the dawning era of big business, Du Pont was experiencing growing pains. Its internal operations had become chaotic, confused, and wasteful. Lammot was one of a number of business managers who early began to seek ways to eliminate these faults in order to achieve a more systematic, coordinated pattern of production.[3]

Altering these long-established work patterns with which everyone had become comfortably familiar over the years would require drastic change. The mills that ran on waterpower had to stay at the water's edge; the greater flexibility of location that steam power would allow did not, in Uncle Henry's mind, outweigh the hazards it presented. Moving mills to other locations to create a systematic, sequential flow of materials was out of the question for many of them had stone walls three to five feet thick, and with deep foundations. And to change the machinery within a mill to perform a function for which the building had not originally been designed was prohibitively expensive and would halt production for too long a time. In short, the plant's layout was becoming obsolete when compared with the newer plants of competitors. A later generation of owners would have bulldozed

ADAMS-SON
N.Y.

The Upper Yard, 1876. An artist's view of the home plant at the time of the centennial. Residences and farm buildings are on the higher land, refinery and charcoal houses on the slope, and the mills for processing powder at creek's edge.

or blown up some of the mills, then put up new ones of lighter and cheaper frame-and-sheet-metal construction, and then arranged them in logical on-line sequence as the process dictated so that materials could move through each step with a minimum of wasted time and effort. But this was 1872; the terms *systematic management* and *production line* had not yet appeared in America's industrial vocabulary; and traditional habits were deeply ingrained. Lammot realized that proving to Uncle Henry that the existing procedure was inefficient and costly was a formidable challenge. It would require a precise description of steps in the process, supported by incontrovertible statistics to show just how inefficient it was.

He set out to do this by first focusing on only one aspect of production, the amount of energy expended by workmen, utilizing animal power and the railway system, to convert 10,000 pounds of raw materials into blasting powder in the Hagley Yard mills. Carefully he measured the distance the ingredients that had to be moved between each mill and the heights they had to be lifted and distances rolled, beginning at the refinery and ending with the finished kegged powder in the pack house. His memorandum indicates that he planned to follow up his "distance and weight" study with one in which he would observe the specialized tasks performed by each class of powdermen in the individual mills where a particular operation was performed. Other matters intervened, however, and this follow-up study was never made. What is noteworthy about this analysis made in 1872 is that Lammot's careful "study of work" was anticipating by two decades the spirit and aims of Frederick W. Taylor, the recognized pioneer in the development of "systematic shop management" and "efficiency engineering" that became the foundation for establishing production standards for men and machines beginning in the late 1890s.

Interpreting this mass of figures compiled from observing the 112 separate movements of materials from refinery to keg mill led him to conclude that a reasonable daily output per worker should be 100 25-pound kegs of powder. Actually it was less than half that amount, sometimes far less. In short, efficiency in the Hagley Yard mills ranged below 50 percent of what should be expected.[4] It has to be assumed that Lammot reported his findings to Uncle Henry and his partners, but nothing has been found to indicate that it resulted in any changes of long-established procedures.

A very significant adoption, though one not mentioned in Lammot's study, was the greater use of steam power in the mills. The 1870 census had shown that there were only three steam engines in operation, but a few years later, when Lammot inventoried the prime power movers in the yards, he listed ten.[5] It had taken nearly twenty years to go from the one engine that Lammot had installed in the refinery about 1852 to three in 1870, so the addition of seven more within the next four years has to be regarded as an accomplishment. It also signaled Uncle Henry's waning resistance to what he judged to be a dangerous innovation. The uncertainty of waterpower, due to the vagaries of weather that caused either high floods or low water or froze the Brandywine, made it an unreliable source of power that too often forced the closing down of the mills. The realization that this increased production costs, at a time when costs were being carefully scrutinized, possibly accounts for Uncle Henry's change of mind about adopting more steam power. Ten years later (1884) he approved a plan to erect a large steam-power plant to operate a number of Hagley Yard mills. This was built and equipped under Frank du Pont's direction. Had Lammot lived six months longer he would have taken particular satisfaction in seeing this signal achievement of his capable assistant.

Whatever innovations were proposed, whether in new types of power or in methods and machinery, had to pass rigorous tests of safety before they were adopted; anything less would have been courting disaster. Invariably it was Lammot, sometimes with Irénée, who worked the new machinery until it was thoroughly tested and the millmen fully acquainted with its workings. "He and Irénée trying out an experimental machine to see if it was safe before allowing the workmen to run it was a common sight, and one quite characteristic of the Brandywine mills," recalled one of the men who worked under his direction.[6] Change, though usually distasteful to Uncle Henry, was approved by him, when urged by Lammot, because he had strong faith in his nephew's

good judgment. Yet with all this preliminary testing and enforcement of safety rules, machines did break down and explosions
and fires took their toll. An account of all the accidents in the
mills since their founding up to the 1870s was compiled by Lammot. All of the known facts about each accident and what was
believed to have caused it were noted. For those occurring during his own years in the mills, he added his opinion as to how
they might have been prevented. This record was picked up and
continued by cousin Frank beginning in 1871 and carried through
1902.[7]

At the time Lammot was making his study to determine the
efficiency of operations in the Hagley mills, the Du Pont Company had to deal with another matter that was to test its technical
competence. This was of such importance, vis-à-vis its role as a
supplier of powder to the army and navy, and demanded so much
of Lammot's time and attention, that he was compelled to put
aside all other matters.

In June 1871 the Navy Department had ordered a thousand
barrels of Mammoth powder (100,000 lbs.). This was the very
dense, large-grain cannon powder that he and Capt. Thomas J.
Rodman had developed for use in the 12- and 15-inch guns shortly
before the Civil War. With their surpluses of wartime powder
much reduced, the ordnance bureaus of the army and navy were
now concerned with obtaining an improved quality of Mammoth powder that would perform with unfailing consistency in
their big guns. Though Mammoth was clearly superior to all other
types of large-caliber powder, recent test-firings had resulted in
such wide variations in initial velocity, in the pressure on the
barrel of the gun, and in the distance the projectile was hurled,
that ordnance officials were not satisfied with its performance. A
recent congressional inquiry into the nation's readiness in the
event of war had brought charges that the powder experts in the
ordnance bureau were not keeping pace with the improvements
being made in the manufacture of large guns. Bureaucratic leth-
argy, if such was the case, was prodded into action by civilian
criticism.[8]

The Navy Department specified that 100 pounds of powder
should hurl a 450-pound projectile at an initial velocity of 1,500

feet, plus or minus 25 feet, and exert no more than 20,000 pounds pressure per square inch on the barrel of the gun. Before filling the order Du Pont was asked by the Ordnance Bureau to carefully analyze the qualities of its raw materials, experiment with their proportions, and modify its manufacturing procedures wherever it seemed such changes would produce a powder that would meet these specifications and give consistently uniform results. Sample batches of powder were to be sent to the navy's testing laboratory at Annapolis and to the army's firing range at Fortress Monroe in Virginia. If the ordnance officers were satisfied with the results, Du Pont would be notified to go ahead and fill the order based upon the sample batch of powder that satisfied the standards they had set.[9]

This effort to improve Mammoth powder was not to be conducted solely by Du Pont but was to be done in cooperation with an Ordnance Bureau officer. The obvious choice would have been Capt. Thomas J. Rodman, but Rodman had died in 1871 and the assignment went to Lt. Comdr. J. D. Marvin, an inspector of ordnance. Marvin had recently returned from Europe, where he had visited arsenals, ordnance works, and powder mills on a special project for the navy. His superiors considered him well qualified to undertake his new assignment and dispatched him to Wilmington in August 1871.

Marvin arrived at the mills anticipating that some preliminary work had already been done, but he was informed that all experimental work of this kind was conducted by Lammot, who was away on a trip and would not return for another week. "Lammot du Pont," he informed his superior, "is pointed to by the other members of the firm as the man who knows everything and who always has charge of all government work." While awaiting Lammot's return Marvin spent some time observing what was done in the refinery and the other mills. His first impression was not good: "From what I can gather I infer that 'rule of thumb' plays a far greater part in the manufacture here than in many of the government works I have visited," presumably those he had recently seen in Europe. In reply, his superior officer reminded Marvin, "You are engaged in a very important work, i.e., to determine how far it is within the power of the manufacturers to produce uniform results by 'rule of thumb,' and how far science may direct and control [said] 'thumb.'"[10] This was a challenge to Lammot's theoretical ideas and technical abilities, and for the next five years he gave much of his time to this task. The record of this work testifies that his approach was much more scientific than traditional rule of thumb.

Marvin worked closely with him and with Eugene and Frank observing, discussing, posing questions, making suggestions, and testing the finished powder samples. Also, for the first time in company history an outsider was hired to do work usually done by a family member. This was William H. Chadwick, a chemist Lammot hired to help in the laboratory and to assist in the experimental work. A small building was made available to Marvin which he used as an office and laboratory where he could work independently, utilizing an array of instruments furnished by the Ordnance Bureau. Here he conducted some experiments on his own, with this reciprocal understanding between himself and his hosts: "The Messrs. Du Pont say they will make all the small samples I choose to ask for, free of charge, if I will give them the results of whatever experiments I may try with them—a proposition I am very glad to consent to." His reports reflect a hardworking officer, ready to go into the mills to observe operations, sharing the same risks as the workmen, and willing to get his hands dirty when necessary.

Early in his stay, which stretched out intermittently over several years, after watching the men at work in the press mill, Marvin reported that "the Du Pont presses enable the manufacturers to produce powder in greater quantities at lower rates than any others in the world, I suspect, and therefore are the best to employ in making powder for commercial purposes. Naturally they are in high favor here, for out of an annual production of 12,500,000 lbs. the government orders are mere drops in their financial bucket."[11] Production of blasting powder on such a large scale did not require the careful control necessary to guarantee military powder that would meet government standards of quality and uniformity. Subsequently Lammot changed the pressing operation in a way that overcame this criticism.

By early summer 1872, after testing a number of sample

batches of powder, each somewhat different in formulation and method of manufacture, the navy gave its approval to go ahead and fill the order for a thousand barrels. These samples had first been test-fired on the company's own firing range located about a quarter mile west of Lammot's home before submission to the Ordnance Bureau, and they seemed to meet all navy specifications.[12] When ready, Du Pont was to ship 500 barrels to the navy magazine on Ellis Island, New York, 300 barrels to Fort Mifflin, Philadelphia, and 200 barrels to the navy magazine in Washington, D.C. The Navy accepted the powder even though its tests showed that the pressures on the gun barrel, on the average, were in excess of its stipulated maximum of 20,000 pounds per square inch. For this failure to fully satisfy its standards, the Navy Department felt justified in asking Du Pont to bear the costs of shipping the powder, which it did willingly. The company's charge for the 100,000 pounds amounted to $23,151, or twenty-three and a fraction cents a pound.[13]

Lammot and Marvin were disappointed that the months devoted to this project had failed to meet all government specifications. Somewhere in their work they had made a "blunder," Lammot noted. An opportunity to find out what the blunder was came about the same time the navy powder was being shipped out. This was an order from the army for a thousand barrels of Mammoth powder with the same specifications as the navy order. Again Du Pont was asked to first prepare samples of powder made with varying proportions of raw materials, and with the addition of other ingredients if experimentation indicated they might improve its performance. Every step, from the preparation of the raw materials through each successive phase of manufacture, was to be reassessed, and where innovations and changed techniques appeared promising they should be tried and the results carefully noted. Lammot kept a careful record of all the experimental work done for these orders and made copies of it for the Ordnance Bureau. Marvin was instructed to stay at the mills and continue as consultant and collaborator in this second attempt to produce the desired quality of powder needed for the large guns.[14]

Of the raw materials, charcoal received first attention. A

Analysis of gases from gunpowder. A page from the laboratory notebook of Lammot du Pont describing the procedure and apparatus used to determine the gases released when black powder is detonated.

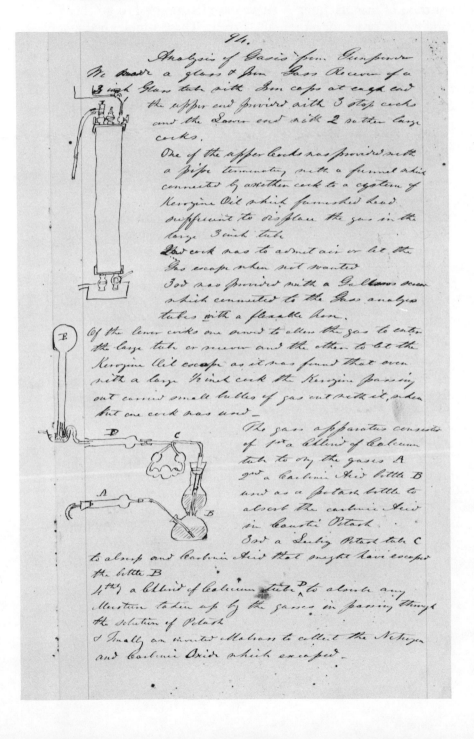

94.

Analysis of Gases from Gunpowder

We made a glass & Iron Gass Receiver of a 3 inch Glass tube with Iron caps at each end the upper end provided with 3 stop cocks and the lower end with 2 rather large corks.

One of the upper Corks was provided with a pipe terminating with a funnel which connected by another cork to a cystern of Kerosine Oil which furnished head sufficient to displace the gas in the large 3 inch tube

2nd cork was to admit air or let the Gas escape when not wanted

3rd was provided with a Gallows screw which connected to the Gass analysis tubes with a flexible hose.

Of the lower corks one served to allow the gas to enter the large tube or receiver and the other to let the Kerosine Oil escape as it was found that even with a large ½ inch cork the Kerosine passing out carried small bubbles of gas out with it, when but one cork was used —

The gass apparatus consisted of 1st a Chlorid of Calcium tube to dry the gases A 2nd a Carbonic Acid bottle B used as a Potash bottle to absorb the carbonic Acid in Caustic Potash

3rd a Leibig Potash tube C to absorb any Carbonic Acid that might have escaped the bottle B

4thy a Chlorid of Calcium tube P to absorb any Moisture taken up by the gasses in passing through the solution of Potash

& finally an inverted Matrass to collect the Nitrogen and Carbonic Oxide which escaped —

number of different kinds of willow and other woods were burned—really distilled—and branches varying in size and age were packed into the kilns in different ways, and charred for varying lengths of time. "Red" charcoal and "black satin" charcoal were produced and their characteristics and effectiveness compared. Descriptively and statistically Lammot evaluated each experiment and gave an opinion on which method had yielded the best results. In conjunction with this work on charcoal he made a survey and count of the willow trees growing in the three powder yards and their immediate vicinities, classifying them as to which were healthy, which were decaying, and which were dead. He noted that the company no longer sent out its own crews of experienced willow cutters in the spring but instead was buying from outside suppliers, a practice he did not like, for it lessened the company's control over the quality of this essential raw material.

Breaking with the centuries-old formula for black powder, Lammot added such substances as sulphate of potash and paraffin to the usual ingredients, trying to find out if these would make the powder burn more slowly and reduce its pressure, while at the same time achieving the desired initial velocity. The results were negative, pressure increased and initial velocity dropped too low. He ran the rolling mills which mixed the ingredients at different speeds and for varying lengths of time, and put in carefully measured amounts of water to get varying moisture contents, hoping to determine which yielded the most thorough, homogeneous mixture of the powdercake. Some batches of powder were rolled on damp, humid days, others on hot, dry days to measure the effects of humidity on the powder mixture.

In the pressing of the batches of powdercake a different degree of pressure was applied to each batch and the pressure maintained for differing lengths of time. Here the purpose was to see which technique would give the powder the desired specific gravity of 1.755. To obtain uniform results, Lammot reasoned that each individual grain should be of uniform density throughout, and he knew this was not being obtained with the type of press plates being used. Powder pressed between plates with perfectly flat surfaces did not receive the same degree of pressure around the edges as that at the center of the plate. Correlated with the problem of obtaining uniform density was the need to determine what shape of grain would present the maximum surface area at the moment of ignition; when solved, the two should assure uniformity in combustion and pressure, so the answer seemed to lie in the design of the surface of the press plates. As it finally turned out, this proved to be the key factor in producing the quality of cannon powder the armed forces were requesting.

After considerable mathematical calculation to determine the surface areas of several sizes of spheres, squares, equilateral triangles, and hexagons, Lammot concluded that a hexagon was the optimum shape for a powder grain. Each plane or facet of it received equal compression, hence it was uniform throughout in density, and it presented the maximum surface area to the igniting agent when fired. With Eugene's help he designed new plates and had ten pairs of them made of brass fashioned at the foundry of Pusey, Jones and Company, Wilmington machine makers and shipbuilders. The entire surface of each plate was stamped with dies in the shape of a dodecahedron, forming a mold with raised ribs. After being pressed between these wafflelike plates the sheets of powder were removed and broken up, the break or fracture lines occuring along the thin edges made by the raised metal ribs. This resulted in grains that were hexagonal in shape in cross section, and after a series of successful test-firings Lammot and Eugene applied for a patent on their new press plate. This was granted, Letters Patent No. 133,522, on December 3, 1872.

Glazing techniques were also reexamined; the amount of powder glazed at one time was varied; the speed of the glazing barrel and the length of time each batch was tumbled were changed with each run, and the quantities of black lead added to coat the grains were altered with each batch. No less than seventeen experiments were tried to determine the best way to dry powder. In one, hot, dry air was blown over it, and in another the air was blown beneath the cloth-bottomed trays that held it. Drying the powder over sulphuric acid in a vacuum and over sulphuric acid in a bell glass receiver were other experiments. Powder trays were shifted to different locations in the dryhouse, some nearer the source of heat, others at measured distances from it. The relation between ventilation and the moisture content was measured in several ways, and drying under different weather conditions was also tried. The old method of open-air drying in sunlight was discarded because of the excessive amount of labor involved and the uncertainty of weather changes.[15] Even the oak barrels in which the powder was to be packed received attention, Lammot specifying that only older, well-seasoned, thoroughly dry oak barrels be used rather than new ones that still had some natural moisture in their staves and heads.

Three batches of powder, each differing in details of manufacture from the other, were test-fired over a period of months during 1873 at the army's testing range at Fortress Monroe. The hexagon-shaped grains fully satisfied all the ordnance specifications of initial velocity and pressure, and gave more consistently uniform results when tested against the older ball-shaped Mammoth powder. In their final form the hexagon-shaped grains were reddish in color, an inch and a half in diameter, and an inch thick with a small hole running through the center; in general appearance they resembled the nuts on a wagon wheel. The army's 1,000-barrel order was filled with the new powder. In November the navy hurriedly followed suit and placed several orders for hexagon powder in anticipation of possible war with Spain over the Cuban struggle for independence.[16]

Upwards of two more years were spent in efforts to perfect and firmly establish the uniform performance of Hexagonal Powder. Lammot stayed with it doggedly, telling his nephew William Kemble, now working at the Wapwallopen mills: "I am still pounding away at my experiments, and have still hopes of success, but the job gets bigger instead of smaller." A few weeks later he made this comment on his progress: "Am busy yet with our experiments, and pressed this afternoon the first lot of new powder (140 kegs) made on a working scale. It will take not less than *2 weeks* to examine it.[17]

Periodically orders came from the navy for 100-barrel lots of the new cannon powder, to be made according to a formula "now known to you as the 'Navy Standard' as to materials, proportions, and manufacture." Finally, in the spring of 1876 the company received this accolade from the chief of the Navy Ord-

Mathematical calculations (from Lammot du Pont's "Notes on Pellet Powder") to prove that hexagon-shaped grains of powder were the most effective for use in large-caliber cannon.

themselves would be comparitively soft.

To avoid these surfaces we must confine ourselves to a figure, which will form a complete surface
These are the Equilateral triangle, Square, and Hexagon.

Let us see what the ratio of periphery of these figures are to their areas

			Periphery	Area
we find in Equilateral triangle circumscribed by $\frac{3}{4}$ circle	"	"	1.95 inch	.183
Square	"	"	2.12 "	.281
Hexagon	"	"	2.25 "	.365
Circle	"	"	2.35 "	.442

From which we see the Hexagon, is much nearer the Circle then any other figure

Hence the horizontal section of these granules should be a Hexagon — and the ribs should be of such a size

as would make the vertical section an Octagon, or the angle a b c should be a right angle and the length of a b should be .2929

What would be the initial surface of this powder when of a Sp. Gravity of 1731

We have $O'k = .375$ or Radius of $\frac{3}{4}$ in circle

$dg = .375$ (one side of inscribed Hexagon) and the area of this inscribed Hexagon $= .365$

$$OZ = \frac{Ok}{\sin O'kO} = \frac{.375}{\sin 22.5° k} = .38258$$

and $dc = 1$ side of Octagon when circumscribed radius is .38258 or $dc = .2929$

and $dk =$ side of small Hexagon $= .1464$

Then Surface of one Granule =

$= 6 \times efgh + 12\, dghi + 2\,($ area small Hexagon of which hi is a side $)$

$= 6 \times .375 \times .2929 + 12 \left(\frac{.375 + \frac{.2929}{2}}{2} \right) \left(\sqrt{(.2929)^2 - \left(\frac{.375 - .1464}{2} \right)^2} \right) + 2\,(.1464)^2 \times 2.598$

$= .659 + 12\,(.2607 \sqrt{.07273}) + 2\,(.0559)$

$= .659 + 12 \times .0703 + .1118$

Or surface of one Granule $= 1.6142$ inches

How many granules to the pound Sp. Gravity of the powder being 1731.

nance Bureau: "The Bureau has lately received from the Naval Experimental Laboratory the reports of the experimental firings of your G. G. Hexagonal. From these it congratulates you on the success you have reached in this powder, and thinks for Naval purposes a better cannot be made." Even in the 100-pounder Parrott rifles the entire charge was burned and gave excellent velocities with low pressures.[18] For the next several decades, until guncotton and smokeless powder were perfected, America's armed forces relied upon Hexagonal Powder for use in large-caliber guns. It was an achievement hard won through repeated trials that demonstrated Lammot's persistence and innovative cast of mind when confronted with difficult problems. The record of his work affords ample evidence that his lively intellect, schooled in physics, chemistry, and mathematics, rejected any "rule of thumb" approach and tackled these problems with a mind molded in scientific discipline.

Lammot du Pont's labo-
ratory. This laboratory-
workshop stood a few
yards to the rear of
Nemours and overlooked
the powder mills below.
It has been reconstructed
and furnished by the
Hagley Museum with
equipment, apparatus,
and chemicals used by
Lammot.

Chapter IX

Competition, Consolidation, and Control

A LETTER from uncle Charles Belin at Wapwallopen to Lammot early in 1870 contained a comment that epitomized the nature of industrial competition prevailing during the last third of the nineteenth century: "I do not think it requires much discernment from anyone to see that centralization is the order of the day, the manufacture of gunpowder included. The control of the coal trade in the hands of a few is already very clearly developed. Financial matters are like military operations, the bigger force runs the day, the small fry will have to clear the track or go to the devil."[1]

This blunt Darwinian dictum was written at a time when there was intense competition among powder producers for the lucrative trade of coal mining companies in the Pennsylvania anthracite district. During the Civil War years a number of small powder mills had been erected close to the mines, and in the postwar years their owners were fighting to retain their business at a time when the market was glutted. The large producers such as Du Pont and the Laflin and Rand Company, which had mills at Kingston and Newburgh in New York State, were also seeking a greater share of the mining business. To achieve this meant the control or elimination of the smaller companies either by drawing them into a cartel, by purchasing them, or by resorting to measures that could force them out of business.

These were the tactics being used to "consolidate" such major industries as oil, steel, sugar, tobacco, whiskey, meat packing, and the railroads. The resulting transformations in size, structure, and methods of business caused the latter decades of the century to be dubbed "The Era of Big Business." To the roster of the industrial giants who were shaping the country's economic future—Rockefeller, Carnegie, Gould, Vanderbilt, Swift, Drew, Havemeyer, Hill, Huntington, and Morgan—the name of du Pont was soon to be added. The planner and executor of the means by which his firm came to dominate the explosives industry was Lammot. The coal region was a primary objective, but concurrent with this was a move toward self-regulation of the powder industry nationwide, and here again Lammot was the moving spirit.

Aggressive entrepreneurs striving for greater power and profits had neither qualms nor doubts as to the right and propriety of the methods they used to secure a dominant place in their particular industry. In common with other businessmen the du Ponts were not restrained by ethical or moral strictures from using their advantages of size, financial resources, technical superiority, and clever negotiating skills. Had they consciously articulated a philosophy to guide their actions they would have affirmed the time-honored ideals of hard work, ambition, thrift, ability, and foresight as the keys to success. The comfortable maxims of Benjamin Franklin's "Poor Richard" and the laissez-faire teachings of Adam Smith, buttressed by the Darwinian thesis of the survival of the fittest applied to economic endeavors, were all the justification needed for their aggressive practices. In time the consequences of some of these practices forced a closer examination of them, and legislation to curb their more harmful aspects was adopted, but this lay decades into the future.

Among Lammot's papers are several memoranda that resemble a military strategist's plans for a campaign of conquest. The clearly stated purpose, the choice of tactics, the careful weighing of alternatives, the opposition to expect, and how to capitalize on final victory, all suggest that he was laying a master plan of attack before his partners. If so, this may have taken place at one of the "think sessions" he had recommended they hold periodically to consider how the family business could be promoted.

The initial objective was to stabilize the powder business of the Schuylkill mining district, a region that embraced Schuylkill, Columbia, and Northumberland counties. The powder business in this district was in a wretched state, resembling the mythic

Augean stables, and just as badly in need of cleansing, in Lammot's judgment. It was oversupplied with powder, much of it coming from a number of small, independent rural mills, all hustling for colliery trade. Price cutting, rebates, and other inducements were used to get orders, and the mine owners played off one supplier against another by claiming his competitors were offering powder at lower prices. A powder manufacturer in Tamaqua described the conditions prevailing in 1872: "It seems as if the very *devil* was among the powder men in this county. Here they are going around pretending that they want to advance the price of powder & the very next minute they will offer 10 to 15 cents less per key to get rid of what powder they may have on hand."[2] With such cutthroat competition it was clearly a buyers' market that did none of the powder producers any good, and there were no signs this chaotic condition would end soon. Decisive measures were needed to bring order and profit out of such deplorable market conditions.

The course of action was obvious: reduce the number of suppliers by buying up or forcing out of business the smaller, marginal powder firms. This would require the collaboration of the larger powder firms doing business in the district, Du Pont and the Laflin and Rand Company. Together they should decide which of the small mills to buy out and shut down and which to take over and continue operating under their individual or joint ownership. As the winnowing and consolidating progressed, these two would also need to negotiate agreements between themselves on production, division of the market, and the fixing of prices to which both would adhere. Lammot's agenda for action is made clear in the introduction to his "campaign" memorandum:

> Propose War—
> General Program—
> Will it pay?
> Is this the best time?
> Are we ready?
> What will we do if successful?[3]

Continuing the military analogy, he noted that the grand objective to be gained was the sale of 190,600 kegs (4,765,000 pounds) of powder—the amount consumed by the Schuylkill district mines between July 1871 and July 1872. Du Pont's share of this market had been 59,600 kegs; Laflin and Rand Company had sold 49,000 kegs; and the remaining 82,000 kegs had been supplied by the small regional mills. Since these last were to be the target of the campaign, Lammot had gathered all the information available about them as to location, proprietor, capital invested, mill equipment, annual output, and principal customers.

Before making any overt moves, Du Pont and Laflin and Rand should invite the proprietors of these small mills to agree to a fixed schedule of prices that would be determined by the two big companies. Implied here was the warning that if price cutting continued the larger firms could outlast and bear losses more easily than the smaller mills. Also, by first inviting the local powdermen into such a cartel, Du Pont and Laflin and Rand would mute the cries of "Combination!" and "Monopoly!" that such action by outsiders would inevitably provoke. A. T. Rand, president of Laflin and Rand, doubted that the invitation would be accepted: "We do not believe the Schuylkill mfrs. will stick long. If they don't it certainly leaves us with a better record than if they are squelched without a trial."[4] No firm pledges to a fixed schedule of prices could be obtained from the independents, so Lammot's campaign got underway.

A salient had already been made by him when he had purchased an interest in the powder plant of H. A. Weldy and Company at Tamaqua in Schuylkill County in May 1871. Henry A. Weldy, a native of Reading and a former railroad worker, in partnership with Conrad F. and Edward F. Shindel, had bought the Edgeworth and Tunnel Mills in 1864 when the wartime demand for powder was strong. Its sales in 1870 had amounted to 25,000 kegs. The Shindels were silent partners who had left the direction of the business to Weldy. Now they wished to sell their interest, and when Weldy learned that Du Pont wanted to establish production facilities in the Schuylkill region he had invited Lammot to visit the plant. For their two-thirds interest, which included fifty acres of cleared ground, the Shindels were asking $30,000, a price Lammot considered too high.

During the ensuing months he had called at the Tamaqua

An advertisement from Beers and Cochran, County Atlas of Schuylkill (Pa.) (New York, 1875) showing the Weldy Mills at Tamaqua. Acquisition of a two-thirds interest in these mills in 1871 marked the beginning of the Du Pont Company's effort to gain control of local powder mills in Pennsylvania's anthracite coal region.

mills several times but it was not until after an explosion in the spring of 1871 that a deal was struck. The Shindels lowered their price to $24,000 and Lammot bought their two-thirds interest, thus giving the Du Pont Company majority control. The firm was to continue to operate under Weldy's name and all parties were pledged to keep secret the new partnership. Rather than Lammot being seen frequently in Tamaqua, he and Weldy arranged to meet in Reading to discuss business matters, and letters between them were mailed in plain, unmarked envelopes. But it was not long before other Schuylkill powdermakers learned of the Weldy–Du Pont partnership, which was to provide the local beachhead from which a campaign of consolidation would be waged.[5]

Buying into the Weldy firm also improved the Du Pont Company's competitive position vis-à-vis Laflin and Rand, its principal rival, yet sometimes ally. Laflin and Rand's initial reaction to it was noted by Weldy: "Rand seemed to be very exercised as to Du Pont's object in coming to this county. He feared it meant fight!"[6] Laflin and Rand already had a foothold there, for in 1869 it had leased the powder plant of Asa G. W. Smith and A. J. Smith at Cressona near Pottsville, the county seat.

The campaign to eliminate the small mills was planned in discussions Lammot had with A. T. Rand during July 1872. First, the Schuylkill region was divided into two geographic zones, one of which was to be an exclusive market area for Weldy–Du Pont, the other for Laflin and Rand. Certain large, longtime customers of each, such as the Reading Coal and Iron Company and the Pardee and Markle mining interests, though in the other's district, were to be reserved, however, to their usual supplier. Targeting the small "enemy" mills, Du Pont, through Weldy, was to try to buy out those operating along the Little Schuylkill River— the Bachert, Ginter, Smith, and Quakake mills; while Laflin and Rand was to go after the mills around Pottsville—those owned by Koch, Wren and Shoemaker, Alspach, and Garbey. For the present the mills in the vicinity of Shamokin, six in number, were to be left alone, but the Big Two were to cut their prices in this area to below cost in an attempt to force these mills to shut down. Lammot had carefully analyzed his costs and had found that the rock bottom price at which he could sell soda or "B" blasting powder was $2.10 a keg; the higher grade saltpeter, or "A" blasting powder, could be sold for $2.60 a keg. With a good idea of production costs of the local, independent mills, he was certain they could not match his prices without suffering serious losses.

All new business captured in this war against the small mills was to be divided proportionately between the Big Two, based upon their sales in the Schuylkill region during 1871. Du Pont's sales for that year had been 43,000 kegs, and Laflin and Rand's 34,000 kegs, so in the allocation of sales quotas in future years Du Pont was to retain this margin of 9,000 kegs.[7]

Lowering prices was to be the first assault weapon, and when this had hurt the opposition Lammot noted what his follow-up would be: "If all had shut down I would [then] advance [the price] 10 cents per keg, until some one started [up again], then I would fall again. Thus if they [had] bought stocks [of raw materials] and tried to start [up] again they would lose money." And there were other measures to be considered: "As chance offered [I] would buy the available H$_2$O powers, and let the rest shut down by hiring [away] their men, which would trouble them not a little. And I think that in less than one year things would regulate themselves." This last could only mean that the Schuylkill district, where nearly seven million tons of coal were being produced annually, would become an orderly, controlled powder market, regulated in the best interests of the Du Pont and Laflin and Rand companies. The fight would cost the big companies some money, $44,000 for Du Pont the first year Lammot estimated; but after that, he assured his partners, the company could anticipate permanently increased profits.

The coal trade was presently in a dull period; coal prices were dropping, and a number of mining companies facing bankruptcy were being taken over by the stronger companies. The latter, Lammot reasoned, would be so glad to buy powder at the reduced prices quoted by Du Pont and Laflin and Rand that they would not think to inquire how the Big Two could undersell the local suppliers so sharply. He assumed that in their eagerness to buy as cheaply as possible they would fail to realize that higher prices would certainly follow once the Big Two had eliminated all their competitors. This was a naive assumption, for in time some of the coal company executives came to see that a powder monopoly was in the making and they tried to thwart it by giving their business to the local producers, some even threatening to set up their own powder mills.[8] Lammot also misjudged the tenacity of some of the independent millowners by thinking they could be eliminated or brought under control within a short time, but this campaign to consolidate extended over a number of years.

Even before the opening salvo of lower prices had been fired, some of the small producers let it be known they would consider selling out. Weldy, a gregarious man who kept himself well informed about his rivals, was Lammot's "intelligence" agent and straw man who negotiated the purchases. Three operators—William Bachert at Switchback, a few miles north of Tamaqua; Philip Ginter on the Little Schuylkill River; and Louis Koch at St. Clair—were ready to sell; Bachert's price was $5,400; Ginter wanted $4,000, and Koch, who had recently had an explosion, was asking $9,000 for his two mills and some adjoining farmland. Ginter had already closed down, and Bachert and Koch were running only half time. The townspeople of St. Clair strongly opposed Koch rebuilding his mill, so he had advertised it for sale, a bad omen of what lay ahead for the local powder producers, noted Weldy: "I can assure you that it looks blue in this region & if it does not sicken the small men, there is nothing that will."[9]

Lammot visited the region in early August 1872, conferring with Weldy and observing firsthand the initial effect of their price cutting. The small millowners were already crying "Monopoly!"—charging that the big firms were trying to crush them! Once they were out of business, they warned, prices would go up. To offset this charge, and to conceal their collusion on establishing prices, Lammot recommended to Laflin and Rand that it and Weldy–Du Pont stage a phony price war by cutting each other's prices—"keeping up the appearance of a fight . . . [thereby] throwing dust in their eyes." To this Rand agreed, but after a month had passed with no reductions made by Laflin and Rand, Lammot reminded him again of the need to give the impression they were fighting each other, and urged that he cut prices ten or fifteen cents a keg, following which Weldy–Du Pont would then lower its prices. In addition to creating the desired impression that they were battling each other, those small mills that tried to meet these very low prices would certainly suffer such losses that they would be forced to sell out or shut down.[10]

As the winter of 1872 approached, several of the small operators came to Weldy at Tamaqua offering their mills at such reduced figures that he advised Lammot to purchase them at once. Some had been hurt not only by the price war but also by the failures of several coal companies that owed them money. One victim was Bachert at Switchback, who now in November was willing to take $4,500 for his mill instead of the $5,400 he had asked in July. The deal was made, Weldy becoming the nominal purchaser, and Bachert was hired to stay on to manage the mill. Subsequently Weldy arranged for Bachert to sound out other small owners and handle the preliminary negotiations in purchasing their properties.

Ginter on the Little Schuylkill wanted $10,000 for his mill and sixty acres of land, too much in Weldy's opinion, but, he warned Lammot, "this matter had better be settled notwithstanding his figure, or else he will give you trouble in the Hazleton region." He also advised Lammot to buy another mill, that of T. H. Bechtel at Mahanoy Plane, near Girardville, even though the asking price of $4,200 was high. Bechtel was an aggressive man who could become a thorn in their side: "I think it best to take it even if we are compelled to blow it up some night to get rid of it. . . . If I had the *say* and the *means* I would buy up the whole of them at once."[11]

Possessing both the "say" and the "means," and with the concurrence of his partners, Lammot provided Weldy with funds to buy Bechtel's and Ginter's mills and that of D. C. Smith at Mintzer's Station on the Little Schuylkill. A bonus that came with Ginter's mill was a large contract he had to supply powder to the Philadelphia and Reading Coal and Iron Company, a contract Weldy would now complete. "Buying up the enemy," in Weldy's words, getting greater control of the trade in this district, was nearing a fait accompli toward the end of 1873. With some satisfaction he reported that the Du Pont–owned mills had supplied approximately three-fourths of all powder consumed in

Schuylkill County during the month of October, and Lammot echoed his satisfaction at this achievement: "It simplifies matters to consolidate all Schuylkill matters into one firm."[12]

Laflin and Rand had been less zealous in buying up its targeted mills in the Pottsville area as agreed to in the understanding Lammot had with A. T. Rand. Much of its local trade was supplied from the Smith mill at Cressona, which it had earlier leased, and from a plant at Moosic near Scranton. At Lammot's urging, in March 1873 it agreed to buy an equal interest with Du Pont in the Laflin Powder Manufacturing Company, which had mills at Laflin in Luzerne County and at Quakake in Schuylkill County. The senior member of this firm was Henry Dwight Laflin, a cousin of the Laflin and Rand Company, who had quit the family firm to go on his own. Lammot's interest in this younger firm was twofold: its mill at Laflin, near Pittston, could compete against the strongly independent Oliver Mills, which had a large share of the powder business in the Luzerne-Wyoming mining district; and the mill at Quakake could readily supply the coal and limestone-quarrying trade in the more southerly Lehigh district. The joint investment made by the Big Two in these mills amounted to $28,000, a five-sixteenths share of ownership, the balance being retained by Laflin and his partners, who continued to manage the mills.[13] This was the first outlay of funds by Laflin and Rand in the joint agreement with Du Pont, and part of the acquisition lay outside the Schuylkill region where the battle to eliminate the opposition was concentrated. Neither Lammot nor Weldy was satisfied with their ally's lukewarm efforts.

A. T. Rand, president of Laflin and Rand, was succeeded by Solomon Turck in 1873. Reviewing for him the plan of collaborative action earlier agreed upon by the two companies, Lammot noted that the Du Pont Company had spent about $78,000 in acquiring small mills, whereas Laflin and Rand had spent less than one-fifth of that amount. Du Pont was bearing too much of the expense of doing away with local competitors yet Laflin and Rand was sharing in the fruits of this victory; it was time Laflin and Rand went after the mills it had promised to buy out. In language that did little to veil the threat, Lammot asserted that if this was not done he would be inclined to put the mills he had acquired up for sale, which would mean a return to the chaotic market conditions that had prevailed before 1872.

In reply, Turck firmly told Lammot that he thought he had acted too hastily in buying up the small mills. If he had held off, bad times and the low price powder was now bringing would have forced the small proprietors to sell out at much less than Lammot had paid them. Further, now that it was known that Du Pont was eager to buy the small mills, that fact itself encouraged some men to deliberately put up new mills as a potential threat to the Big Two, confident that the latter would buy them out on very profitable terms. Turck was offering this advice just one month after the onset of the Panic of 1873, the beginning of the general economic depression that afflicted the country for the next six years.[14]

The impasse was resolved in some conversations Lammot subsequently had with Turck in the Laflin and Rand Company offices at 21 Park Row in New York City. Turck was made to see the continuing need to be more aggressive in stifling competition if the two companies hoped to gain full control over the Schuylkill district trade. It was again agreed that Laflin and Rand would try to acquire certain mills around Pottsville, and the two companies jointly would buy or lease other mills near Shamokin and in neighboring Northumberland County. This understanding was not to preclude either from buying or leasing other mills solely on its own when it thought advisable to do so.

But Laflin and Rand's commitment was not strong, for by the end of 1875 it had spent only $40,000 compared to Du Pont's $120,000 in "buying up the Enemy." When bringing this to Lammot's attention, Weldy enumerated other complaints which reveal that though the Big Two were temporarily allied in a common cause, efforts had surreptitiously been made to take advantage of each other. Weldy charged that Laflin and Rand's local agents were quoting prices below those fixed by Lammot and Turck; they were offering secret rebates, giving larger allowances for returned empty kegs, and wooing some of Weldy's best customers by making gifts of whiskey.[15] Accusations of this kind were repeated frequently against each other by agents of both concerns during the years of their tenuous alliance. At the top level, Lammot and Turck promised to make their subordinates abide by the agreements they had made, but violations continued to recur sporadically on both sides. On the central matter of pursuing their campaign of liquidation and consolidation, Turck expressed a philosophy more temperate than Lammot's: "I am one of those who would rather sell less powder at remunerative prices than much powder at little or no profit. Nor have I any desire to do more business than our competitors. I feel that this world is big enough for all, and I know that we can take nothing out when we leave it. I also know that should we fight we cannot fight always, and for that reason we should adjust our little differences amicably."[16]

Lammot's reaction to this seeming weakening of purpose is not known, but on his next visit to New York he most certainly had some earnest talk with Turck, reviewing their mutual gains thus far and revivifying his faltering zeal by persuasive argument. From the considerable correspondence exchanged during the twelve years of their association, it is evident that Turck came to have an earned respect for Lammot's judgment and he was generally willing to follow his lead. But there was nothing sycophantic in this relationship. When they disagreed Turck frankly stated his views without reserve, inviting Lammot to rebut his arguments if he could, for only in this way could differences be reconciled and decisions affecting their mutual interests be made wisely. As we shall see, this forthright exchange of views evolved into policies which were to shape the course of the American explosives industry.

Turck acknowledged Lammot's greater experience in manufacturing explosives, his technical competence, and his shrewd business sense. Their association became much closer after Lammot established the Repauno Chemical Company in 1880 to produce dynamite and industrial chemicals. Turck, representing Laflin and Rand's part ownership of this new firm, became its vice-president and a member of its board of directors. His recognition of Lammot's superior judgment is evident in a letter in which he had stated some opposite opinions to those held by Lammot: "Don't let anything I may say or write annoy you in the least. You are the captain of the ship and I have full confidence in our commander. I know that it would be impossible for you or anyone to please all the conflicting interests. Do what to you may seem right and best for the interest of Repauno Co. and I am with you."[17]

Consolidation continued throughout the remainder of the 1870s with more of the small mills in the Schuylkill district brought under the umbrella of Du Pont and Laflin and Rand, jointly or individually. Hard times forced some owners to capitulate; some went into bankruptcy and were liquidated at sheriffs' sales; others suffered explosions, and, lacking funds to rebuild, either shut down or sold out or leased their buildings to the Big Two. Those that continued to operate lost customers as the smaller collieries shut down or were taken over by the larger mining companies. The latter contracted annually for sizable quantities of powder at very favorable prices, and the small powder men had not the production capacity of the Big Two nor could they meet their low prices. In 1876 powder prices dropped to $1.90 a keg, then to $1.60 in 1877, and in 1878 the price fell as low as $1.47. Regularly, as the end of each year drew near, Lammot and Turck would assess market conditions; they would then decide what prices they would quote their major customers on the upcoming year's contracts, and what prices would be charged the smaller purchasers.[18]

Underselling competitors was the most effective weapon in their arsenal, but other means were also used to hamstring enemy operations. Some of these took the form of subtle or indirect industrial sabotage. One was to prevent experienced powder workmen from being employed by rival companies. Henry Dwight Laflin at the Quakake mill had to fire one of his better men for drunkenness, but rather than have him remain in the coal region where he could disclose Laflin's production methods to a rival powdermaker who might hire him, Laflin gave him $150 to "go west"—to Leadville, Colorado, where he could get a job in some new powder mills just starting up. In another instance, when Weldy learned that a capable millwright named Nye had been approached to install machinery in a new powder mill being built at Orwigsburg, he asked Lammot if he could find a job for Nye at Repauno "to put him out of this part of the country." A place was found for Nye at Repauno, where he went on Lammot's payroll at the beginning of July 1882.[19] Some promoters planning to erect a mill near Shamokin offered a Weldy millwright named Pelton a hundred dollars to draw the plans for their mill. Pelton informed Weldy of the offer, and his rejection of it, which led Weldy to remark, "This man Pelton we have kept for the last year just tinkering around to keep him out of harm's way."

Suppliers of machinery to the Weldy–Du Pont mills were threatened with the loss of their business if they furnished powder mill equipment to competing firms. The Tamaqua foundry and machinery supply firm of Carter, Allen and Company was bluntly told by Weldy that he would take his business elsewhere if that firm bid low on supplying machines for a new mill being put up near Ashland. As a result Carter, Allen's bid proved too high for the new firm. And to keep secondhand machinery out of the hands of potential competitors Weldy bought it at sales and auctions, even though he did not need it, and put it in storage.[20]

A running dispute with Laflin and Rand Company over shutting down a mill at Ashland that had been jointly purchased with Weldy–Du Pont illustrates another way in which competition was curbed. The previous owners, named Goyne and Reilly, both experienced powdermen, had been hired to stay on and run the plant. Laflin and Rand wanted to shut down the mill because it was making little profit, and Goyne and Reilly were being paid too much. Weldy took an opposite view. "By keeping the mills running we keep two dangerous men employed who otherwise would give us more trouble & make us lose more money than their wages amount to."[21] In short, it was to the Big Two's advantage to pay these men good salaries as employees rather than have them go back into business for themselves or sell their technical know-how to rival powdermakers.

More blatant and rather reprehensible practices were sometimes resorted to. A letter addressed to one of Weldy's workmen from a party planning to put up a mill near Womelsdorf in Berks County was intercepted and read by Weldy who feared possible loss of his employee. When a new firm, the Mahoning Powder Company, tried to make a delivery to a colliery customarily sup-

plied by Weldy, the powder was rejected, because, as Weldy revealed, "We had his mine boss fixed." From repeated allusions to
it, the soliciting of payments from powder suppliers by mine
superintendents who did the buying was a common practice. If
the supplier did not come across, he lost the business. This happened to Weldy, who found himself shut out after he stopped
making his usual payment of ten cents a keg to the boss at another colliery, who then switched to Laflin and Rand.[22]

By 1878 most of the small mills had either been purchased,
bought into, leased, or forced to close down by the Big Two.
The near monopoly they enjoyed moved Turck to recommend
to Lammot that they raise powder prices: "Now that we have
got Koch and Garbey out of the way, would it not be well to
advance the price of powder throughout the anthracite coal regions on May 1, 1878 to $2.20 or $2.25 per keg? What say
you?"[23] The campaign Lammot had begun six years earlier to
"regulate" the powder trade of the Schuylkill region, though taking longer than he anticipated, was now an accomplished victory.
Weldy's sales for 1879 amounted to nearly 90,000 kegs, in addition
to another 47,625 kegs he sold in the Lehigh mining district.
And profits were good, averaging $30,000 annually, one-third
of which went to Weldy and two-thirds to the Du Pont Company.[24]

About this time Lammot prepared a list of the powder mills
that had been acquired, and sketched a "genealogical tree" showing the Du Pont Company's growth from 1802.[25] For fifty-six
years Du Pont had remained rooted on the Brandywine in Delaware at Eleutherian Mills, the Hagley Yard, and the Lower Yard,
shown as the trunk of the tree. The first primary "branch" shooting off from it had appeared in 1858, when Lammot had put the
Wapwallopen mills into operation. A second primary branch began with the purchase of the two-thirds interest in the Weldy
Company in 1871, and growing from this were the subsidiary
branch mills, those taken by Lammot in his recent war to bring
stability and profit into the powder business of the Schuylkill
region. A minor foray into Montgomery County in 1874 had
resulted in the purchase of several small mills near Sumneytown
on Perkiomen Creek. Powder had been made here by Pennsyl-
vania-Germans during the American Revolution, and small-scale

Du Pont Company "genealogical tree." Growth of the company by acquisition of other black powder and high explosive companies is depicted in this drawing by Lammot du Pont c. 1880.

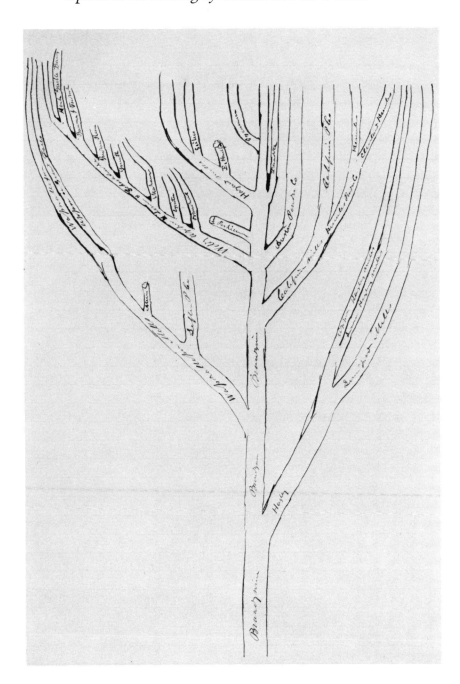

production had continued well into the nineteenth century. This acquisition was shown as a stubby branch shooting off the main Du Pont trunk. But several other small mills on Perkiomen Creek had successfully resisted intermittent attempts to take them over and continued to compete for the slate and limestone-quarrying trade in Montgomery, Bucks, Lehigh, and Northampton counties.[26]

A branch that Lammot repeatedly tried but failed to "graft" onto the family tree was the plant owned by Gen. Paul A. Oliver at Laurel Run near Wilkes-Barre. Sometimes a collaborator, but more often a competitor of Du Pont and Laflin and Rand, he fought for a fair share of the powder trade in the upper anthracite district and sometimes invaded the Schuylkill market. He was determined and independent, a maverick who, backed by executives of some of the larger coal companies, was able to withstand the Big Two's pricing agreements, quotas, and division of the market. On one occasion Lammot accused him of putting an extra pound or two of powder in each keg to boost his trade. Wishing to get back into the coal business at a time when bankrupt mining properties could be bought very cheaply, Oliver offered his mills to Lammot for $275,000, but this was too high a price and made at a time when demand for powder had fallen off.[27]

A drastic price-cutting war took place in 1877 which Lammot thought Oliver could not survive. But Oliver's coal company supporters, aware of the monopoly being forged by the Big Two, came to his aid and helped him repel the attack and stay in business as a competing producer. It was not until 1903 that the Oliver branch sprouted from the Du Pont Company tree when Oliver, then in his seventies, sold out to Lammot's son Pierre S. and his nephews Alfred I. and T. Coleman du Pont, who had taken control of the Du Pont Company the previous year. Under their direction all of the mills in Pennsylvania that Lammot had acquired during the 1870s, plus such several later acquisitions as Oliver's, were organized into a separate subsidiary named E. I. du Pont de Nemours and Company of Pennsylvania, with Lammot's brother-in-law and confidant Henry Belin, Jr., its president.[28]

Concurrent with the near monopoly attained in the anthracite region of Pennsylvania during the seventies were attempts to
organize all the country's powdermakers into a cooperative body
that would work together to advance their mutual interests.
Lammot was a central figure in this effort to stabilize the industry
and put an end to the cutthroat competition that was benefiting
none of the powder producers. It is to this that we now turn our
attention.

ARCHITECT OF THE POWDER TRUST

It was a matter of first importance that took Henry du Pont to
New York City during the last week of April 1872 to meet with
the heads of the country's other major powder companies. Their
purpose was to try again, following earlier attempts that had all
ended in failure, to bring about closer cooperation and united
action in solving the problems besetting the industry. The meeting place was the office of the Du Pont Company's New York
agent, Furman L. Kneeland, at 70 Wall Street.

The agenda listed familiar matters that had plagued the
powdermakers for a number of years:

> 1. Putting an end to the price-cutting wars that had taken
> the profits out of the business
> 2. Regulating output to market demand to avoid overpro-
> duction
> 3. Establishing sales quotas in principal markets for the co-
> operating companies
> 4. Gaining control over, or eliminating, companies that did
> not collaborate in these self-regulatory measures
> 5. Finding a way to minimize the bad effects of government
> dumping of surplus Civil War powder
> 6. More effective lobbying with Congress to assure favor-
> able tax treatment

Some of these issues were identical to those Lammot was dealing
with in the anthracite region. Here, however, the program was
to be nationwide in scope, the major firms in the industry joining
together to police themselves for their mutual benefit.

Collaboration among the powder companies had ample

precedent. Du Pont and the Hazard Powder Company had agreed upon the prices they would quote the Crimean War belligerents in the 1850s. They had consulted one another on prices to charge the Union government during the Civil War; and the industry, electing Lammot as its spokesman, had sought favorable tax treatment from Congress. And there had been lobbying efforts to prevent the Ordnance Bureaus from dumping their millions of pounds of surplus powder on the open market in the postwar years. When these efforts had failed, the companies had collaborated again in negotiating favorable terms when taking some of this surplus off their hands. And to put an end to price wars waged by their agents and commission merchants in some of the metropolitan markets, in 1866–67 eight of the powder companies had made a gentleman's agreement establishing fixed schedules of prices and pledged that their sales representatives would adhere to them.[29]

But these instances of working together had been fitful, forced by unusual circumstances or temporary crises, and once the crisis had passed cooperation and good will disappeared, soon to be followed by recriminations and charges of broken pledges. The sharp competitive practices bred by the postwar depression and intensified by the economic uncertainties at the beginning of the seventies had finally convinced several of the leaders of the industry that a more permanent, durable arrangement had to be hammered out and an organization created to formulate and enforce agreements if the explosives business was to prosper. This was the objective to which the powder company executives addressed themselves when they met in Kneeland's office on April 23, 1872.

Four years before this meeting, in a conversation with Henry M. Boies of the Laflin Powder Company, Lammot had stated his views on the advisability of establishing just such an "Association of Powder Manufacturers" and he had offered suggestions on its structure and functions. Shortly after this meeting Boies wrote Lammot, reviewing their discussion, and setting forth in a clarifying memorandum the principal measures which they had considered necessary to safeguard "a business so exposed to injury on all sides as this, few more important to the well fair [*sic*] of the State. . . . Almost without influence with the government to which it is essential, it has been legislated out of a larger part of its trade without a word of complaint, and now each individual interest seems determined to involve the whole business in ruin. . . . In union there is strength!"[30] Boies asked Lammot to go over the recommendations contained in his five-page memorandum outlining the structure and the powers of an organization he chose to name "The National Board of the Powder Manufacturers of the United States." Selecting the right name for such an organization was very important, cautioned Boies, for it had to be wholly free of the odium of "Rings" and "Combinations." Acknowledging that his proposals were essentially those that Lammot had proposed in their earlier conversation, if Boies's version of them now met with Lammot's approval, he asked that Lammot discuss them with his partners and with officers of the Hazard Powder Company. If acceptable to them, Boies was reasonably certain that the Laflin Powder Company, of which his father, Joseph M. Boies was the president, would also favor the proposals and agree to join to put them into effect. Once the large companies had committed themselves to forming such an association, the smaller companies should be invited to join.

The du Pont–Boies plan bears examination, for though it was premature in 1868 the association created in 1872 in Kneeland's office bears such a close resemblance to it that one must conclude that this earlier plan could have served as a blueprint for those who founded the Gunpowder Trade Association. The general objects in forming such an association, read the du Pont–Boies preamble, were to protect powder manufacturers against injurious legislation; collect information and statistics that would be useful to all its members; expand the business both at home and abroad; and prevent ruinous competition in prices. Each firm joining the association would be entitled to a number of votes equivalent to the number of rolling mills it operated, except, because of their size, the Du Pont Company which would be limited to fifteen votes, and the Hazard Company and Laflin and Rand Company which would have fourteen votes each. The association would be governed by a board of directors composed of one member from each participating firm, and the directors would meet in New York City twice a year. A president, vice-president, secretary, and treasurer were to be elected for one-year terms by the directors. An executive committee consisting of the president, vice-president, and treasurer, plus two other directors, would act on behalf of the board of directors between its scheduled meetings.

The key working figure in the organization was the secretary. He was to have no affiliation with nor any financial interest in any of the powder companies, but was to be paid out of the association's treasury. Treasury funds would come from membership dues levied against each member company at the rate of $100 for each vote to which it was entitled. The members would also be required to deposit bonds in the association treasury to the amount of $2,000 for each vote they held, such bonds to be forfeited by those companies that refused to abide by the decisions of the board of directors. The secretary was to be in charge of the association's New York office, receive and reply to communications from the member firms, send out meeting notices on order of the president, investigate charges and complaints and report on these to the executive committee. All his files, records, and correspondence were to be open to inspection by the member companies. Boies proposed for the secretary's post, rather oddly, "some bankrupt business man of large experience."

The directors, or the executive committee, were authorized to set a schedule of prices for powder in any marketing area at the request of any member, giving due weight to the wishes of other members competing in the same locality. Should any member company sell below these rates, after investigation and verification by the secretary, the president and executive committee would review the evidence, and if satisfied that there had been a price-cutting violation, they could fine the offending member fifty cents to a dollar for every keg sold below the established price. Fines collected would go into the association's treasury. Where a charge of price cutting could not be proved, the accused member could be requested by the secretary or executive committee to swear in an affidavit that he had not violated the price code, and if he agreed to do so, that settled the matter. If, however, he declined to take such an oath, he would be considered guilty as charged and fined accordingly. This fixing of price schedules and their enforcement was the real raison d'être of the association, for only through self-regulation could the retaliatory price wars that had been destroying the industry's profits be halted. "This organization," Boies confidently asserted to Lammot, "can effect its object without restricting a healthy competition." There was no recognition by Boies that it could also become a combination in restraint of trade.

The confidence these younger men had that the senior members of their firms would give serious consideration to their proposals was unfounded. Age and longer experience in the business world had made their elders cynical and skeptical of the pledged word of competitors; one acted according to his own best interests. The record of broken agreements was a sorry one, and there was no reason to believe this plan proposed in 1868 would prove an exception. And company heads such as Uncle Henry, long accustomed to absolute authority in company affairs, could not easily be persuaded to relinquish any measure of control over their operations to an association made up of competitors, even though it had been created to promote the best interests of all involved. Du Pont, well entrenched as the recognized leader in the industry, financially strong, and with a far-flung network of agents, was in an advantageous position to wage its competitive battles free of restraints imposed by membership in such an organization. These were most likely the considerations uppermost in Uncle Henry's mind as he discussed with Lammot the value of such an organization when it was again proposed in 1872. But both had been too busy to have a full exchange of views on the matter in the weeks just before the April 1872 meeting.

Securing adherence to a fixed schedule of prices, to production limits, and to sales quotas was made difficult because of the diverse ways powder was marketed. Very large sales to such enterprises as railroad contractors or mining companies were usually by contract with the manufacturer. But sales were customarily made through an agent strategically located in one of the larger marketing areas, a city or town with good transportation facilities. Powder shipped to him was stored in a magazine in a safe,

isolated place, the magazine sometimes put up at the manufacturer's expense, sometimes erected by the agent. In the latter case
the manufacturer would pay a monthly storage fee for his powder kept there. Some agents made outright purchases of powder;
others took it on consignment and reported their sales periodically to the manufacturer after deducting their commission, which
varied at times from 4 to 6 percent.

An agent's reports listed his customers, amounts sold, and
the prices. He reported his inventory of the types and quantities
of powder still on hand. Covering letters told of the sales activities of rival agents and market conditions and contained other
pertinent information he thought the producer would like to have.
Some agents handled powder made by more than one producer.
Some of these gave allowances for advertising and supplied window display cards. Agents serving a large marketing region appointed subagents to cover the outlying areas. These sold to small
retailers and to the consumer in some instances at prices set by
the principal agent and were paid the usual commission.

At times when powder was yielding good profits this system
was disrupted by intruders, jobbers who bought large quantities
of powder from the manufacturer at discount prices and then
peddled it at cut-rate prices from wagons traversing the agent's
territory. Agents and subagents retaliated by reducing their prices,
by offering rebates, and then by paying a premium for empty
kegs returned to them. And the manufacturer who had supplied
the jobber would receive letters of complaint from the agents
hurt by the transaction.

But the persistent problem affecting the marketing of powder was the mutual suspicion that each producer was trying to
steal a march on his competitor, that agents were encouraged and
aided to go after a larger share of the market by fair means or
foul. Gentlemen's agreements were no longer honored—there
was need for something more binding, an organization with enforcement powers.[31]

A particularly savage and widespread price-cutting war, and
disagreements over sharing the trade in a number of markets,
had existed between the Du Pont Company and Laflin and Rand
Company in 1871 and early 1872. A. T. Rand, head of the latter

since 1869, was considered the instigator of the conflict by Uncle Henry, who charged him with breaking their gentlemen's agreements and waging an aggressive campaign aimed at monopolizing the market. Rand's predecessor, Joseph M. Boies, head of the Laflin Powder Company before it had merged with Smith and Rand, had been a more amenable person whose relations with the Du Pont Company had been generally harmonious. Now, after failing to convince Rand that his tactics were hurting the entire industry, Uncle Henry declared, "We have concluded to meet them fair and square every where and 'let the Devil take the hindmost!'"[32]

The challenge was apparently carried to Rand by Lammot, who spent four hours closeted with him in his New York office on April 5, 1872. What passed between them is not recorded, but a few days later, giving poor health as his reason, Rand went on a long vacation to Bermuda; subsequently he was replaced as president by Solomon Turck. One of Rand's associates, Henry M. Boies, coauthor with Lammot of the 1868 association plan, might very well have provided Lammot with some telling arguments that led Rand to capitulate. The other Laflin and Rand officers and a number of stockholders disagreed with Rand's policies, preferring conciliation and cooperative measures that would put an end to the profitless conflict. This readiness to cooperate was also shared by the officers of the Hazard Powder Company, the third largest company. Added to the Du Pont Company's threat of all-out war, his serious split with the other officers of Laflin and Rand must have convinced Rand he should step down. His associates, wrote Kneeland, who was privy to Lammot's four-hour session with Rand, "are ready to concede a great deal, & will endeavor to maintain prices & the majority of stockholders desire a new departure." With Rand out of the picture the time was right for organization.

Kneeland, a central figure in Du Pont's financial and marketing operations, tried to overcome Uncle Henry's reservations about cooperative action by calling attention to what was happening in other industries: "The white lead men, linseed oil men, shot manufacturers and nail manufacturers have all adopted . . . [associations] . . . after having worked for the public till they became tired. The state of the market appears favorable to such a course . . . it appears to me a favorable arrangement for *you*."[33] He could not know how accurate this prophecy was to be.

Overproducing, and the need to get rid of powder surpluses by underselling one's competitors, was regarded by Kneeland the dangerous reef on which this mutual undertaking could founder. He did not foresee any surpluses occurring for the rest of 1872; output could be paced to demand, but should there be signs of a glut, a resolution adopted by the manufacturers binding all of them to cut back their output on a proportionate percentage basis would restore the balance. The quantity each company could sell would be calculated on the number of kegs each had sold in the last twelve-month period, with each then allocated an equivalent percentage of the total sales made by the entire industry. As demand increased, the sales quota of each company could be adjusted upward proportionately. Voting on issues before the association should be according to the size of each company, with Du Pont, Laflin and Rand, and Hazard each having three votes, Oriental Powder Mills two, and the Zenia, American, and Austin companies one vote each; if the California Powder company, a large West Coast producer, should join, it would have two votes. It is of special interest that five days before the organization meeting held on April 23, Kneeland, in a letter that confirms Lammot's role as architect of the plan, addressed this request to Uncle Henry: "I wish you would draw up Articles of Association according to your Mr. Lammot du Pont's ideas; it will save time, as there will be a great deal to do and little time to do it in."[34]

Irénée, Lammot's older brother, who has left scant written record of his career in the company or any opinions on its policies, responded to Kneeland expressing hope, but with some misgivings. The plan had both advantages and disadvantages; it might work for a time, but, sharing his uncle's skepticism, Irénée believed that once there was a glut of powder all agreements would go out the window. All the powder producers outside of the association, mostly younger, smaller companies, would first start cutting prices, and the companies in the association would have to follow suit to hold their customers. Nevertheless, although previous efforts had been fruitless, he would like to see the attempt at regulation tried once again; and as for those who might try to scuttle it, the Du Pont Company should "turn on them & show them no mercy."[35]

This prevailing willingness to "give it another try" was the coalescing spirit that brought the company heads together in Kneeland's office on Tuesday morning, April 23, 1872. Uncle Henry and Kneeland represented the Du Pont Company; Joseph M. Boies and T. C. Brainerd the Laflin and Rand Company; Thomas S. Pope and A. E. Douglass the Hazard Company; Arthur Williams and J. M. C. Armsby the Oriental Powder Mills; Addison G. Fay the American Powder Company; and Addison O. Fay the Miami (Ohio) Powder Company. Not present, but pledged by letter to join them, was Linus Austin of the Austin Powder Company.

Lammot had been slated to be his firm's representative, but on April 17 a tragedy had occurred at Wapwallopen which made him rush there to take charge, for Uncle Charles Belin was distraught and threatening suicide. Belin's only son, John, though a good swimmer, had drowned in the Susquehanna River when the flatboat on which he was crossing to the other shore took on water. This startled his team of horses, and as he tried to quiet them he was knocked overboard unconscious. His body was lost in the roiling freshet and not recovered for over a week. Lammot directed the search, posting paid watchers on bridges downstream and offering a reward for recovery of the body. The mills had been immediately shut down by the frantic father. Lammot took command, got the plant running again, instructed a replacement for John, and did his best to comfort his bereaved uncle and aunt. These tasks kept him at Wapwallopen until April 27, compelling him to miss the meeting of the twenty-third in New York, which Uncle Henry at the last moment had decided he should attend.[36]

This first meeting was to consider the general recommendations on how the powdermen should organize themselves, and, second, to draw up a schedule of prices governing powder sales throughout the country. Kneeland outlined the formal structure and functions of the associations, which, in light of his asking for Lammot's ideas on this subject a week earlier, certainly reflected Lammot's thinking. And, to expedite the most urgent need, Uncle Henry then moved that a committee be named to draw up a price code to be submitted at the next meeting, which was to be held the following Monday, April 29.

At this second meeting in Kneeland's office Lammot was present, replacing Uncle Henry, for he had been able to leave Wapwallopen after getting the plant working once again. He was unanimously elected president of the Gunpowder Trade Association (G.T.A.) a position to which he was annually reelected until he declined renomination in 1880. The other officers were A. E. Douglass of the Hazard Company, vice-president, and Edward Greene of Laflin and Rand, secretary-treasurer. The "Articles of Association" proposed the previous week by Kneeland were adopted, the preamble to which stated that the purpose of the organization was to ensure "an equitable adjustment of prices and terms for sales of powder throughout the United States." In all matters to be voted upon the seven companies forming the G.T.A. were entitled to a number of votes according to their size:

Du Pont Company	10 votes
Hazard Company	10 votes
Laflin and Rand Company	10 votes
Oriental Powder Mills	6 votes
Austin Powder Company	4 votes
American Powder Company	4 votes
Miami Powder Company	4 votes
Total	48

Other powder companies would be invited to join, and a firm could withdraw after giving thirty days' notice of its intent.

The Association was to meet quarterly, but a smaller five-member Council on Prices was created to meet weekly, or at the call of the president, to hear complaints of violations of the price schedule, which the Association then adopted and ordered to go into effect May 1. All communications were to go through the secretary, who was to investigate complaints and present them to the council if he thought they were valid. If the member firm charged with the violation did not like the council's decision, it could appeal the matter at the next general meeting of the association for a final adjudication. (At a later date, in March 1876,

Organization of the Gunpowder Trade Association, 1872. Page 1 of the minutes of the organizational meeting. Lammot du Pont was president of the G.T.A. until 1878.

CONFIDENTIAL.

AT an adjourned meeting of the Manufacturers of Gunpowder, held at the office of Mr. F. L. Kneeland, 70 Wall Street, New York, at 10 o'clock A. M., Monday, 29th April, 1872 :

PRESENT.		REPRESENTING.
Mr. LAMMOT DuPONT,	- - -	E. J. DuPont de Nemours & Co.
Mr. F. L. KNEELAND,	- - -	
Mr. A. E. DOUGLASS,	- - -	The Hazard Powder Co.
Mr. THOS. S. POPE, -	- - -	
Mr. J. M. BOIES,	- - -	The Laflin & Rand Powder Co.
Mr. EDWARD GREENE,	- - -	
Mr. C. O. FOSTER, -	- - -	The Oriental Powder Mills.
Mr. I. M. C. ARMSBY,	- - -	
Mr. A. G. FAY, - -	- - -	The American Powder Co.
Mr. A. O. FAY, - -	- - -	The Miami Powder Co.
Mr. A. E. DOUGLASS,	- -	The Austin Powder Co.

On motion of Mr. A. E. Douglass, Mr. Lammot DuPont was called to the Chair, and Mr. Thomas S. Pope was appointed Secretary.

On motion of Mr. F. L. Kneeland, the scheme for an Association of Manufacturers of Gunpowder, which had been considered at the meeting of 23d April, 1872, was called up, and on motion of Mr. A. E. Douglass, the Association was agreed to, and the following

ARTICLES OF ASSOCIATION

unanimously adopted :

WE, the undersigned, Manufacturers of Gunpowder, for the purpose of ensuring an equitable adjustment of prices and terms for sales of powder throughout the United States, hereby agree to the subjoined Articles of Association, to which we severally pledge for ourselves, and all under our control, rigid and honorable adherence.

1st.—This Association shall be called "THE GUNPOWDER TRADE ASSOCIATION OF THE UNITED STATES," and comprises all manufacturers of Gunpowder in the United States, who now or hereafter may be admitted thereto ; the present organization being composed of the following manufacturers, entitled to representation and vote at all meetings of the Association, as follows :

E. I. Dupont de Nemours & Co..Ten Votes.
Hazard Powder Company..Ten Votes.
Laflin & Rand Powder Company..Ten Votes
Oriental Powder Mills...Six Votes.
Austin Powder Company...Four Votes.
American Powder Company..Four Votes.
Miami Powder Company..Four Votes.

2d.—The officers of this Association shall be a President, Vice-President, Secretary, and Treasurer, to be elected by ballot on the first meeting of this Association, and annually thereafter, and who shall hold office until others are elected in their stead.

3d.—It shall be the duty of the President to preside at all meetings of the Association, and on the written request of two members thereof, to call special meetings of same. In case of his absence, the same duties will devolve upon the Vice-President. The Secretary shall attend all meetings of the Association, keep full record of their transactions, and issue such notices to the associates as the properly authorized officers may direct. The Treasurer shall have the custody of all funds belonging to the Association.

a penalty of one dollar per keg was levied against the guilty firm for every keg sold below the fixed price, the fines collected going into the Association's treasury.) Funds needed to cover the association's expenses were to be assessed by the council on each member in proportion to the number of votes it held.[37]

It was not feasible to have only one set of prices for the entire country, for this did not allow for differences in transportation costs and local market conditions, so the country was divided into seven marketing zones and a schedule of minimum selling prices drawn up for each. Sales quotas for each member firm in the G.T.A. were determined by its estimated production for the year 1872, each firm then being given a quota corresponding to the percentage its production bore to the industry's total output (total output for the year 1872 was estimated at 1,500,000 kegs):

Du Pont	566,000 kegs, or 37%
Laflin and Rand	316,000 kegs, or 21%
Hazard	180,000 kegs, or 12%
American and Miami	50,000 kegs, or 3.3%
Austin	40,000 kegs, or 2.7%
Oriental	30,000 kegs, or 2%

Thus the G.T.A. firms' aggregate production totaled 1,182,000 kegs, or 78 percent of the national output, and firms outside the association, it was calculated, would produce 318,000 kegs, or 22 percent. By this apportionment the top three combined could sell 70 percent, and the smaller companies inside and outside the G.T.A. would share the remaining 30 percent of all powder sales. It was agreed, however, that if the Big Three oversold their annual quotas, the four smaller companies in the association would have their quotas increased proportionately; and if the smaller companies sold beyond their quotas, they would have to buy powder equal to the excess from the Big Three.[38] Not included in any of these arrangements, however, either as a marketing area to be shared or governed by the G.T.A. price schedules, was the Pennsylvania anthracite region. Du Pont and Laflin and Rand had reserved this as a special market for their own penetration and control.

Price list, Gunpowder Trade Association. Prices of various kinds of powder (25-lb. kegs) at which member companies agreed to sell their products in 1872.

They recommend the adoption of the following prices at the places respectively named, to-wit :

	RIFLE.	SALTPETRE. MINING AND BLASTING.	SODA. MINING AND BLASTING.	FINE SPORTING. ADVANCE ON NEW YORK LIST OF
Chicago, Illinois	$6.50	$4.25	$3.75	2 cts. per pound.
St. Louis, Missouri	7.00, less 5 per cent. to city trade	4.50 net	4.00 net	4 "
Cincinnati, Ohio	6.50	4.25	3.75	2 "
Xenia Mills, Ohio	6.50	4.25	3.75	2 "
Indianapolis, Indiana	6.50	4.25	3.75	2 "
Evansville, Indiana	6.75	4.50	4.00	3 "
Milwaukee, Wis	6.50	4.25	3.75	2 "
Detroit, Michigan	6.50	4.25	3.75	2 "
Louisville, Kentucky	6.50	4.25	3.75	2 "
Wheeling, W. Virginia	6.65	4.50	3.85	3 "
Lafayette, Indiana	6.50	4.25	3.75	2 "
Marietta, Ohio	6.65	4.50	3.85	3 "
Steubenville, Ohio	6.65	4.50	3.85	3 "
Cleveland, Ohio	6.30	4.05	3.55	1 "
Bridgeport, Ohio	6.65	4.50	3.85	3 "
Columbus, Ohio	6.60	4.50	3.85	3 "
Pomeroy, Ohio	6.75	4.50	4.00	3 "
Ironton, Ohio	6.75	4.50	4.00	3 "
Toledo, Ohio	6.40	4.15	3.65	2 "
Alton, Illinois	7.30	4.80	4.30	5 "
Du Quoin, Illinois	6.75	4.50	4.00	3 "
Rock Island, Illinois	7.00	4.75	4.25	4 "
Davenport, Iowa	7.00	4.75	4.25	4 "
Moline, Illinois	7.00	4.75	4.25	4 "
Keokuk, Iowa	7.00	4.75	4.25	4 "
Burlington, Iowa	7.00	4.75	4.25	4 "
Quincy, Illinois	7.00	4.75	4.25	4 "
La Salle, Illinois	6.75	4.50	4.00	3 "
Des Moines, Iowa	7.00	4.75	4.25	4 "
Cedar Rapids, Iowa	7.00	4.75	4.25	4 "
Sioux City, Iowa	7.25	5.00	4.50	5 "
Omaha, Nebraska	7.00	4.75	4.25	4 "
Kansas City, Missouri	7.50	5.00	4.50	6 "
Leavenworth, Kansas	7.50	5.00	4.50	6 "
St. Joseph, Missouri	7.50	5.00	4.50	6 "
Hannibal, Missouri	7.25	4.75	4.25	5 "
Memphis, Tennessee	7.00 less 5 per cent. to city trade	4.50 net	4.00 net	4 "
Paducah, Kentucky	7.00	4.50	4.00	4 "
Nashville, Tennessee	6.50	4.50	4.00	2 "
Vicksburg, Mississippi	7.25	4.75	4.25	5 "
St. Paul, Minnesota	7.25	5.00	4.50	5 "
Minneapolis, Minnesota	7.25	5.00	4.50	5 "
Dubuque, Iowa	7.00	4.75	4.25	4 "
Plattville Mills, Wis	7.00	4.75	4.25	4 "
Buffalo, New York	6.25	4.00	3.50	1 "
Troy, New York	6.25	4.00	3.40	1 "
Albany, New York	6.25	4.00	3.40	1 "
New Orleans, Louisiana	7.25 less 5 per cent. to city trade	5.00 net	4.50 net	5 "
Mobile, Alabama	7.25			5 "
Atlanta, Georgia	7.00	5.00	4.50	4 "
Chattanooga, Tennessee	6.50	4.50	4.00	2 "

The structure, functions, and regulatory powers of the G.T.A. resembled the proposals Lammot and Boies had put forth in 1868. Now, recognized as a leader in the industry, as its most active promoter, with definite ideas of how regulation could be made effective, and as the representative of the company without whose participation any cooperative scheme had little chance of success, it is not surprising that Lammot was elected the first president of the Gunpowder Trade Association.

The minutes of the G.T.A. meetings, along with surviving copies of Lammot's presidential reports and his correspondence with other members, provide insight into the day-by-day bread-and-butter problems and how they were resolved. At the quarterly meeting in August 1872, marking its first three months of life, Lammot expressed guarded satisfaction that it was working well. He commended the Council on Prices for its masterly handling of regulating prices and its good judgment in speedily adjusting them where justified. Not all member firms had benefited equally during these trial months, and Lammot praised them for their forbearance in taking no actions that could jeopardize the functioning of the organization. Where they existed these inequities had to be eliminated—"The sooner the disease is taken in hand the more easily it will be managed."

He appealed to the membership to put an end to the perennial suspicion that each company was undercutting its rivals by lowering prices and giving rebates or special credit terms. The fault here lay with the selling agents who acted too independently; they had to be brought more firmly under the control of the manufacturers and made to adhere to G.T.A. regulations. Second, more adjustments in some price schedules were necessary so that the "western mills" (Ohio Valley producers) were not penalized by the higher freight rates they had to pay for powder shipped eastward. And, third, some solutions had to be found for the problems created by the dual system of selling powder through commission agents and sales made directly from the factory to large customers located in an agent's territory. Lammot offered several proposals to correct this situation and asked his confreres to consider these matters before acting upon them at the next meeting. To tighten the association, he asked for the adoption of by-laws that would further clarify and strengthen the Council on Prices' authority, "as they know better what will be for the benefit of the Association." His closing words reflected satisfaction with what had been achieved at the end of three months: "Let me express my belief that the Association has worked much more smoothly and better than any of us had a right to expect."[39]

The workings of the Association, however, did not always run smoothly, and needed frequent lubrications of compromise, concession, threat, and diplomatic tact in the effort to achieve united, mutually beneficial action. The ideal of sacrificing a measure of individual company liberty for the good of the entire industry was severely strained during the business decline that began in 1873, a year in which total powder demand fell off by 300,000 kegs. Accusations, investigations, and adjudications were numerous. They dealt with price cutting, exceeding quotas, rebates and freight allowances, excessive numbers of agencies, special deals to large customers, and the invasion of other companies' sales territories. For most of these infractions the manufacturers blamed their overzealous agents; each was out to earn as much as he could in commissions, and it was a recurring problem to keep them bound by G.T.A. regulations.

In an exchange of letters dealing with charges of price cutting, Arthur Williams of Oriental Powder wrote to Kneeland, Du Pont's New York agent, stating his company's support of the G.T.A. and its method of dealing with insubordinate agents: "We believe it is the best policy to impress our agents that all members of the G.T.A. are friends acting together for mutual interests, and not, that we are suspiciously watching each other. . . . We hold our agents squarely up to their agreements and if any kick over the traces we apply the remedy."[40] It would be difficult to assess how generally successful the manufacturers were in enforcing adherence, and, conversely, to what extent they secretly abetted their agents' "illegal" methods of securing a larger share of the business, despite disclaimers of any cheating to the G.T.A. officials.

Companies outside the G.T.A. that tried to remain independent in policy and action were subjected to varied treatment. A nonmember, the Warren Powder Company, located in Warren,

Maine, in 1876 was asked to keep its prices in line with the G.T.A. price schedule for the New England area. When it refused, a two-man committee was named by the G.T.A. to call upon the Warren Company officers to try to persuade them to comply. When the Warren people remained adamant, the G.T.A. representatives then offered to buy their mills, meeting with them several times to negotiate the purchase, but to no avail. This was reported to the G.T.A. at its April meeting in 1876, the negotiating committee stating it was "difficult to deal with that Company."

Two of its weapons, persuasion and purchase, having failed, the Association thereupon decided to use its third—pressure. Authority was given to two New England firms, Oriental and American, to sell powder in a 100-mile region circling the Warren plant, its primary market area, at prices below Warren's prices. Contrary to what the G.T.A. anticipated, there was no quick capitulation; Warren fought back and stayed alive for another seven years, but finally had to shut down early in 1883, bankrupt and with a considerable inventory of powder on hand.[41]

Another outsider, the Lake Superior Powder Company located in Marquette, Michigan, was another firm subjected to G.T.A. pressure. Beginning in 1868, it had become the principal supplier of blasting powder to the iron and copper mines in northern Michigan, selling an average of 35,000 kegs annually by 1870. Prosperity led it to expand its territory in 1877 into the coal regions of southern Illinois, where it ran into competition with G.T.A. firms already serving that market. After it refused to withdraw and confine its sales to the iron and copper regions, the G.T.A. named a committee to investigate the possibility of purchasing the Lake Superior Company. When the committee reported that $26,000 would be needed to gain controlling interest in the firm, it was authorized to try to buy the necessary stock. But all offers were rebuffed by the Lake Superior officers and their friends who owned a majority of the stock.[42]

During the latter half of 1877 the G.T.A. companies put the squeeze on by selling to many of Lake Superior's customers at prices barely above the cost of production. Within a few months some of its stockholders, fearing bankruptcy, became more amenable to offers to purchase their shares, and blocks of stock began to change hands. By the spring of 1878 all of the Lake Superior stock, 2,000 shares, were owned by the Big Three and the Gunpowder Export Company:

Du Pont	457 shares	$ 7,997.50
Laflin and Rand	457 shares	7,997.50
Hazard	457 shares	7,997.50
Gunpowder Export	629 shares	11,007.50
Total	2,000 shares	$ 35,000.00

The purchase agreement allowed the Lake Superior Company a quota of 15,000 kegs to be sold yearly in the mining district, and the Big Three were to divide the remainder of the business among themselves. Laflin and Rand was allotted an annual quota of 5,500 kegs with the balance of the trade going to Du Pont and Hazard. All of the other G.T.A. companies were to stay out of the Great Lakes district for a period of five years. By its own shares, those of the Hazard Company which it had secretly purchased in 1876, and from its part ownership of the Gunpowder Export Company, Du Pont was now clearly the majority owner of the Lake Superior Powder Company. A short time later, at Lammot's instigation, the Lake Superior Company began producing nitroglycerine compounds and dynamite, for these were now preferred over black powder by the copper and iron mining companies in the district.[43]

Among the companies later admitted to G.T.A. membership the largest was the California Powder Works, which had a dynamite plant near San Francisco's Golden Gate and black powder mills at Santa Cruz. In 1869 Du Pont had quietly bought an interest in this firm, and by June 1876 had increased its stock holdings to 3,333 shares, a one-third interest. The following year it enlarged its investment to give it nearly 44 percent ownership, and an influential voice in its management. Under the leadership of Capt. John H. Baird and James Howden, a chemist, the California company had been one of the first in the United States to produce nitroglycerine compounds and dynamite. Uncle Henry's adamant opposition to the new "patent" explosives suggests that Lammot had to argue very persuasively to convince him that the Du Pont Company should buy into the California firm. The continued manufacture of black powder at its sprawling Santa Cruz plant and the handsome profits it posted each year may have softened his uncle's resistance.[44] By the mid-1870s the company was aggressively pushing its products in the Mississippi Valley region and becoming a threat to the eastern producers.

Before its joining the G.T.A. early in 1875, Lammot and Kneeland had met with the officers of the California company and negotiated an agreement that barred sales of powder by the G.T.A. companies in the far western markets and similarly prohibiting the California company from making sales in the East. In between lay a vast middle zone, the Rocky Mountain region embracing the states and territories of Utah, Montana, Wyoming, Colorado, and New Mexico, where mining operations and railroad construction were using great quantities of explosives. This lucrative market was to be "stabilized" by what Lammot called the "Neutral Belt Agreement." This agreement established fixed schedules of prices for various zones in this neutral montane region which the G.T.A. companies and the California company were pledged to observe. The G.T.A. penalty of one dollar per keg was to be levied against firms found guilty of selling below the fixed price.

The California Powder Works agreed not to ship east of the Neutral Belt, in return for which it was to have sole right to sell in California, Oregon, Nevada, Arizona, Idaho, Washington, and Alaska. But special concessions were made to Du Pont, Hazard, and Oriental, which were allowed to sell limited quantities of powder in these states and territories. The Neutral Belt Agreement ran for five years, not always harmoniously, and was renewed early in 1880 for another five years when Lammot negotiated new terms with the California company. In this second agreement dynamite and nitroglycerine compounds were included in the price schedules and the allocation of markets.[45] This came on the eve of Lammot's withdrawal from the family firm to strike out on his own as a producer of high explosives.

By these agreements the stabilizing influence of the G.T.A. had now extended nationwide. A major competitive struggle had been averted, and in the rapidly developing Neutral Belt region all the companies in the G.T.A. were free to go after business, bound only by the Association's price schedules. The Du Pont Company benefited most from this arrangement. The interests of the California Powder Works, of which it owned more than two-fifths, had been protected and advanced; Du Pont could still sell considerable powder in the California market by the quota allowed in the agreement; and, by its acquisition of the Hazard Powder Company in 1876, it in effect had acquired the quota assigned that company in the expanding western markets. Not immediate, but a delayed benefit of great importance to Lammot, was the purchase of the California Powder Works' high explosives subsidiary, the Hercules Powder Company in Cleveland, Ohio, in 1881. The Hercules plant became an ancillary unit to the Repauno Chemical Company, which he had established a year earlier. With dynamite now beginning to outsell black powder three to one, Lammot had become convinced that the future of the industry would be in high explosives, not black powder.[46]

The G.T.A. had come under greater domination by the Du Pont Company in the centennial year when it secretly purchased the third member of the Big Three. Since the death of its founder, Col. Augustus G. Hazard, in 1868, the Hazard Powder Company had been without a capable, aggressive executive leader. An explosion at its Hazardville, Connecticut, works in 1871 had done serious damage, and with the falling off of earnings in the depressed years that followed, the stockholders became increasingly discontented and inclined to sell out.[47] Lammot knew the current Hazard officers, A. E. Douglass and Thomas S. Pope, from frequent business contacts, particularly in the G.T.A., where both held office at different times. Hazard's New York City office was at 88 Wall Street, a few doors from Du Pont's at 70 Wall Street, and its mills were located at Scitico and Hazardville, Connecticut.

Before making an offer to buy, Lammot had carefully inventoried the Hazard mills and put a value of $341,200 on them. Other Hazard assets brought the total purchase price to $789,000, which sum the Du Pont Company agreed to pay in six annual payments of $131,500 each. Thomas S. Pope was named vice-president with overall general direction and was instructed by

Lammot to keep him fully informed of all Hazard operations. Pope was to represent Hazard at all G.T.A. meetings, but he was to take his cue from the Du Pont representative and vote accordingly. No word of the change of ownership was to be made known; it was to be a closely kept secret, with Hazard carrying on its business as usual, maintaining its own identity and competitive stance within the framework of G.T.A. regulations.[48]

A potentially serious threat to the G.T.A. had appeared in 1874 when a maverick officer of the organization broke away from it, started his own mills, and set out to capture all the trade he could by offering powder below Association prices. This was Dr. Thomas C. Brainerd, a medical man with Civil War experience who had married into the Laflin family and had become secretary of Laflin and Rand Company; he had also served for a time as secretary of the G.T.A. Brainerd was ambitious to become president of Laflin and Rand after the death of A. T. Rand, but when passed over by the stockholders, who selected Solomon Turck to head the company, Brainerd had angrily resigned. He bought a mill near York, Pennsylvania, and soon was cutting prices in the coal regions and as far west as Chicago and St. Louis. The member companies of the G.T.A. retaliated by lowering their prices, and a price war was on.[49]

Though never financially sound, and forced to borrow heavily, Brainerd carried on his "raiding" throughout 1875, capturing such large customers as the Reading Railroad Company, to whom on one occasion he sold 20,000 kegs at $2.05 a keg. His old company, Laflin and Rand, tried to buy him out, but with no success, after which it dangled before him the prospect of a remunerative position in the G.T.A., and in this he showed some interest. Turck consulted Lammot, as president of G.T.A., with the query, "Would you consent to this, and if so, how could we use him?"[50]

Lammot's response was a cleverly conceived, expansive, four-part plan that would remove Brainerd from the American powder business, counter a looming threat of Canadian powder firms invading the American market, and, in reverse direction, open up the Canadian market to American producers. His proposals, presented to the G.T.A. at its meeting in March 1876, recommended that

1. Brainerd's York mill be purchased by the G.T.A. and closed down

2. A company be created by G.T.A. to handle the export of American surplus powder for sale in Canada

3. Brainerd be made president of this new company and paid an annual salary by G.T.A.

4. The newly formed company then to set about acquiring a Canadian powdermaking firm to gain entry into the Canadian market

Undertakings such as the digging of the Welland and Lachine canals, railroad construction, mining operations, and public works projects were consuming vast quantities of powder and earning good profits for the Canadian powder manufacturers, Lammot informed his associates. The Hamilton Powder Company in Ontario had paid out dividends rising from 25 percent in 1873 to 38 percent in 1875, and plans underway to build a rail line across Canada to the Pacific had brightened the prospects of that country's powder producers.[51]

His recommendations were accepted. Brainerd's mill was bought for $70,000, plus the assumption of some of his debts. To spearhead the move into Canada, the Gunpowder Export Company was organized with Solomon Turck at its head and Lammot its vice-president. This company was capitalized at $200,000, most of which was subscribed by the Du Pont Company (340 shares), Hazard Company (225 shares), and Laflin and Rand Company (220 shares), with the remainder taken up by the officers of these and other G.T.A. firms as personal investments. Brainerd moved to Montreal as representative of the Gunpowder Export Company and soon commenced negotiations for the purchase of the Hamilton Powder Company, the only incorporated powder company in Canada, which had plants at Cumminsville, Ontario, and Windsor, Quebec.

Toward the end of 1876 a deal was consummated and both plants were brought for $108,000, some of the funds coming from the Gunpowder Export Company, and the balance from individual heads of the G.T.A. companies. The Hamilton Powder Company name was retained with Brainerd as its president and Lammot a director. At his urging both plants began making dynamite and soon a third plant was added at Beloeil, Quebec.

Brainerd submitted periodic reports to Furman L. Kneeland, secretary of the Gunpowder Export Company, but copies routinely went to Lammot as spokesman of the controlling stockholder and for his role as originator of the Canadian enterprise. In all important matters, both technical and managerial, Brainerd consulted Lammot; borrowed money from him for personal needs; and turned to him for support when other officers of the parent Gunpowder Export Company sometimes questioned his integrity and found fault with his management.

Soon after securing an exclusive contract in 1877 from the syndicate building the Canadian Pacific Railroad to supply all its powder needs, Brainerd was visited by agents of the British Dynamite Company of Glasgow. They wanted to buy the Hamilton Powder Company and asked at what price would its American owners sell and retire from Canada. Brainerd responded with a courteous negative—it was not for sale—and he did not summon its board of directors to discuss the matter as he assumed the refusal would meet with Lammot's approval.[52]

A Canadian competitor, the Acadia Powder Company of Halifax, which supplied explosives to the coal and gold mines in the maritime provinces of lower Canada, began selling in the Quebec and Ontario markets and set up a new mill midway between Montreal and Toronto. Brainerd counterattacked this invasion of his territory, first by hiring away Acadia's most experienced powderman at triple the wages he was receiving and aggressively retaliating by pushing Hamilton's sales in the maritime provinces. The Acadia people in a short time found they had neither the resources nor the will to withstand such an assault, and after several meetings with Lammot's special negotiator, Arthur Williams, secretary of Oriental Powder, Acadia's president, John P. Mott, convinced his associates it was best policy to sell the business to the Hamilton Powder Company. The sale was made late in 1882, $74,000 being paid for the Acadia Company, two-thirds of which were supplied by Lammot from his private funds. His appreciation for Williams's successful handling of the deal was expressed in a check of a generous amount that overwhelmed the recipient: "I was perfectly thunderstruck," Williams responded, "when I looked at your valuable gift and cannot realize that my services were worth any such sum. . . . I hope that I may be in the future of some substantial service to you. . . . I shall be at your disposal at any time."[53]

Lammot's confidence in the future of the Canadian explosives industry is apparent in the size of his own investment in the Hamilton Powder Company, which amounted to $211,000 of the company's obligations in the form of stocks, bonds, and notes. Eighteen months after his death Hamilton's board of directors made this entry in their minutes for the meeting held on September 21, 1885: "This company owes its present satisfactory position largely to the plans and efforts of the late Mr. Lammot du Pont."[54]

Expansion into Canada to manufacture and market explosives was the first move of the Du Pont Company beyond America's borders, and it marked its beginnings as an international business enterprise. Lammot's initiative inaugurated a pattern of

Concluding a deal. The figures of this cartoon are not identified, but the man at the right smiling and smoking a cigar is certainly Lammot du Pont.

expansion that characterized the company's later development into the world's largest chemical corporation, with plants, offices, and affiliates located in many other countries. This achievement was the work of his three sons, Pierre, Irénée, and Lammot II, who served successively as company presidents from 1915 until 1940.

The eight years Lammot served as president of the Gunpowder Trade Association developed his executive abilities, tested his integrity as arbiter and compromiser, and strengthened his determination to make the explosives industry a profitable well-regulated enterprise. His leadership and the benefits it brought them won the confidence and support of his associates who annually reelected him president until he declined the office in 1880. By this time Du Pont clearly dominated the American powder business. In G.T.A. affairs it held the majority of votes, it was given larger production and sales quotas, and the offices of the G.T.A. were usually held by its men or those allied with it. Yet in the early stages of this transformation of an industrywide association into an organization controlled by one company, the relations between the individual members comprising it had to be premised on cooperation and rooted in good faith, otherwise it would have been short lived. The ambitions of the smaller companies had to be respected if the destructive price-cutting wars of past years were not to be repeated. This demanded the collaboration of all G.T.A. members at a time when the worsening condition of the economy intensified the desire to put one's own interests uppermost in order to survive.

All of Lammot's experience had been as a partner in the country's largest and oldest powdermaking firm. His outlook was one that favored mergers and consolidation resulting in larger companies that were more efficient, economical, and profitable. But as head of the G.T.A. in its formative years he had to counterbalance this aim by a concern for the welfare of the smaller firms who could wreck the G.T.A. if they thought they were not being accorded fair treatment. Their interests had to be aligned with those of the larger firms in promoting the growth of the industry and in mutual protection against rivals outside the G.T.A. and newcomers to the industry who might threaten the hegemony of the Association.

Lammot's incumbency produced a stable, self-regulated industry, expanding domestically, pushing more aggressively into foreign markets, and earning decent profits. By the end of the 1870s the Gunpowder Trade Association had also become synonymous with the Du Pont Company. Sidestepping the use of the word *monopoly*, Lammot acknowledged that "the G.T.A. is only another name for Du Pont and Co., and if abandoned I think it would be well to hold monthly meetings of Du Pont and Co.'s principal agents and parties when trade could be arranged as well as now. Whatever is Du Pont's interest will be done even if the G.T.A. dissolves."[55] The single remaining major competitor was Laflin and Rand, and relations with it were collaborative rather than competitive.

Consolidation, the genesis of a monopoly, had come about by Du Pont lending badly needed capital funds to other companies; by acquiring stocks in or making total purchase of the assets of others; and by supplying technical advice and improved machinery to some that turned to it for assistance. Though not originally conceived to serve this purpose, the G.T.A. had become the agency by which much of this absorption had been achieved. Beginning in 1880 consolidation broadened to include the manufacture of high explosives, which Lammot had been urging Uncle Henry to get into for several years but with no success except for some moderate investments of funds in other firms that were producing nitroglycerine compounds and dynamite at a comfortable distance away from the Brandywine. The failure of uncle and nephew to agree on this matter was one of several reasons Lammot withdrew from the family firm in 1881.

The sketch of the Du Pont Company's "genealogical tree" made by Lammot is not dated, but it could very well have been drawn when he was in a reminiscing mood at the time he was considering separation from the family firm. Shooting off from the trunk he shows a second primary branch with subbranches bearing the names of powder firms outside of the Pennsylvania anthracite region partly or wholly owned by Du Pont. Only Laflin and Rand, a few small independent black powder plants, and a large high explosives producer, the Giant Powder Company located in California, remained free of its control. This tabulation, based upon his sketch and chronology of acquisitions, shows Du Pont's affiliates and subsidiary companies:

Company	Location	Date Acquired	% Ownership
Austin Powder Co.	Cleveland, Ohio	1870	34
California Powder Works	Santa Cruz, Calif.	1869–1877	44
Sycamore Powder Mills	Nashville, Tenn.	1873–1876	50
Gunpowder Export Co.	New York City, N.Y.	1876	c. 75
Hazard Powder Co.	Hazardville, Conn.	1876	100
Brainerd's Powder Mill	York, Penna.	1876	100
Hamilton Powder Co.	Hamilton, Ontario	1876	c. 70
Lake Superior Powder Co.	Marquette, Mich.	1878	c. 80
Oriental Powder Mills	South Windham, Me.	1879	67
Hercules Powder Co.	Cleveland, Ohio	1881	100
Acadia Powder Co.	Halifax, Nova Scotia	1882	100[56]

The voluminous correspondence in Du Pont Company archives and in Lammot's own papers make it quite clear that, aided by Furman L. Kneeland, Du Pont's New York agent, Lammot was the moving spirit fostering expansion and consolidation. Uncle Henry, who by nature moved more slowly and cautiously, relied heavily upon their recommendations. He recognized their grasp and intimate knowledge of the industry and the advantages to be derived from their associations with other powder company officials. Possessing a forceful, somewhat austere personality, and, by family custom, having ultimate authority as the senior partner, his was the decisive voice that determined company actions. But more and more he had come to respect Lammot's judgments and delegated to his nephew the power to act upon them. In numerous matters Lammot was his uncle's alter ego, his attorney in fact, his signature equally binding the company to agreements and contracts with others.

Considerable travel was involved in many of these dealings, for Uncle Henry was never comfortable away from his home ground on the Brandywine. Outwardly taciturn, distant, and reserved, he preferred to remain in the small stone office that was company headquarters located a few steps from his home. Here he absorbed himself in directing routine operations, keeping a watchful eye on finances, and personally handling most of the routine company correspondence, writing late into the night by candlelight. His devotion to the minutiae of business, even when confined to his bed by illness, is portrayed by his wife Louisa in

Henry du Pont (1812–1889), "Uncle Henry," senior partner and head of the Du Pont Company from 1850 to 1889.

a note to sister-in-law Sophie at Upper Louviers across the Brandywine: "It would amuse an outsider to see the way in which
Henry's illnesses are conducted & the constant stream of clerks,
office boys, etc., which is kept going on all the time. Letters,
checks, despatches, etc., carried on through headaches, rheumatism, colds and other ailments, which are generally supposed to
exempt people from work."[57]

Next to business, Uncle Henry's greatest interest was in the
company's extensive farming operations, particularly raising cattle
and growing wheat, to which he gave a good deal of attention.
On his routine inspections of the farms on horseback or by carriage, a dog or two—whippets and greyhounds—invariably accompanied him. His fondness for dogs once prompted a business
caller from Wilmington to remark that Uncle Henry's office floor
was not covered with carpet, but rather carpeted with greyhounds! This senior partner favored the life of a country squire,
a gentleman farmer–industrialist, with one foot planted in field
and garden and the other in the mills, anchored to the family
homestead and company headquarters where he considered his
presence indispensable. Small wonder then that he had come to
place such reliance upon Lammot, traveling, investigating, supervising, negotiating, and exercising authority over all company
matters outside of Delaware.

Chapter X

Uncle Henry Challenged

THE DEATH of his brother Irénée in September 1877 intensified the incipient discontent Lammot had kept suppressed
for some time. A new partnership agreement would now have to
be drawn up, and Lammot saw this as the opportune time to
propose changes in the company's management and financial
structure. Now forty-six years of age, with twenty-seven years'
experience in the explosives business in which he had earned recognition as a leading figure, he had become restive under the
restrictions imposed by his subordinate status to his uncle. His
horizons and his understanding of the changes taking place in
industry had been broadened by his wide-ranging contacts and
involvement in the busy work-a-day world. The Du Pont Company had grown into a multimillion dollar enterprise with mills
and sales agencies nationwide, and though organized as a partnership, all real authority still remained with the senior partner.
Since he had replaced Lammot's father as such in 1850, Uncle
Henry's one-man domination of the firm had never been challenged until Lammot did so after his brother's death.

During the fall months of 1877 he drew up a long memorandum that contained the changes he thought should be incorporated into the new partnership agreement. Couched in respectful
language, the memorandum was revised several times and submitted to some of the other junior partners and to his brother
Fred, in Louisville, before being presented to Uncle Henry at
the end of the year. Lammot's major proposals concerned the
making of company policy; a reorganization of management;
better compensation for the junior partners; and a more equitable distribution of the firm's capital among all partners com-

Eleuthère Irénée du Pont II (1829–1877), Lammot's older brother. Loyalty to family rather than personal choice kept him in the powder-making business.

mensurate with their years of service and contributions to the company's success. The moderate tone of his memorandum—it was not a "Young Turk's" scornful rebellion against authority— is evident in its salutation: "It is the *duty*, in my opinion for our Senior to allow the junior members a little more power, and to use his influence to keep matters straight while he is yet in the prime of life, otherwise it may be too late. And it is the duty of all his nephews and sons to urge and impress on him the necessity of this step."[1] Uncle Henry was sixty-five.

In what Lammot might have considered a "Magna Carta" from which all else would follow, he recommended that the making of company policy should be shared by all the partners. This had been Uncle Henry's prerogative, sanctioned by observance and family custom since their grandfather's day. Now, after free and open discussion, final decisions should be made by each partner having a vote, and the majority should prevail. To make this more palatable to Uncle Henry, Lammot suggested that in the event all the junior partners voted unanimously, on a matter which the senior partner opposed, the decision would be postponed for three months and then a second vote taken. If all the junior partners still remained united in their position, and Uncle Henry still opposed, then he should yield and accept their opinion. This was really a very modest concession for there was scant likelihood that his two sons, Henry Algernon and William, recently made partners, would remain opposed to their father. Lammot's purpose was to force recognition that his uncle's authority was no longer absolute; that it should be shared with others; and after allowing time for further study, if he was still in the minority, he should yield to their wishes. Such a procedure would generate a stronger sense of responsibility for the company's success among the younger men and would induce feelings of self-respect and pride in what was accomplished.

Specifically, Lammot outlined areas of company operations for which each partner should be responsible:

Lammot:	General management of all powder plants not in Delaware, with Henry A. du Pont as adviser
Eugene:	Manufacture of all powder in the Brandywine mills; preparation of materials, refinery, charcoal making, etc., assisted by Henry A. du Pont

Henry A.:   Office, correspondence, agents, purchase of raw materials.
                       To employ extra clerk to keep strict statistical accounts so
                       that all managers can be kept currently informed on state
                       of business
F. G. du Pont: Repair of mills and machinery; supplies of kegs, lumber,
                       iron, oil, etc.
William du Pont: Farming and agriculture, animals, renting of all properties
                       in Delaware including farms, tenement houses, and cotton
                       mills; transportation

To make this allocation of duties acceptable to Uncle Henry, who
might view it as leaving him with little more to do than scratch
the ears of his favorite greyhound, Lammot added this reassuring pledge: "Nothing in the above shall be interpreted to exclude
Henry du Pont from an overruling control in any or all the above
branches of the business." Veto power was to be his.

This plan of Lammot's recognized that with extensive company growth and its attendant complexities there had to be better, more efficient ways to handle its multifarious activities.
Traditional practices, one-man direction—the candles and quill
pen on Uncle Henry's desk—belonged to an earlier, simpler age
of business enterprise; in a fast-moving, increasingly competitive
era of big business they no longer sufficed. A business controlled
by one family needed infusions of new blood and new ideas to
be innovative and stay in the running.

Greater responsibilities merited better salaries. Those being
received by the junior partners, Lammot informed his uncle, "are
entirely out of the times," and were being eroded by higher living
costs. When his annual salary had been $3,000, and his family
smaller, he had been able to save. But now, even though modest
increases had come, rather belatedly, his salary could not cover
the expenses of his growing family nor provide some of the
amenities that would make life pleasanter for them. The partners'
salaries, however, should not be equal; those who risked their
lives daily doing the dangerous tasks in the mills should receive
more than those who did not, and for his uncle's guidance he
proposed this schedule of annual salaries: Henry, Henry A.,
and William du Pont should receive $20,000. Lammot, Eugene,
and F. G. du Pont should receive, respectively, $8,000, $7,000,
and $5,000. By this schedule Lammot would be the highest paid

member of the firm, if Uncle Henry divided the aggregate of $20,000 for his branch of the family equally between himself and his sons, which was not likely.

Those who traveled on company business, Lammot noted, were never fully reimbursed for their expenses, nor did they receive any extra compensation for the discomforts endured and the enforced absences away from home. For the period 1873 through 1876 he calculated he had averaged annually 32,000 miles on the road, and for none of these years had he been reimbursed more than $1,200 for expenses. Entertainment expenses and the cost of suitable travel clothes had come out of his own pocket. Clearly larger salaries and more generous expense accounts were needed.

Before writing his proposals, Lammot, apparently with the help of the chief clerk, had penetrated Uncle Henry's exclusive preserve, the company's financial records. From these he learned that the firm's average annual profit over the past five years had been $407,833, a yield of 12.22 percent on the capital investment. After a sum to maintain the sinking fund at $25,000 had been deducted from the profits, the balance had been distributed as earnings among the partners proportionate to the number of shares each held. What the stock ledger revealed about the apportionment of shares left Lammot dumbfounded and angry. At the end of 1877 the apportionment of shares was this:

Henry du Pont	106 shares	$ 2,647,875
Lammot du Pont	17 shares	431,460
Eugene du Pont	6 shares	147,487
Francis G. du Pont	1 share	35,841
	130 shares	$ 3,262,663

Five years earlier, in 1873, Uncle Henry's shares had numbered eighty; where had the additional twenty-six shares come from? The answer seemed to be that the senior partner had performed some financial legerdemain. Without informing the other partners or the executors of Irénée's estate of his intent, he had purchased Irénée's twenty-two shares worth $491,000, and had added them to his own eighty shares. This was a violation of the partnership agreement of 1858, which was still in effect, and this

stipulated that in the event of the death or withdrawal of a partner from the company, the remaining partners should have equal
opportunity to purchase his shares. A second figure brought another shock; the number of shares credited to Lammot in 1873
had dropped from twenty-two to seventeen shares at the end of
1877! Had Uncle Henry also arbitrarily transferred five shares
belonging to Lammot to his own account without informing
their owner? Eugene's six shares and Frank's one share remained
unchanged.

Before confronting the senior partner with a demand for an
explanation, Lammot examined the ledgers again to determine
the amount of withdrawals each partner had made from their
respective stock accounts during the past five years, for this would
reveal the current portion of ownership each held in the firm.
Uncle Henry had withdrawn a total of $333,943; this sum, di-
vided by his eighty shares, meant that each share had diminished
$4,174.30 in value. Lammot had withdrawn $121,489, which
meant that each of his twenty-two shares had dropped $5,522.24
in value. On a comparative basis Lammot had withdrawn $1,348
more per share than Uncle Henry for a total of $29,684. Round-
ing this off to $30,000, he figured that his capital stock account
should not be reduced proportionately more than $30,000 be-
low his uncle's. The excessive number of shares now held by his
uncle was giving him an undue portion of the profits, and he
would continue to benefit unfairly until there was a more equitable distribution of capital ownership. The pending new partnership agreement would be the instrument by which this could
be accomplished.[2]

To curb this shift toward total control of the company by
one branch of the family, Lammot recommended that when a
partner died leaving male heirs, enough funds of the partner's
estate should remain with the firm to entitle one of his male heirs
to become a partner and manager. This would insure "that at all
times the three male branches of the family should be equally
represented." This proved to be a prescient proposal. Twenty-
four years later it made possible continued family ownership of
the business by some younger members of the family when the
older partners were thinking of selling out.

Company funds had been used to acquire extensive properties and land to which title had been made in Uncle Henry's name. In Lammot's judgment ownership of real estate purchased with company funds should be vested in the company, not held by a single partner. Accordingly he suggested that the Delaware legislature be petitioned to pass an act enabling E. I. du Pont de Nemours & Company to hold such real estate, and then have all the deeds to the properties retitled and registered in the company's name. Lammot could hardly have been unaware that what Uncle Henry had done was a repetition of what his own father, as senior partner in the 1840s, had done when he too had purchased a number of properties with company funds and had them titled in his name. He had been forced to turn the properties over to his brothers, Henry and Alexis, as trustees, at the insistence of the other partners when he had retired from the firm in 1850.

In his memorandum, really a preliminary draft of a new partnership agreement, Lammot included several other proposals. One stipulated that the partners meet at least once a month regularly to discuss current matters of business. Another asked for a better, systematic keeping of records, the prompt making of all entries, and that all partners have equal access to the books. Single expenditures made by a partner in managing his department should be limited to a thousand dollars; anything above this would have to be approved by the other partners.

Before submitting his memorandum to Uncle Henry, Lammot sent a copy to his brother Alfred Victor in Louisville asking for his opinion. Fred's response had these cogent suggestions:

> 1. Discard or tone down what might be offensive to "our Senior's pride"—those parts which are not essential to the existence of the firm.
> 2. Some articles could more appropriately be considered as by-laws. Separate them into a body of by-laws, but keep them as brief as possible, otherwise Uncle H. will not read it with the care necessary.
> 3. Consider carefully this matter: "What will be the value of the large amount of property outside of Uncle H. in hands of E. I. du Pont & Co. if a rupture occurs? And [if this happens] will not all blame you alone?"

Fred's cautionary advice—avoid offending, distinguish the really important from the less, and anticipate possible harmful consequences—reflects a thoughtful, detached point of view, one that, while favoring change, sought to preserve harmony; otherwise family unity and the family business could be in danger of collapse.

Copies of the memorandum were also given to cousins Eugene and Henry Algernon for their opinion. Eugene's only comment was that the profits be divided equally among the partners, not proportionately according to the shares held by each. Henry Algernon favored equal salaries for all the partners, and being a horselover with a stable of horses at his Winterthur farm, he asked that he and brother William, and Lammot if he wished, be allowed rations for their horses and feed for their cattle from the company farms. Sending a preliminary copy of his proposals to cousin Henry Algernon dispels any suspicion that Lammot was secretly trying to rally the other junior partners to oppose the head of the firm. The two Henrys were close and their interests mutual, so it is likely that Henry A. showed his father his copy of Lammot's memorandum. If cousin Frank made any comment there is no record of his response.[3]

Henry Algernon's recent affiliation with the firm after fifteen years in the army may have caused Lammot to have some disquieting thoughts about who would succeed Uncle Henry as head of the company. Was the father grooming his son as his successor? An indication of the father's thinking was evident as early as 1858 when Henry A. was still a cadet at West Point. In a letter he had informed his son that some day the responsibility for caring for his mother and sisters would rest upon him. The powder company was the source of their livelihood, and its continuation would probably require him to give up his military career and return home to take a hand in running the business: "It will devolve upon you hereafter, to represent my interests in the business & to assist your cousins in carrying it on."[4] Now in company employ since 1875, the colonel had not been assigned any of the dangerous, grubby work in the mills where all the other junior partners had served their apprenticeships, but was ensconced in the office assisting his father. His first duties had been a correspondence clerk, for "my father was unwilling to let any part of the business go out of his hands, and for a long time that was all I did."[5] In time he was entrusted with company transportation matters, and in 1878, under Lammot's aegis, was named president of the Wilmington and Northern Railroad.

Lammot has left no record of any thoughts he may have had on the matter of a successor to Uncle Henry. If he gave it any thought he had every reason to believe that his years of hard work and dedication to the business, added to the stature he had gained in the industry, would make him the obvious person to head the firm. He would have been more than human, however, had he not felt some misgivings. Blood ties, nepotism, and Uncle Henry's desire to have his branch of the family perpetuate its control of the company could turn a blind eye to Lammot's justifiable expectations. We can only speculate with what equanimity the latter contemplated his future when he prepared the final draft of his proposals to reorganize the company.

Accompanied by a covering letter giving his reasons for requesting that a new partnership agreement be written, Lammot sent the memorandum to his uncle in December 1877. Succinctly he listed these reasons: (1) A partner, his brother Irénée, had died. (2) Eugene and Frank had never signed the existing agreement made in 1858. (3) Henry A. and his brother William were about to be admitted as new partners. (4) The 1858 agreement suited the size of the company at that time, but the firm had grown enormously since then and it now also controlled outside companies. The fundamental document that determined its operations needed updating to meet these new conditions.

His closing statement sounded a call for family unity, forbearance, and the cooperation of all the partners in working for the common good. The object was to work harmoniously together to provide decent livings for their families, and to transmit to the next generation the business of E. I du Pont de Nemours & Company.[6]

No written response from Uncle Henry has been found. It is possible that after reading the memorandum he decided to give it the silent treatment, thinking the business of reforming the company would disappear from Lammot's mind under the pressure of so many other matters demanding his attention. Or, in his cautious, deliberate manner of carefully turning over a problem to look at it from all possible angles, the senior partner may have been taking time to ponder the full intent of his nephew's proposals and what their consequences might be if adopted. The two men had frequent contacts in the company office so it can be assumed they discussed the matter, but if notes of their conversations were made they have not survived.

After marking time for four months waiting in vain for a response, frustrated and angered by his uncle's apparent indiffer-

Du Pont Company Headquarters. Erected in 1837 by Alfred Victor du Pont, this small stone building located near the Eleutherian Mills residence was used as company headquarters until 1891.

ence, Lammot decided the only course of action left to him was
to resign. So on a Sunday morning early in April 1878 he wrote
this letter of resignation: "I tender herewith my resignation as a
partner in the firm of E. I. du Pont de Nemours & Co. to take
effect after the 1st of July or 31st of December of this year, at the
option of you and Eugene. . . . It takes no little thought and is a
responsibility that should not be suddenly taken, to leave a home,
the home of your father; to leave a business, the business of my
life, and one whose prestige stands 2nd to none in the country;
to abandon all friends, family, wealth & position to take your
wife and family of little children and leave for an uncertain and
unknown future. This is my only excuse for causing you so much
extra trouble, but it cannot be helped."[7]

This was a most difficult letter for Lammot to write, for the
emotional strain of putting into words the feelings that stirred
deep within him is evident. At forty-seven years of age it meant
giving up a well-established career; uprooting his family and
moving away from their comfortable Brandywine home, leaving
relatives and friends; and in the seventy-six-year history of the
Du Pont Company he would be the first member of the firm to
break away, severing the tightly knit family-company bond. What
his withdrawal would mean to the future of the company could
hardly have failed to cross the minds of Uncle Henry and the
other partners.

We do not know how Mary felt about her husband's decisions, whether she advised against it, or whether, conforming to
our (possibly mistaken) stereotyped conception of the Victorian
wife, she dutifully suppressed her own opinions and meekly ac-
quiesced in his decision. If our perception of their relationship is
accurate, we believe Lammot would have unburdened himself to
her, recounting his reasons for severing ties, and she would have
agreed even though it would be a painful wrench to separate
from family and friends and leave their beloved Nemours.

When she learned of his intent, Lammot's mother, Meta,
living a few miles away at Goodstay, feared it would cause ill will
and create a rift in the close-knit clan. The marriage of Willie,
Uncle Henry's younger son, was to take place soon after Lammot had sent his letter of resignation, and when Meta heard that

he was not going to attend the wedding she chided him gently: "Now dear son, do not think of staying away from it. It would give great offense to all the family if you were not there. Everyone would think there was some terrible cause, or a quarrel, and make a coldness and ill feeling with some one of them. Tis wrong and useless to offend people, with your eyes open to the danger. If it is the expense of a suit of clothes (tho' I should not be particular in your place), I will cheerfully give you $100 for it. Anything to avoid blame being attached to my beloved son."[8] Whether his adoring mother's entreaty, buttressed by the offer of a new suit of clothes, persuaded him to be a guest at Willie's wedding, is not known.

More than a month went by before Uncle Henry made any direct response to Lammot's memorandum. This came in a brief note in which he suggested that the firm's excess capital be apportioned among the partners pro rata according to the number of shares each had held under the old partnership. He said nothing about Lammot's other proposals.[9]

Lammot regarded this as a sop, altogether unacceptable, for it confirmed his belief that his uncle could not face up to making the fundamental changes that threatened to diminish his authority, and possibly reduce his income. Lammot's patience snapped, and on a hot August night he forced a showdown in an outburst of impassioned language, repeating in bitter, angry words that he was getting out of the company!

The confrontation penetrated his uncle's stubborn stance, for the following morning he sent Lammot a letter, conciliatory in tone, reproachful of his nephew's intemperate manner, but asking him to reconsider his decision to resign:

> Referring to our conversation of last night, I would say that as you absolutely refused to give your reasons for the course you propose, and as I am thoroughly ignorant of having given you any cause for such a step, I am totally at a loss to understand your motives. But as your uncle and friend, as well as your partner, I must entreat you to do nothing hasty, nor commit yourself to any course of action such as you propose. It could be of no benefit to you & would be a very serious injury to the du Pont family. . . . I think you owe it to your family to weigh all matters thoroughly

in connection with this matter, & I feel sure that whatever cause or grievance you may have, it is not well founded & can be readily explained if a chance is fairly given for explanation.[10]

On reading this Lammot must have been amazed at his uncle's failure to comprehend his reasons for resigning. Either he had not carefully read his December memorandum, or, if he had, had failed to grasp its import. He may have filed it away as something which, in time, would blow over and be forgotten. After "sitting on" the proposals for months without making any response, Uncle Henry's conciliatory request that they now talk things over calmly so that he might understand the causes of his grievances must have appeared ludicrous to Lammot. His uncle was either insensitive, obtuse, or had finally come to realize what the loss of his nephew would mean to him and the firm.

Lammot replied, stating the sorrow and feelings of trepidation that assailed him on breaking relations: "The severing of family ties and leaving behind the results of a lifetime, often brings my heart into my throat." But he was remaining firm in his resolve. As to his uncle's plea that he still did not understand Lammot's reasons for leaving, he noted: "Now Uncle, you knew sufficient of the troubles and difficulties of the matter, as they were all handed you in writing in the proposed Articles of Copartnership. These, instead of being frankly discussed and modified by the views of all the partners, were copied almost without modification, and, as what *I demanded*—then given to be signed. Is this fair or right to the others? Have not six months of the copartnership passed and not one word from you on the subject? How can I interpret this but that you prefer my retirement?"[11]

An immediate reply from his uncle denied that he had failed to give serious attention to Lammot's proposals. He had written a new copartnership agreement using Lammot's memorandum as his guide and had shown it to Lammot who apparently was satisfied with it. Subsequently the other partners had read it and then met in his office to discuss it. There were no dissenting opinions, but when he had asked them to sign it, he reminded his nephew, "You know how that was received," implying that Lammot had objected to his handiwork, and had stormed out of the meeting in anger. His uncle defended his position in this conflict that had set them against one another:

> I was perfectly satisfied to have the new articles in the shape you and the others wanted them and the failure in getting them signed is not due to me. I cannot in looking back carefully through all our intercourse as partners, relations, and neighbors see any just cause for the umbrage you seem to have taken against me, and I assure you that I have always had the kindest feelings toward you; that I deeply deplore the morbid feelings you seem to entertain towards me, which I feel are not founded on any action of mine to which you should take exception. You have never stated any cause of grievance, till this letter states it about those articles of co-partnership. You say "that instead of being frankly discussed by the views of all the partners they were copied almost without modification." You will remember that you, Eugene and Frank discussed it and agreed what your views were; we discussed it afterwards, I representing my two sons, and I agreed to it for them and myself, and that was all that could be required.[12]

If Uncle Henry was accurate in describing what had happened, one is puzzled by Lammot's refusal to sign the newly drafted agreement which, according to his uncle, incorporated the reform measures he had proposed. His papers throw no light on this, but it may have been that on further careful reading he had found one or more of his key proposals omitted. And had the other partners really been encouraged to freely criticize and offer their own suggestions to the senior partner's draft, or had Uncle Henry handled this in cursory, rubber-stamp fashion, confident there would be no opposition to his wishes? There is also the likelihood that by his manner, facial expression, and tone of voice in which he presented the agreement to the other partners, that he did so in a pejorative manner—these were Lammot's *demands*—the ultimatum of a disgruntled partner who, for the present, had to be placated. Uncle Henry's attitude may have been one of feigned acceptance of Lammot's proposals—adopt some of his milder reforms and in time the rest would be forgotten and the business would continue in the good old proven, comfortable way. Uncle Henry knew there had to be a measure of acquiescence, much as it hurt his authoritarian spirit, for if he failed to bend he would lose Lammot's services, and this he was loath to contemplate. And, as patriarch of the family, it would sadden him to see its unity broken.

In truth, too, Lammot did not want to leave, but he could not retreat from the position he had taken. A fundamental restructuring was needed if Du Pont was to retain its dominance of the explosives industry. Now, with his uncle professing his intent to make some changes but with Lammot's skeptical disbelief that he would really do so, how could the impasse be resolved? Could some compromises be arranged that would satisfy both and restore harmony? A groping toward accommodation, a desire to get back on a friendlier footing, pervades the notes that passed between them from late summer 1878 until spring of the following year. Lammot did not resign but stayed on the job. A friendlier tone in their exchanges evinces a desire to heal the breach, and their conversations in the office may have brought about a rapprochement that promised to heal wounds.

Uncle Henry suggested to Lammot that he assume the presidency of the Hazard Company and take complete charge of its manufacturing and marketing operations. In his opinion, after a month or so in Hazard's New York city office, Lammot would only have to spend two or three days a month on Hazard business, so his active role in the parent company would not be diminished.[13] There was little inducement in this, however, for since Du Pont's quiet acquisition of Hazard in 1876 its officers had been reporting to Lammot who was responsible for all plant operations outside of Delaware. His uncle may have misjudged Lammot as ambitious to be formally titled, wielding executive authority, but such would have been an empty formality. For the first time during his long tenure as senior partner Uncle Henry sent Lammot a preliminary draft of the company balance sheet and inventory for 1878, and asked if he had any suggestions concerning it. There was also some talk about adding a private office to the company headquarters building for Lammot, and engaging a confidential clerk to assist him. These, and other concessions seem to have kept the rift from widening, but they did not altogether satisfy Lammot, and at the end of April 1879, he told his uncle that he would retire at the end of the year.[14] For

General Inventory of E. I. du Pont and Company, December 31, 1878. Compiled by Lammot du Pont when he was at odds with Henry du Pont over financial matters, management, and division of profits.

General Inventory of E J du Pont & Co
Dec 31st 1878

Gunpowder Mills	(N°3)		393	300	00
Wooden Mills	(N°3)		128	423	60
Mill Sites	(N°3)		57	430	09
Farms	(N°3)		286	652	43
Houses & Lots &c	(N°3)		90	344	90
Wharfs Middletown & Wilm	(N°3)		26	885	69
Heller Tract at Wap.	(N°3)		2	100	00
Powder Magazines & Lots (N°4) including &c &c			359	624	25
Shares & Bonds (N°5)			920	848	69
Bills Receivable (N°6)			154	831	05
Bonds Receivable (N°7)			5	519	45
Nitrate of Soda 1.473.220 lbs p (N°8)					
Sulphur (9) 430,500			7	792	50
Crude Saltpetre 1.300.880 lbs p (N°10)					
Muriate of Potash 1015400 N°11			11	423	25
Charcoal Wood (12)			9	028	62
Wap. Inventory (13)			61	092	78
Due to Wap. (13)				392	80
H A Wiley omitted entries (N°14)			35	181	31
Sea Inventory N°2 omitting Gunpowder at Brazos & Agencies			95	584	01
Cost Price of Hazardville			883	310	45
Ledger accounts to our credit			905	071	80
Factory to our credit			621	512	94
Total liabilities less stock & Property & Sons			2 822	311	57
Total amt less Powder in Agencies & on Brandywine					

the present he confided to no one a plan taking shape in his mind to launch an enterprise of his own. Everywhere production of black powder was being cut back as dynamite was capturing market after market. Users were finding that one pound of it was equivalent to three pounds of black powder! The future of the explosives industry was in high explosives, a fact which, "of course, draws our grave thoughts to the matter," Lammot informed a business acquaintance.[15]

Chapter XI

Repauno

Dynamite had been introduced into the United States in 1867 when the Giant Powder Company in San Francisco began manufacturing it under license of patents held by the Swedish explosives engineer Alfred Nobel. Its production was very hazardous, the first stage of which was the combining of nitric and sulfuric acids with glycerine to form liquid nitroglycerine, a highly sensitive, unstable compound. This was as far as the original discoverer, Ascanio Sobrero, professor of industrial chemistry at the University of Turin, Italy, in 1846 had developed it. He had considered it a laboratory curiosity far too dangerous ever to be produced for commercial use.

Other chemists carried on experiments with nitroglycerine during the 1850s seeking safer ways to manufacture, transport, and detonate it, but it was not until 1864 that this was accomplished by Nobel, who was granted Swedish and British patents for the new explosive which he named dynamite. His success came with the discovery that nitroglycerine would remain inert when absorbed in a type of earth called kieselguhr until it was detonated by a blasting cap, which he also invented and patented. Under a royalty arrangement the American rights to manufacture under these patents were granted the California Giant Powder Company, and within a short time its dynamite, even at the initial high price of $1.75 a pound, began winning customers who found it much more effective than black powder in most mining and excavating operations.

To meet this competition, the largest producer of black powder on the West Coast, the California Powder Works, based in San Francisco, with mills at Santa Cruz, began producing a high explosive called "Black Hercules." This consisted of nitroglycerine absorbed in black powder rather than kieselguhr, but in use it was soon found that black powder was not a very satisfactory absorbent material. In its place the California company's chemist, James Howden, concocted a better absorbent, or "dope," and produced a variant form of dynamite consisting of nitroglycerine (40%), potassium nitrate (31%), magnesium carbonate (10%), sugar (15.66%), and potassium chlorate (3.34%), which was marketed under the name "Hercules."

Howden died before obtaining a patent on his explosive, but in 1874 a patent for "Hercules" dynamite was issued to Joseph W. Willard, another officer of the California Powder Works. The Giant Powder Company regarded this as an infringement upon the Nobel patent for which it held the American rights and it instituted suit against Willard and the California Powder Works.

The Du Pont Company had a 40 percent interest in the California Powder Works, a major supplier of black powder and dynamite to construction projects and mining operations in the western and Rocky Mountain states.

Litigation dragged on through the courts for a number of years during which time each of the companies increased production of their respective brands of dynamite, competing against each other, and against the black powder manufacturers, for the trade of the booming mining operations in the far western and Rocky Mountain states. Both firms also went after the trade of the midwestern and Atlantic states, the California Powder Works sending Willard to Cleveland to set up a branch dynamite plant, appropriately named Hercules, and the Giant Powder Company establishing a rival plant at Kenvil, New Jersey.[1]

These developments had been warily watched by the black powder manufacturers. In the beginning years a number of disastrous explosions had convinced some of them, including Henry du Pont, that dynamite was much too dangerous to ever pose a real threat to black powder. Despite this, about 1869–70, when the California Powder Works was still primarily a black powder producer just edging into dynamite, Uncle Henry had agreed to a modest investment of Du Pont Company funds in the west coast concern, presumably upon Lammot's recommendation. This proved to be such a good investment that Uncle Henry's objections to high explosives gradually diminished, and by September 1876 he was willing to buy an additional thousand shares in the California firm, but surreptitiously. The purchase was made in the name of his daughter Sophie, recently married to an architect, Theophilus P. Chandler, and living at Ridley Park, Pennsylvania, midway between Wilmington and Philadelphia. Within the next five years Du Pont's holdings in the California company increased to a total of 6,500 shares with a book value of $234,336, but on which Lammot placed a market value of $760,500, or $117 per share. Total profits earned by the firm in 1881 amounted to $402,166, approximately 40 percent of which was paid in dividends to the Du Pont Company.[2]

Lammot was the liaison between the two firms. His correspondence with Bernard Peyton, the California company's superintendent, and later president, reveals a familiarity with all its operations. Peyton's letters show a turning to Lammot for advice and guidance on matters of policy, finance, transport and marketing, and for some technical assistance in certain aspects of dynamite manufacture. Lammot had a copy of Nobel's and other high explosive patents and kept abreast of developmental work being done in dynamite manufacture. In his laboratory-workshop he performed experiments with sulphuric and nitric acids and glycerine, dynamite's components, and recorded his observations and results in laboratory notebooks.[3]

An instance of Peyton seeking Lammot's advice occurred in the summer of 1876 when his company was thinking of setting up a plant to produce its own nitric and sulphuric acids rather than continue to buy from outside suppliers. After stating his estimate of costs, and the anticipated savings from this change-over, Peyton asked du Pont's opinion before going ahead with the project "because some members of your firm are specially qualified to advise upon the matter."[4] In this same letter Peyton noted that the dynamite presently being produced at his plant consisted of 85 percent nitroglycerine and 15 percent light carbonate of magnesia, the latter proving to be a much better absorbent than kieselguhr or any other material. This information was of particular interest to Lammot because carbonate of magnesia was one of the chemicals he believed could probably be extracted from the soda lakes he had recently acquired in Wyoming.

His interest in the lake deposits as a source of a raw material for making dynamite could only have been whetted by Peyton's endorsement of carbonate of magnesia as the preferred absorbent of nitroglycerine. This was also the verdict of J. W. Willard at the Hercules plant in Cleveland who, after testing many other substances, reported to Lammot that he had produced "the best form of dynamite known" when he used carbonate of magnesia as the absorbent.[5]

In a letter accompanying a copy of a heavily statistical annual report of the California Powder Works for 1877, which also included many details on plant operations, Peyton concluded: "I do not, of course, expect you to wade through the sea of figures, but thought that Mr. Lammot might, some evening, glance over them and then point out to me where improvements could be made." Lammot responded to this promptly, offering his opinion of a site Peyton had selected for a new mill, and making suggestions for some mechanical improvements. He also described some recent tests he had conducted of methods and ingredients used in making Hercules dynamite which confirmed his belief that the process did not infringe upon the Nobel patents held by the Giant Powder Company.[6]

Lammot's help was also sought by Peyton to intercede with the railroads to carry dynamite from the California plant to the construction projects and the numerous mines and diggings being worked in the shadows of the Sierra, the Rocky, and Wasatch mountains. Freight agents of the Union Pacific Railroad, the principal carrier, refused to handle it because they considered it too hazardous. Lammot wrote directly to the president of the Union Pacific Railroad, Sidney Dillon, explaining to him that Hercules dynamite was the most stable of all dynamites and was perfectly safe to carry by rail if normal handling precautions were observed. His letter on this matter clearly marks Lammot as a convert to dynamite, for he informed Dillon: "You must be aware (which I as a powder manufacturer do not like to acknowledge) that these high explosives are now a necessity for hard rock, and in driving tunnels where the rock is confined they do more execution and less drilling than powder does. Many gold, silver and lead mines are now worked at a profit by the use of these explosives that could not with common powder. Hence their transportation becomes a necessity, particularly where the development of the country is to be desired. Hence its safe transportation cannot fail to interest you and your road." Dillon forwarded the request to his district superintendent at Omaha, Nebraska, but that gentleman, after weighing the risks involved, decided that all high explosives were too hazardous to ship by rail. He refused all requests to carry them and instructed all his agents to do likewise. This meant that for a number of years dynamite had to be delivered by wagon teams, pack mules, and where possible, by river boats. In early 1881 Lammot was still pushing this matter with the Union Pacific, advising Dillon where cars carrying high explosives should be placed in a freight train, and how they could be shielded against rifle shots fired at them.[7]

Lammot had thus come to know a great deal about dynamite well in advance of his decision to leave the Du Pont Company. In his usual thorough approach he had read, studied, and experimented with its chemical components and had become fully aware of the dangers involved in processing them into nitroglycerine. Converting that compound into a safe, commercial explosive depended upon a precise amount of it being absorbed in the most suitable absorbent material. He had observed it being made on visits to the Hercules plant in Cleveland, where his mentor was J. W. Willard, its superintendent. The overall layout of a dynamite factory, the placement of the several structures, their design and materials of construction, and the machinery and equipment contained in them were all matters with which Lammot had now become familiar when he began putting down on paper his plans for the construction of a high explosives plant in the fall of 1879.

The inhabitants of Wilmington and northern New Castle County were understandably alarmed when they read a news item in the Wilmington *Every Evening* of November 4, 1879, stating that nitroglycerine mills were being built about a mile and a half from the powder mills on the Brandywine. One building was well under way, others would soon follow, and a spur rail line would connect the new plant with the Wilmington and Northern Railroad. Its exact location was not given by the paper, but it appears to have been upstream in a rural area between the villages of Greenville and Centerville, uncomfortably close to cousin Henry Algernon du Pont's Winterthur property.

The newspaper announcement is the only known source of information on this development. Lammot's and Uncle Henry's papers, and those of the company, contain no mention of the new plant. There is little doubt that it was begun at Lammot's instigation but then quickly abandoned under pressure from Cousin Henry, Uncle Henry, and other neighboring property owners. Convinced by this time that dynamite was a superior explosive for many blasting purposes and aware of the profits it earned, Uncle Henry was now at last disposed to have the company get into high explosives, and Lammot was the obvious person to direct the new undertaking. But another site for the plant, at a safe distance from the black powder mills, had to be found. This decision coincided with, and may have been hastened by,

word from Solomon Turck of Laflin and Rand, who informed
the Du Pont Company that his firm was going into the dynamite
business. Turck suggested that this be a joint enterprise with Du
Pont and Hazard having an equal interest with Laflin and Rand.
It was better to cooperate than compete against each other, as
regulation of the black powder industry by the Gunpowder Trade
Association had proved, but his firm would nevertheless go it
alone even if Du Pont and Hazard did not accept his invitation.[8]

Turck's offer was accepted and within a few weeks a preliminary agreement was reached in which the Big Three black powder manufacturers united to organize a high explosives firm of
which Lammot would be president. He would be responsible for
erecting the plant and getting it into production at the earliest
possible date, sometime early in 1880. By its secret ownership of
the Hazard Company, Du Pont would in fact be two-thirds owner
of the new company. And from its inception Lammot began
marshaling his own personal financial resources in anticipation
of acquiring part of the Du Pont Company's interest in it for
himself.

The new venture he was to direct provided a welcome
emancipation for Lammot. It allowed him to move out from his
uncle's shadow and to assume the executive responsibilities for
which his thirty years in the explosives industry had prepared
him. With a confidence grounded in experience and accomplishments, psychologically he was ready and eager to assume leadership of the new firm. It would outwardly preserve the appearance
of unbroken family harmony and avoid the unpleasant publicity
that would have attended any disclosure of his serious differences
with his uncle. These were now moot, for to all outward appear-
ances the move into high explosives would be seen as another
step in the Du Pont Company's continuing growth, and as Lammot had been the most aggressive promoter of this expansion it
was obvious he should be given direction of the new venture.

As head of the new firm, unhampered by a too cautious
conservatism, he was free to introduce his own ideas of company
organization and management. He could employ capable associates from outside the family circle and more readily experiment
with processes and machinery that gave promise of improving its
position vis-à-vis its competitors. His break from total, one-family

control of all operations was essential to the success of a company in an era of large and complex competing organizations. In the firm he began creating he broke the old company mold and introduced a pattern of organization and a strategy of operations that were to influence the leadership his sons and nephews gave the Du Pont Company when they took control of it shortly after the turn of the century.

A number of possible sites for the new plant were examined by Lammot during the closing weeks of 1879 before an isolated spot on the New Jersey shore of the Delaware River was selected. This was a 750-acre expanse of bottomland drained by Repaupo Creek near its confluence with the Delaware River, an area known as Thompson's Point, in Gloucester County. The nearest community was Gibbstown, and directly across the river on the Pennsylvania side was the riverfront city of Chester which had good shipping facilities by water and rail.

From the outset Lammot realized that he needed the help of someone with experience in selecting the best location for a dynamite plant, so he enlisted the aid of J. W. Willard of the Hercules Company plant in Cleveland. Willard recommended his nephew, Charles A. Morse, who had done work of this kind. Morse was hired in November and for the next four months he assisted Lammot. Together they examined the New Jersey site, surveyed and purchased it, and then set about having the land cleared and a wharf constructed. They planned docking facilities and looked into railroad connections, gauged river depths and highwater levels, and decided upon safety measures. One drawback to the site was the absence of trees of any size that could serve as buffers in the event of an explosion. Morse examined all bids submitted by contractors and interviewed the first employees hired to work for the Repauno Chemical Company, the name Lammot had given it. Repauno rather than Repaupo was chosen to avoid confusion with a nearby rail stop named Repaupo, and because it had a more euphonious sound.[9] The area had once been the site of a Lenape Indian village. Caches of artifacts were found when a number of burial mounds were unearthed, a discovery that delighted Lammot who added them to the Indian materials he had been collecting over the years.

Solomon Turck of Laflin and Rand Company was kept advised of developments as the plant was built, Lammot sometimes deferring action until he had obtained Turck's opinion. As a one-third partner Turck visited Repauno a number of times during its construction and these visits strengthened the friendship between the two men and increased Turck's confidence in Lammot's ability to head the new enterprise. Turck suggested that one of his employees, Samuel T. Appolonio, move into the vacancy caused by Morse's departure in March 1880 and be made works manager, Turck assuring Lammot that Appolonio would "devote his entire time to the new company. . . . he will make us a good man."[10] The appointment proved to be an excellent one, for Appolonio took on many assignments, handling them with initiative and efficiency that earned Lammot's approval and relieved him of many routine chores.

Other appointments were made, again with Willard's help. One was Harry W. Norcross, an employee of Willard's at the Cleveland plant, who was put in charge of the nitroglycerine and dynamite operations and subsequently made superintendent of Repauno. A second was Herbert G. Chase, a Willard relative, who was first the bookkeeper and later general assistant to the superintendent. Searching for a man with good credentials in both the theoretical and technical aspects of high explosives chemistry, Lammot recruited Walter N. Hill from the U.S. Naval Torpedo Station at Newport, Rhode Island. He had first met Hill when the latter had testified as an expert witness in a court case, and Lammot was so impressed that he promptly offered Hill the position of chief chemist at Repauno.

During the early months of construction Lammot commuted daily from home, first stopping at the Chester post office to pick up mail from Post Office Box 33, which he had rented. The river crossing was made by rowboat for a time, but in March 1880 a second-hand steam yacht, thirty-seven and one-half feet long, with an eight-foot beam and a four-foot hold, was bought from Enoch Moore, Jr., a Wilmington boatbuilder, for $761.50. Christened *Repauno*, this vessel became the principal transportation link, carrying people and supplies across the river for a number of years. Some items came from Wetherill and Company of Chester, who furnished steam engines, boilers, and copper vats.

Pusey and Jones Company, shipbuilders and manufacturers of papermaking machinery in Wilmington, furnished acid pots, distillers, and tanks. Other equipment came from the Hercules plant in Cleveland, and some was made in the Du Pont Brandywine machine shop under Eugene's and Frank's supervision, following sketches and specifications supplied by Lammot.

A visitor with a special interest in the Repauno plant was Bernard Peyton of the California Powder Works, who came east in January 1880. His main purpose in making the trip was to meet with Lammot and the attorneys defending his firm in the patent infringement suit that had been brought by the Giant Powder Company. The Du Pont Company's 40 percent ownership of Peyton's firm would be seriously affected if the California company lost the case, so Peyton and Lammot met with George Harding, a New York lawyer who, by no strange coincidence, also happened to be a legal counsel to the Du Pont Company. Harding apparently advised that an attempt be made to settle the case out of court, possibly by a pooling of patents, before it came up for final adjudication, which was scheduled in a forthcoming term of court. This was also very important to the future of Repauno, for without a settlement of the patent dispute its process for manufacturing dynamite could also be challenged as an infringement upon the Nobel patents held by the Giant Company.

To resolve the matter, Lammot accompanied Peyton when he returned to San Francisco in mid-February 1880. Negotiations of this nature could not be carried on by letter or telegram, and long-distance lines had not yet spanned the continent, so a meeting with the heads of the rival Giant Company for the purpose of working out an amicable arrangement prompted Lammot to make the seven-day trip west in the dead of winter. San Francisco was observing Washington's birthday the day he arrived, Monday, February 23, with all business houses closed, so nothing got done. After dinner at his hotel, the Palace, "the largest in the world," he had been told, he had several visitors. One was the Du Pont Company's San Francisco agent, John Skinker; also Evan and William Coleman, relatives through his brother Bidermann's wife, and four officers from the California Powder Works. It was midnight before he got to bed, he wrote his wife, but "only to kick all night as I missed the motion of the cars," referring to the six nights he had spent riding in the Union Pacific's sleeping cars.

The next morning he visited the dynamite plant of the California Powder Works, following which he was taken to lunch at the exclusive Pacific Club. Here it was pointed out to him that of the forty-nine men dining there, thirty-one were millionaires! "I really think California can produce more of them in less space than any part of the world," he wrote to Mary. One wonders if he had any fleeting regrets that he had not followed his youthful impulse back in 1849 when he had almost joined the "gold rush" in search of his own quick bonanza. That afternoon was spent with the head of the Giant Powder Company, Albert Dibblee, discussing how the patent suit might be settled out of court. Dibblee was a polite listener to Lammot's proposals, but he could say nothing affirmatively until he discussed the matter with his directors, and this could not be done for several days. Lammot was not optimistic of the outcome, for in a postscript of his letter to Mary he advised, "You can tell Uncle Henry that the result is extremely doubtful, they have not given an answer to any of my arguments, or, in fact, made any reply."[11] When the patent suit went to court later in 1880 the Giant Powder Company lost the case. The patent that it claimed was being infringed upon—a reissue of the original Nobel patent—was declared invalid because it claimed more than the original patent had granted. With the dispute thus settled in their favor, the California Powder Works—and Repauno—could now continue operations free of the threat of a damaging lawsuit.

The Atlantic Giant Powder Company at Kenvil, New Jersey, the subsidiary of the California Giant Company, remained a serious competitor for the dynamite trade of the eastern part of the country. To bring it under control, the Du Pont Company, Laflin and Rand, and Lammot personally, began buying stock in the rival concern. Within two years they had acquired a one-third ownership and were able to reorganize it, renaming it the Atlantic Dynamite Company. An agreement was made by the participants that licensed each to manufacture dynamite under the patents held by the others. As "conscience money," or to assure continued peace within the industry, it was also agreed that the Atlantic Dynamite Company would receive 45 percent of all profits upon the combined sales of all the parties to the agreement as a royalty on all its patents, and in settlement of all claims for past infringements. The dynamite companies were also brought into the Gunpowder Trade Association, pledged to honor fixed price schedules, quotas, division of sales territories, and the same "neutral belt" stipulations that governed the black powder trade. In forging these arrangements that effectively stabilized the high explosives industry, Lammot was the pivotal figure. His confidence in the future of dynamite was shown by the amount of his personal fortune he invested in it. His aim to become a one-third owner of Repauno was opposed by Uncle Henry, but after a bitter confrontation extending from March to October 1882 Lammot became a coequal owner with Du Pont and Laflin and Rand. This was done when he finally cut his ties with the Du Pont Company, and in paying him for his share in the family business Uncle Henry agreed to transfer to him securities in a number of firms, including a thousand shares of Repauno stock valued at $120,000. A summary of his assets at the beginning of 1884 shows that his largest single investment was in the Repauno Chemical Company, $212,163, and the second largest in the Atlantic Dynamite Company, $178,526.[12]

Getting Repauno built and into operation was Lammot's most pressing task, one to which he could easily have devoted all his time, but this was not possible. Although he had notified his uncle that he was withdrawing from the Du Pont Company at the end of 1879, it was not feasible to abruptly drop the numerous company responsibilities he had been handling. None of his cousins was yet ready, by experience or inclination, to assume his demanding work load; and other than himself, Uncle Henry was the only one fully informed about all the ramifications and the status of current and pending developments. The senior partner, now sixty-eight years old, and anchored to his office by a self-imposed burden of myriad details that he would not delegate to others, habitually avoided direct personal contacts with the outside business world and relied upon Lammot to act in his stead. Lacking Lammot's open, gregarious personality, Henry was aloof and ill at ease among strangers when away from his own domain, and he was unequipped temperamentally or by experience to take on the many tasks that someone would have to assume if Lammot's departure was sudden. Nature and circumstance had fashioned Lammot for a career in the broader currents of American industry, Uncle Henry for the more placid, quieter pools of the Brandywine.

Lammot was well aware he could not just drop these unfinished matters and give all his time to Repauno. After thirty years as a key man in the family firm he could not turn his back on it and just walk away. The successful completion of some of these matters would also affect his own future and his personal fortunes. Consequently, for the next several years he gave time to Repauno and to looking after a number of important Du Pont Company affairs.

The scope of his work load was made clear in a letter to Uncle Charles Belin at Wapwallopen early in May 1880 at an extremely busy time when Repauno was just about to go into production. Lammot's letter was in response to one from his uncle seeking clarification of his status as head of the Wapwallopen plant. A Thomas Scott had recently been appointed manager of the mills there, and Belin felt the new man would usurp his authority. Lammot chided him for being too sensitive about the matter—Scott had been sent to assist him, not replace him—Belin should rest confident that he was still in charge.

Then in a mood of mild reproach at his uncle's concern over a seemingly petty problem, and to contrast it with the tasks presently confronting him, Lammot invited Belin to "forget yourself for a few minutes and put yourself behind my spectacles and see what you would do in my place." There followed this enumeration of the more important tasks on his agenda:

1. Looking after 58 pairs of rolling mills at many locations outside of Delaware and attending to their machinery. Of all these Uncle Henry had only seen the four at Wapwallopen.
2. "Contrary to the wishes of my senior I have gone into the high explosives business which has been sapping the foundations of the black powder trade."
3. With no previous experience in this line of manufacture

have begun building a chemical plant to produce nitric and sulphuric acids, nitroglycerine, and dynamite.

4. Has two "heavy lawsuits" on hand, and is commencing a struggle with the Giant Powder Company.

5. Continues to attend to the relations between the powder companies in the Gunpowder Trade Association at the insistence of its members, though he no longer heads that organization.

6. Gives support to Thomas C. Brainerd, head of the Canadian Hamilton Powder Company, because "no one else will except my friend Solomon Turck," president of Laflin and Rand.

7. Is winding up a struggle with the Reading Railroad Company for control of the Berks County Railroad, a feeder railroad to the Wilmington and Northern Railroad.

8. Helps Col. Henry A. du Pont in running the Wilmington and Northern Railroad, and is now electing "a new board that he can work with smoothly."

And, as a gentle parting reprimand, Lammot chided his uncle, "Now uncle, if you had these matters on hand I think they would keep even you busy."[13] Lammot was never to be totally free from parent company involvement; and for the next four years he found it obligatory, and advisable, to share his time and energy between this "unfinished business" of the Du Pont Company and the enterprise he was launching at Repauno.

The Repauno Chemical Company was formally incorporated and granted a charter by the Delaware Superior Court on June 17, 1880, all the required legal papers and formalities being taken care of by cousin Victor du Pont, a Wilmington attorney. The charter licensed it to make, buy, sell, compound, and refine chemical explosives, cartridges, fuses, and primers. Its initial capital of $300,000 was to be furnished by the Big Three black powder companies in equal amounts of $100,000 each, subject to the call of the president, Lammot, through the secretary-treasurer, his cousin William, younger son of Uncle Henry. The total stock was not immediately subscribed to but bought in blocks over the next several years. Uncle Henry's caution, maybe a lingering doubt about Repauno's future, saw the Du Pont Company's paid-in capital amounting to $85,000 by the close of 1881, eighteen months after the plant had commenced operations on May 30, 1880, under Lammot's watchful eye.

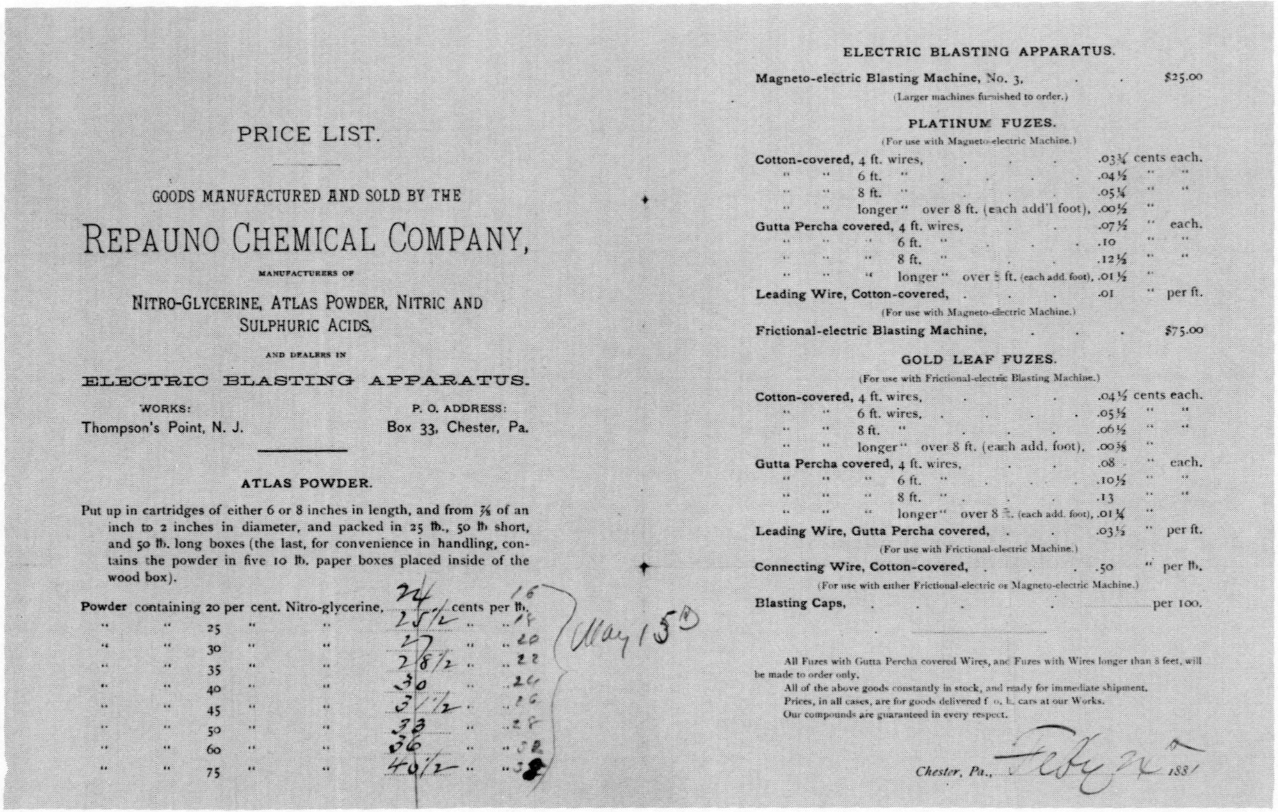

PRICE LIST.

GOODS MANUFACTURED AND SOLD BY THE

REPAUNO CHEMICAL COMPANY,

MANUFACTURERS OF

NITRO-GLYCERINE, ATLAS POWDER, NITRIC AND SULPHURIC ACIDS,

AND DEALERS IN

ELECTRIC BLASTING APPARATUS.

WORKS: Thompson's Point, N. J.

P. O. ADDRESS: Box 33, Chester, Pa.

ATLAS POWDER.

Put up in cartridges of either 6 or 8 inches in length, and from ⅞ of an inch to 2 inches in diameter, and packed in 25 ℔., 50 ℔ short, and 50 ℔. long boxes (the last, for convenience in handling, contains the powder in five 10 ℔. paper boxes placed inside of the wood box).

Powder containing 20 per cent. Nitro-glycerine,		cents per ℔.	
" " 25 " "		"	"
" " 30 " "		"	"
" " 35 " "		"	"
" " 40 " "		"	"
" " 45 " "		"	"
" " 50 " "		"	"
" " 60 " "		"	"
" " 75 " "		"	"

ELECTRIC BLASTING APPARATUS.

Magneto-electric Blasting Machine, No. 3,	$25.00	
(Larger machines furnished to order.)		
PLATINUM FUZES. (For use with Magneto-electric Machine.)		
Cotton-covered, 4 ft. wires,	.03¾	cents each.
" " 6 ft. "	.04½	" "
" " 8 ft. "	.05¼	" "
" " longer " over 8 ft. (each add'l foot),	.00½	"
Gutta Percha covered, 4 ft. wires,	.07½	" each.
" " " 6 ft. "	.10	" "
" " " 8 ft. "	.12½	" "
" " " longer " over 8 ft. (each add. foot),	.01½	"
Leading Wire, Cotton-covered,	.01	" per ft.
(For use with Magneto-electric Machine.)		
Frictional-electric Blasting Machine,	$75.00	
GOLD LEAF FUZES. (For use with Frictional-electric Blasting Machine.)		
Cotton-covered, 4 ft. wires,	.04½	cents each.
" " 6 ft. wires,	.05½	" "
" " 8 ft. "	.06½	" "
" " longer " over 8 ft. (each add. foot),	.00⅜	"
Gutta Percha covered, 4 ft. wires,	.08	" each.
" " " 6 ft. "	.10½	" "
" " " 8 ft. "	.13	" "
" " " longer " over 8 ft. (each add. foot),	.01¼	"
Leading Wire, Gutta Percha covered,	.03½	" per ft.
(For use with Frictional-electric Machine.)		
Connecting Wire, Cotton-covered,	.50	" per ℔.
(For use with either Frictional-electric or Magneto-electric Machine.)		
Blasting Caps,		per 100.

All Fuzes with Gutta Percha covered Wires, and Fuzes with Wires longer than 8 feet, will be made to order only.

All of the above goods constantly in stock, and ready for immediate shipment.

Prices, in all cases, are for goods delivered f. o. b. cars at our Works.

Our compounds are guaranteed in every respect.

Chester, Pa., 1881

Repauno Chemical Company price list, February 1881. Use of the term dynamite *by Repauno at this time would have been an infringement on Alfred Nobel's patent.*

The first bucket of nitroglycerine, some of those present later recalled, was carried to the mixing house in a copper bucket by Lammot, a hazardous "first," but one he characteristically would have insisted upon. No mention is made of his experiencing a "nitroglycerine headache," one of the painful accompaniments suffered by workers handling nitroglycerine. An improved conveyance for transporting it to the mixing house where it was blended into the absorbent material was soon designed by Lammot. This was a "spider," a two-wheeled cart with extended arms on which could be hung eight buckets of nitroglycerine.[14]

The isolated location of the plant, with its fifteen buildings, some barricaded, widely dispersed, allayed the fears of nearby residents about the likelihood of damaging explosions, but there were others who did suffer immediate damages. These were the commercial fishermen who caught and impounded the prolific runs of sturgeon and shad up the Delaware River in the spring of each year. Waste acids from the nitrating house drained into an impounding area just below the plant and killed an estimated 15,000 fish, a loss the fishermen put at $10,000, but for which they later accepted $4,000 in settlement. The accident made apparent the need to find a better way to get rid of the spent acids, and the immediate solution was the Delaware River, a capacious sewer. But steps were taken to find a way to recover the waste acid water, to fortify and strengthen it, and use it over again in the nitrating process. Such a recycling process would keep most of the harmful acids out of the waterways and improve the economy of Repauno's operations. It required continued, patient laboratory work by Lammot and his chemist Walter Hill to bring this to the practical "works" stage, but this promising improvement in the technology of high explosives manufacture was to bear tragic consequences.[15]

Choosing a name under which to market Repauno's first dynamite was not difficult. A week before the first batch was made Solomon Turck offered two suggestions drawn from classical mythology: "How would Atlas suit you for a name? You know old Atlas carried the world on his back. Second, how would Ajax do? You know that Ajax was a better man than Hercules!"[16] "Atlas" was chosen as the first brand name, and it was marketed in varying strengths containing from 20 percent to 75 percent nitroglycerine, and priced accordingly. It was, however, advertised as a powder, not dynamite, for Lammot was aware that until the patent litigation with the Giant Powder Company was finallly settled the premature use of the word *dynamite*, coined by Nobel to identify the high explosive made under his patents, might prejudice the outcome of the litigation. So at the outset Repauno marketed its dyanmite as a new class of high explosive powder. The first sale, 250 pounds of 40 percent Atlas Powder, went to the quarries of Thomas Leiper on Crum Creek near Chester, and the second shipment to quarries near Port Deposit in Maryland. Repauno also sold nitric and sulphuric acids to manufacturers and to other chemical concerns, and offered blasting machines and caps, leading wire and fuzes to detonate the charges.

In a little more than a year following Repauno's start-up, Lammot added "Hercules" as a second brand by negotiating the purchase of the California Powder Works' Hercules plant near Cleveland. To bring it under Repauno's aegis rather than have it as a rival for the trade of the Ohio Valley and the Neutral Belt region to the west was in accord with his belief in the advantages of consolidation and controlled competition. The acids used at Hercules could be supplied by Repauno at lower cost than what was being paid to the local Cleveland acid suppliers, and, very important to Lammot's mind, Willard, whom he regarded as the ablest man in the business, would be retained as the Hercules plant manager.

The San Francisco officers of the California Powder Works raised no objections to the sale of their Cleveland plant to Repauno. The president, N. G. Kittle, and secretary, John F. Lohse, even if they had been opposed to it, would have realized that opposition was fruitless; the Du Pont Company, which owned two-fifths of their firm, was also the majority owner of the Repauno Company, an overwhelming combination of negotiating power. The purchase included patent rights and use of the Hercules trade name, and Willard and his staff were to be transferred to the Repauno payroll. The transfer of ownership, as had been done in the purchase of the Hazard Company five years earlier, was not to be disclosed; Hercules was ostensibly to continue operating as the eastern branch of the California Powder Works and to market its Hercules powder in competition with Repauno's Atlas. Other brands—Ajax, Giant, and Rend Rock—were added to Repauno's brands in later years.

The fiction of Hercules as a bona fide competitor was not long maintained, however, for in March 1882 the Hercules Powder Company was chartered in Delaware to operate the Cleveland plant. Lammot was its president, cousin William du Pont its secretary, and the by-laws adopted for its management were identical to those in the Repauno charter. In effect, it was a subsidiary of Repauno.[17]

BREAKING TIES: REMOVAL TO PHILADELPHIA

After a year of commuting by carriage, train, and boat between Wilmington, Chester, and the Repauno plant, with frequent trips to Philadelphia, in 1881 Lammot decided to move his family to Philadelphia and to locate the main office of the Repauno Chemical Company in its business district. He and Mary were now the parents of eight children, the newest arrival being a boy born the previous year and given his father's name. It is likely that Mary's relatives, the Mathieus and the Graffs, Philadelphia residents, directed them toward West Philadelphia and Powelton Village, a community of tree-lined streets and commodious homes not far from the new location of Lammot's alma mater, the University of Pennsylvania at 34th Street and Woodland Avenue. Many of the residents in Powelton were professional and business people—doctors, lawyers, bankers, successful business men, and some of the more affluent academics. Public and private schools were not far distant, and, an important consideration to Mary, there were churches within walking distance.

Two properties at the intersection of 35th Street and Powelton Avenue, a three-story house on a large corner lot and a vacant lot across from it were up for sale, and in June 1881 Lammot purchased both for $43,000, paying $24,000 down and assuming a mortgage for $19,000. The house needed enlarging and renovating to accommodate his growing family and to pro-

Mrs. Lammot (Mary Belin) du Pont (1839–1913).

vide living quarters for a governess and several servants. Lammot engaged his cousin-in-law, architect Theophilus P. Chandler, who had designed the buildings at Repauno, to draw the plans and supervise the remodeling. The extensive renovations cost $19,000 and took five months to complete. Toward the end of the year his mother noted that "Lammot has all his family gathered under roof, in a house without mantelpieces, but I believe in other respects habitable."

Though he was moving only thirty miles, Lammot's departure grieved his mother. She felt she was losing a devoted son, the last of her brood to leave the Brandywine, although she corresponded regularly with her sons Fred and Bidermann in Louisville. They came to see her at Goodstay several times a year, in the summer months Bidermann usually bringing his large family north to vacation in Delaware and at Cape May. In the weeks immediately prior to Lammot's leaving, Meta could not bring herself to talk about the pending separation, not even to her daughter Victorine, who was visiting her at the time. Victorine learned of it from her brother Fred only after she had returned home to New York City. To her Aunt Sophie (Mrs. S. F. du Pont) she expressed misgivings about the move: "Yes, indeed, the saddest event is Lammot's going. It would have been painful enough if he stood alone and was exiling himself but all those children to be taken to a city life, to be deprived of the health and advantages country living gives to youth is terrible. Five boys to grow up in town, he little knows what he is doing, poor Lammot. The blow is so terrible to Mother she cannot speak of it."[18]

Mary, too, had doubts about raising her children in the city, and in a letter to Aunt Sophie soon after getting settled in her new home, she gave way to homesickness: "My heart often yearns after the dear old Brandywine and all my loved friends there." More cheerfully, she was glad her kinfolk, the Graffs and Mathieus lived in the city, where she and Lammot had taken a pew at St. James Episcopal Church at 22d and Walnut streets, where the minister was a Dr. Henry J. Morton, whom she liked. Getting her family ready to go into town for services every Sunday morning, however, proved too much, and within a year the family began attending St. Andrew's, an Episcopal church closer to home. Here, Mary noted, "we are so large a family that we readily fill two pews." But the family also retained its pew at the more fashionable St. James in the city.[19]

Lammot continued to travel a good deal, but when in the city his evenings were usually spent with his family, "our happiest time," said Mary, "surrounded by our five oldest children who are now old enough to be very companionable." In July 1882 their father took Pierre, then twelve, and Sophie, eleven, with him on a combined business and pleasure trip, going first to the Hercules plant at Cleveland, then to see Niagara Falls, down the St. Lawrence to Montreal, headquarters of the Hamilton Powder Company, and then home by way of Lake George and a boat ride down the Hudson River. The youngsters had a good time and had much to tell their mother and brothers and sisters, for this was their first extended journey away from home. Part of their itinerary was a retracing of their parents' honeymoon trip seventeen years earlier.[20]

In the eyes of young Pierre his father, over six feet tall, was "the tallest man on earth," and it came as a disappointment to the boy when he learned this was not so. Papa, at fifty, had fine straight hair brushed straight back from his forehead, and his side and chin whiskers were always neatly trimmed. His eyes were gray, and he wore rectangular steel-rimmed glasses on a straight nose, a feature which Pierre saw differed from his own, which was slightly hooked. His father's hands were large and well proportioned with large straight fingers and nails, all denoting considerable physical strength. Papa was gentle and considerate with his family, and although a firm, determined personality, he never scolded or spoke harshly to his children. When they squabbled among themselves his corrective reminder was, "Let dogs delight to bark and bite, but little children should never fight." Visiting relatives sometimes let it be known that they thought Lammot and Mary spoiled their children.

Pierre thought the guiding principle in his father's life was the Golden Rule, and he neither exacted nor desired return for the good works he did. He approved the moral teachings of the Bible—they were the precepts for the good life—but he was skeptical of much religious dogma and critical of the organized church. His attendance at Sunday church services was spotty, and then only out of a desire to please Mary and because he was expected to set an example for his children. More often he enjoyed his Sunday mornings playing quoits, croquet, or badminton with friends, when, as Pierre remembered, "Mother and the seven aunts, self-appointed dragons and religious guardians, were at Church."

His own enthusiasm for athletics led Lammot to encourage his children to become involved in sports. Some learned to swim at an early age; dancing lessons were de riguer for the girls; all learned to ride bicycles and some enjoyed riding horses. But not Pierre, who had such an instinctive dislike for the animals that he prevailed upon his sister Louisa to take his place at riding lessons. His father enrolled him at a Philadelphia gymnasium, but this was short lived, for Pierre declared he was too clumsy to benefit from the instruction.[21]

Having just settled into their new home in December 1881, Lammot and Mary did not return with their family to the Brandywine for the customary New Year's Day gathering. This was Lammot's first absence from the traditional du Pont family festivities, and his mother, now in her mid-seventies, lamented it as a further sign of the dispersal of her close-knit family. In a dark mood, feeling that she might not live to see another new year, Meta professed to her sister-in-law Sophie, "I had a sad New Year's, wanting the sight of Lammot. For fifty anniversaries I had always seen him, but never shall again." In more cheerful vein she later told Sophie, "Lammot came down and dined with me on Saturday, which was a great pleasure to me." But such happy occasions came too seldom for Meta, so after a long spell of not seeing her son or his family she went on an "expedition" to Philadelphia, "a great event for me now," she told Sophie. "I concluded to summon up my courage for the journey. They were all well, but I had the disappointment of not seeing Lammot—he had gone to New York. The next time I go up I shall have to make an appointment."[22]

Lammot rented an office on the fifth floor of the Peter Wright Building, 305 Walnut Street, in the heart of Philadelphia's banking, insurance, and business district for Repauno's headquarters. He engaged George H. Kerr, a young law clerk and court stenographer, in March 1882 to handle the correspondence and manage the office when he was at Repauno or off on one of his frequent trips out of town. Kerr's first impression of Lammot was his striking resemblance to Abraham Lincoln. Six feet two inches tall, large boned, weighing over two hundred pounds, shoulders slightly stooped, he walked rapidly, his head thrust forward, giving the impression of an athletic young man half his age. Beginning to show flecks of gray, his hair was parted on the right, but, unlike Lincoln's, was neatly combed lying close to his head. In profile the resemblance was closer, the slant of his jaws, and his chin whiskers and sideburns giving him a Lincolnesque look. Kerr noted that his employer had the habit of trimming them with a pair of scissors as he carried on a conversation with business callers. On occasion, when it was quiet in the office and he was in a relaxed mood, Lammot would regale Kerr, whom he nicknamed "Senior," with stories of his experiences in the powder business.

Kerr's first assignment was to equip and brighten the appearance of the office for which Lammot gave him a thousand dollars before leaving on a trip to Salt Lake City. On his return Lammot surveyed the new furnishings—desks, chairs, file cabinet, a Number 2 Remington Standard typewriter (a writing machine just coming into use), a handsome blue rug, and freshly painted bright colored walls—then asked Kerr if he had any money left. When Kerr answered "No," Lammot replied, "I didn't think you had. You're certainly hell for pretty!" To blunt his mild censure of such extravagance, he then made out a check for another thousand dollars, telling Kerr to cash it, buy a safe for the office, and put in it whatever money was left over to take care of future petty cash expenses.

Lammot considered the typewriter an interesting novelty as a "writing machine" but left its operation entirely in Kerr's hands. He claimed that it demanded accuracy in spelling, something he had never mastered, a fault tacitly confirmed by Kerr when typing the final copies of Lammot's hand-written drafts of letters and memoranda. Scratchy pen points exasperated him. "They get their legs crossed," he would complain as he tossed the offending pen across the desk to his secretary to replace the nib. Lammot had been among those who first appreciated the convenience of the telephone. He had had one installed at Nemours in June 1878 and continued as a subscriber to the Delaware Bell Telephone Exchange, paying twenty dollars annually, until moving to Philadelphia.[23] It is reasonably certain that he had telephones installed in the Repauno office and at his new residence soon after locating there.

One morning after immediate matters had been taken care of, Kerr was surprised when Lammot pulled out a box of cigars, took one for himself, passed the box to him, then, puffing on his cigar, Lammot leaned back in his chair and announced, "Senior, we are not going to work this morning. I am going to tell you stories." For several hours he talked of episodes still fresh in his memory—events in the mills at Brandywine and elsewhere, the important changes that had taken place in the technology of explosives, his trip abroad to visit European powder mills in 1858, and the saltpeter mission to England in 1861–62, an account which Kerr, in his reminiscences written fifty-five years later, attempted to repeat verbatim.

One incident vividly recounted by Lammot was an attempt to rob him of a payroll he was carrying to the Wapwallopen mills. The proprietor of a country inn where he sometimes stayed overnight on such trips learned that he carried the payroll with him. On retiring for the night Lammot found the key to his room missing and the bolt on the door would not slide into the socket, so he wedged a chair under the knob of the door and placed his valise under the bed. During the night he was awakened by the sound of the door being quietly opened. Through half-closed eyes as he watched a form creeping toward his bed he silently bunched the bed covers into his hands. When the figure reached under the bed, Lammot hurled himself onto the intruder, and in a smothering embrace carried him kicking and squirming from the room and threw him down the stairs! The next morning the innkeeper was nowhere to be found, and, in a laughing conclusion, Lammot told Kerr he thought the would-be-thief might still be running.

The secretary remembered business meetings where discussions became warm and tempers sometimes flared, at which point Lammot would lean back in his chair, bite the end off a big black cigar, and with eyes twinkling, begin to tell one of his stories. His humor cleared the tense atmosphere, soothed tempers and calmed hurt feelings, and by the time he had finished his listeners were in better spirits and talking civilly once again.

Kerr was in Lammot's employ for only two years, but in that time he came to know him as a kindly dispositioned man coupled with a firmness of character and gifted with personal magnetism. The workmen at Repauno, now numbering about two hundred, liked him, and he knew many of them by name. The enterprise had not yet grown so large that a management hierarchy prevented direct contacts between employer and workers, and Lammot spent much of his time at the plant. In his recollections Kerr characterized him as always fair in his dealings, sometimes to the point of doing himself an injustice, and summed up his admiration for his employer with these words: "If ever a man gave his fellow men a square deal it was Lammot du Pont."[24]

Though he was now the president of both Repauno and Hercules, Lammot owned only ten shares of Repauno stock in his own name. Indirectly, as the owner of approximately one-sixth of the Du Pont Company, he did have a stake in the new companies for, as previously noted, two-thirds of their capital had been furnished by Du Pont and one-third by Laflin and Rand. Now, with the acquisition and chartering of Hercules in March 1882, he judged it the appropriate time to approach Uncle Henry with a request that he be allowed to buy half of the Du Pont Company's interest in Repauno, which would make him an equal one-third owner along with the Big Two of the explosives industry. If his uncle and junior partners would agree to this he was ready to pay the value of Repauno's shares as currently shown on its books. He proposed that the purchase price be deducted from the amount due him in the forthcoming settlement of his account when he formally withdrew as a junior partner in the Du Pont Company. In round figures his one-sixth share in the family business amounted to approximately $440,000, far more than the cost of a one-third interest in Repauno. Not explicitly stated but implied in his request to Uncle Henry was the likelihood that if his offer was turned down he would give up the presidency of Repauno, relinquish oversight of the many Du Pont Company matters still in his hands, and seek employment elsewhere, perhaps affiliating with a rival firm.[25]

Uncle Henry was quick to respond. He assured Lammot that he wanted him to remain at the head of Repauno and to continue to watch over all the Du Pont Company's interests in other high explosives firms. He was willing that Lammot should become a part owner in Repauno, but not to the extent of a one-third interest for that would jeopardize the Du Pont Company control over the new venture. To allow this would give Lammot and Laflin and Rand Company, if they joined together, majority control of Repauno by their combined ownership of two-thirds of its capital. This would be contrary to the long-recognized policy of the Du Pont Company to always seek majority control of every enterprise in which it had a financial stake. His uncle reminded Lammot that "no one was more fully alive to the importance of this than yourself whilst associated with us." Then, in a plea that must have come at great sacrifice to his pride, he asked Lammot, "Cannot you be induced to let things remain as they were before you severed your connections with us? There is a wide field for work, and of a kind in which you have filled your lifetime, why look up another occupation now?"[26]

Uncle Henry's reluctance to consent to Lammot's acquisition of a one-third interest in Repauno was his fear that in the event of a dispute over some aspect of policy or operations Lammot and his friend Solomon Turck, head of Laflin and Rand, would ally themselves against him. The estrangement that had developed between uncle and nephew during recent years gave credence to this possibility. He was also aware of the mutual regard Lammot and Turck had for each other, the latter usually deferring to Lammot's leadership and supporting the initiatives he proposed in the conduct of their mutual interests.

Lammot was so incensed at his uncle's refusal that he rewrote his reply three times before he had a version that satisfied him. He deplored his uncle's insinuation that he, Lammot, after so many years of loyal service to the Du Pont Company, might not continue to support him: "Do you suppose my one third would not be voted in your interest? And if you have not sufficient confidence in my sustaining you after 31 years trial . . . is it not sufficient that you have a ⅔ interest against my one third? Does Du Pont Company with $3,000,000 in black powder begrudge to sell me $90,000 in high explosives?" Under the present capital arrangement his share of the profits that Repauno might make in the future was too little to support his large family. From his long experience making explosives, he warned that for some years to come it could be expected that large portions of the earnings would have to be spent on improvements and rebuilding after explosions. Large sums of money would be needed to finance experimental research before Repauno could excel its competitors. He hesitated spending other persons' money on experiments that might, or might not, yield good results. Since he would be responsible for directing this research he felt that some of the "risk" capital should come out of his own funds. He considered his request for a 33 percent share of Repauno justified and reasonable, and he reassured his uncle that he could always rely on his support—was he not also a du Pont?[27]

But Uncle Henry remained adamant. However much he would like to oblige Lammot, it was not good business policy to yield financial control over an enterprise in which Du Pont had invested so heavily. He had full confidence in his nephew's loyalty, but, presciently, he asked, "What about those who may come after you, your executors for instance, would they take the same view of matters that you do, or in unison with us?" Astonished by this, Lammot scorned it as a lame pretext and reminded his uncle that his sons were still young boys—"I really doubt if you are in earnest in fearing them more than myself. After my *death* could you not *buy* them *out*?" Angrily, he announced that he was resigning as president of Repauno and Hercules effective May 1, 1882—a successor should be sought without delay.

His uncle's response was polite but unyielding on the surrender of majority control over Repauno, and he reiterated once again, "It is precisely the position you have always maintained yourself while associated with us." While he regretted Lammot's resignation, it had not surprised him. Then, revealing Lammot's suppressed dissatisfaction and the strained relations that had existed between them in the years preceding Lammot's announcement in 1878 that he was getting out of the Du Pont Company, Uncle Henry went on to say, "Your brother Irénée told me time and again that you talked of leaving us, and it grieved him sorely to hear you say so. He spoke to me often about it but always said he trusted it would not happen whilst he lived."[28] It will be remembered that Lammot had waited the better part of a year after Irénée's death in the summer of 1877 before he tendered his resignation to his uncle. This he had done reluctantly, feeling frustrated because the senior partner had shown no serious intent to make the needed changes in company affairs that Lammot had urged him to consider.

The letters that passed between uncle and nephew in the spring of 1882 were so heated and vehement that Lammot wrote his own rather than entrust them to his secretary. And Uncle Henry stuck to his customary habit of writing his own letters instead of using the services of a correspondence clerk. Some old wounds were opened, one of which was Lammot's accusation that his uncle had forced his own sisters, Eleuthera and Sophie, to sell him their shares in the family business. He charged him with ingratitude toward "two old ladies whose money stood by you for nearly a half century." Uncle Henry disclaimed this as untrue, telling Lammot he was letting his emotions run away with him, and that he misinterpreted his letters, taking offense where none was meant.[29]

Word of their dispute was now circulating within the family, bringing distress to its members, who were hopeful that it could be settled before an irreparable breach occurred. Henry Belin, Jr., Lammot's brother-in-law, the Du Pont Company's principal agent in the anthracite region based in Scranton, was worried by the split and hoped that concessions on both sides would lead to a reconciliation. He offered his services as mediator, saying, "It may seem officious to you, my desire to interfere in this matter, but the results look so serious to me, both to the old concern and to you and your family that I feel justified in wanting to interfere." Brother Fred in Louisville advised Lammot to lay off work for six months and take a rest. He urged him to "invest your money in government bonds that can be sold any day that you want to start something." On a visit to the Brandywine the previous winter Fred had been told by Uncle Henry that he hoped Lammot could be prevailed upon to stay as head of Repauno. Fred had gained the impression that it was not Uncle Henry, but his sons Henry Algernon and Willie, who were most opposed to Lammot being sold a one-third interest in Repauno.[30]

Lammot had a different temperament from his brother; this matter was too pressing to stay unresolved while he took a prolonged vacation to deliberate on how to plan his future. The only holiday he allowed himself was the two-week trip in July with his two older children, Pierre and Sophie, to Cleveland and Canada, and this was a mixed business and pleasure trip. About this time, however, Uncle Henry's attitude toward his request began to soften and negotiations were begun that seemed to promise a satisfactory solution that would avert the threatened schism.[31]

What brought about a change of heart in his uncle can only be surmised, for Uncle Henry rarely revealed his inmost thoughts on sensitive matters. He may have realized that if he failed to grant his nephew's request, Lammot was now determined to sever all ties with the old firm and Repauno and might set up a rival high explosives company of his own. Or he would possibly ally himself with a major competitor, the most likely being Laflin and Rand. He may also have come to see the justice in Lammot's wish to become a co-owner of Repauno, which he, more than anyone else, had been responsible for founding and had directed for over two years. It had been Lammot's initiative that had taken Du Pont into high explosives, and the profits Repauno was earning were proving it to have been a very good move. And Uncle Henry may finally have come to realize that Lammot could no longer continue in the role of a subordinate. He had outgrown the status of junior partner; what he had accomplished over thirty years had brought him to the point where his self-esteem would not let him accept anything less than executive leadership. Becoming a one-third owner would sanction his authority as head of all Repauno operations, permit him greater independence in determining policy, and allow him to organize its management and operations in ways he thought most efficient. Motivating this, of course, was the urge to make money, to accumulate wealth sufficient to allow his family to live well, and to leave enough of a patrimony to his children to ensure their financial security.

The sense of obligation to provide well for his offspring had intensified as his family had grown in size. Twelve years earlier, in 1870, when he and Mary had only three children, Isabella, Louisa, and Pierre, his need to amass a fortune had seemed less pressing: "In this world a man cannot get more than his bellyful and keep his back warm. We [the du Pont partners], having enough for this, only want to leave our boys as fair a name and as good a business as our fathers left us. . . . I am in no immediate want of Bread and would rather lose 10 or even $100,000 than injure the future of our business. . . . Our object is not entirely to make money at present."[32] Now, a dozen years later, with seven more children to care for, and fully aware of the hazards of his occupation, Lammot's principal concern was for the well-being and security of his large family.

During the summer months of 1882 arrangements were made whereby Lammot would relinquish his one-sixth ownership in the Du Pont Company, valued at $440,000, and would receive in exchange a portfolio of stocks, bonds, notes, and a lump-sum cash payment, which in aggregate value equaled the value of his stock account. Foremost in this exchange were a thousand shares of Repauno stock which, with interest added, had a value of $120,726. This is what he had sought, and securing it made him an equal one-third owner along with the Du Pont Company and Laflin and Rand Company. A financial stake in the subsidiary Hercules Powder Company was obtained by receiving 334 shares of its stock with a value of $40,743. The boom in mining and construction taking place in Canada made ownership of Hamilton Powder Company stock very attractive to Lammot, so he asked for and received in the settlement forty-one shares of its stock valued at $15,375, along with bonds and notes of that company worth $47,750. These added to Hamilton securities he already owned, and others purchased from Laflin and Rand, Hazard, and Oriental Powder, gave him control of the Canadian firm. The other securities turned over to him consisted of shares and bonds of the Mineral Spring Coal Company and the Lehigh-

Luzerne Coal Company, both located in the anthracite district, and shares in the Elizabethport Wharf Company in New Jersey, all of which had an aggregate value of $39,850. There remained at the end of 1882 a balance due him amounting to $103,545, which was paid to him in cash during the first half of January 1883.[33]

It had taken nearly five years for Lammot to dissolve his connections with the family firm and to switch his interest in black powder manufacture to the production of chemicals and dynamite. Both his associates and his rivals in the industry found it hard to believe that he had deserted it for the new high explosives. His friend Linus Austin, head of Austin Powder Company in Cleveland, chided him: "I am sorry that since you have engaged in the high explosives business you have lost your taste for the more conservative and reliable black powder." Then, since he had neither seen nor heard from Lammot for quite a while, he ruefully added, "But it seems that your old friends who still swear by the old article are too old fogyish to retain your regard."[34]

Another die-hard champion of black powder was Paul A. Oliver, proprietor of the Oliver Mills, one of the few producers in the anthracite region who had successfully resisted being taken over by Du Pont. In his opinion high explosive compounds were, "wretched stuff on the market in competition with decent and respectable black powder that will do more work for a given amount of dollars and cents." He found it hard to believe that Lammot had gone into this business, for "I had always considered you the champion of black powder." And brother-in-law Henry Belin, Jr., credited his affluence to Lammot: "Some of our friends in the business do not seem to appreciate what a bonanza the black powder trade is in the coal fields. That it is such a bonanza is chiefly due to the care you have always taken with it."[35]

Evidently not yet aware, or not really believing, that Lammot was dissolving his connection with the Du Pont Company, his friend Henry A. Weldy in Tamaqua informed him that some new powder mills were being erected in the Schuylkill district. It looked like a stiff price war would soon be fought: "If we wish to hold our trade we must meet them in price every time, and when it commences I want *you* on my side of the house." Another coal region producer who appreciated Lammot's role in promoting and making the black powder business so profitable was H. D. Laflin, whom he had helped to set up at Quakake, Pennsylvania. Laflin wrote thanking Lammot for the help and advice given to him over the years, and he hoped that "although you are now devoted to high explosives, please do not forget your very grateful little friend in the good old fashioned *Black Powder*." And, by coincidence, on the very day Lammot finally cut his ties with the Du Pont Company, his uncle Charles Belin at Wapwallopen wrote him telling of a new firm that was about to start making black powder in his neighborhood. The new competition should liven up the business, but, he concluded, "as you are no longer interested in black powder—you can laugh!"[36]

Thus, for Lammot, the requiem for black powder had sounded. From now on his career would be spent supervising the production of high explosives made from chemicals in a plant he optimistically anticipated would some day be the largest in the world.

Chapter XII

A Broken Column

LAMMOT'S OPTIMISM about Repauno's future was well founded. It was launched at a time when the country was emerging from the depressed seventies and the economy was on a gradual upswing. Reassured by the government's return to a gold standard, financiers and business men were more readily investing in new industrial plants and equipment, and this provided employment for many who had been thrown out of work in the years following the market crash of 1873. Industrial production, heavy construction, railroad building, tunneling, urban spread, mining, and the newer extractive industries such as oil and cement were expanding vigorously, creating an increased demand for explosives. Ready to supply them with dynamite were the strategically located powder agencies of Du Pont, Laflin and Rand, and the California Powder Works. With such a network of sales outlets already in existence, Repauno had a decided advantage over its competitors, a factor that contributed to its subsequent domination of the market.

At Gibbstown more ground was acquired for the erection of additional buildings. Production had risen from 500,000 pounds in 1880 to 3,000,000 pounds the following year, a sixfold increase. Workmen's homes were put up near the plant and a workmen's clubhouse established, a marked innovation at that time. Lammot had been among the first in Delaware to subscribe to the new telephone service, and telephones were early installed at Repauno. A separate building well equipped as a chemical laboratory was erected for the testing, experimental, and development work that he and Walter N. Hill, plant chemist and superintendent, carried on. Later designated the Eastern Laboratory, this facility was the first of its kind to be housed in its own building and predated by twenty years the Du Pont company's pioneer experimental station begun in 1903 at "Rokeby," a converted textile mill located in Henry Clay Village close to the Brandywine powder mills.

Safety and economy were watchwords in Repauno's operations. They were most evident in the wide dispersal of the buildings and in the high earth bunkers surrounding some of them. The number of workmen allowed at one time in buildings where hazardous work was done was limited, and wherever it could be done mechanization began to replace hand operations. In the most dangerous operation, nitrating the glycerine, there was considerable loss of nitric and sulphuric acids. With Hill, Lammot sought ways to recover and regenerate these acids so they could be used over again. Many months were spent experimenting in the laboratory, but it was late March 1884 before they felt ready to test their method of recovery in the nitroglycerine house.

At the end of the day, Friday, March 28, 1884, workmen

Laboratory at Repauno Chemical Works, erected c. 1880–81 by Lammot du Pont. It was later expanded into Du Pont Company's Eastern Laboratory in 1902, center of research in explosive and industrial chemicals.

had drawn off the last charge of nitroglycerine and placed it in a lead-lined tank for storage overnight. The following Saturday morning Lammot had a 10 A.M. appointment with A. S. Ackerson, a Laflin and Rand official, and was talking with him and Hill in the laboratory when a workman rushed in excitedly exclaiming that something was wrong in the nitroglycerine house. Lammot and Hill ran to the building where an ominous sight met them. The tank of nitroglycerine was decomposing and fuming—2,000 pounds of lethal explosive! Frantically they tried to "drown" it by tapping it off into an adjoining tank of cold water, but aware that it could explode any moment, Lammot ordered Harry Norcross and his men out of the mill, and he and Hill followed a few seconds later. They had gone about ten feet when it blew apart, hurling timbers and machinery and ripping up the earth embankment that surrounded it.

Lammot and Hill were killed instantly by the tremendous concussion and buried beneath the avalanche of earth and debris. Norcross and his men, about thirty feet away, were struck and killed by flying timbers and metal shards. Lammot's visitor, Ackerson, had left the laboratory and was approaching the nitroglycerine house when it exploded, the shock breaking his neck. One of the workmen, Louis Ley, was alive when taken from the wreckage but lived only a few minutes. Norcross's body was mutilated but the others showed few marks of injury. Doctors had been summoned but there was little need for their services by the time they arrived on the scene.[1]

Frank and Eugene du Pont were the first family members to reach Repauno. Frank described the accident to a third brother, Alexis, and, as far as could be ascertained, the cause of the explosion. Responsibility was placed upon Norcross's men working in the nitroglycerine house. They had apparently failed to keep the mixture sufficiently cool as it was being nitrated, and when it started to fume, an ominous sign, they should have immediately discharged it into a nearby tank of water. Instead, they had panicked, with one racing off to get help from Lammot and Hill. Their desperate, last-second efforts had come too late.

Frank reviewed these final moments with the experienced superintendent of the Cleveland Hercules plant, Joseph Willard, and he agreed that had the workmen responded more speedily to the mounting danger the accident could have been averted. Sensitive and articulate, Frank was deeply saddened by the sudden death of his cousin and mentor:

> Just look at the results of this explosion, Lammot 9 children [Mary was carrying their tenth child, born two months later]. Norcross to have been married on Thursday. Ackerson, a husband of one week; the two men who worked the N.G. both to be married shortly. I tell you this thing is heart rending. All our little differences with Lammot have vanished. I can bring myself only to remember the many, many pleasant hours I have spent with him, and the assistance he gave me from his experience when I first came here. I have scarcely had another thought but of him since the accident. He was universally beloved, and many letters have poured in condoling us on our loss. Men came from Cleveland, Canada, Cincinnati and the West, as well as from the North to be present at his funeral.[2]

Mary, grief stricken, left with nine children, the oldest sixteen years, was outwardly calm, but praying that no harm would come to the child in her womb. She would have found scant comfort in the fatalistic philosophy of an explosives manufacturer, a friend of her husband's; indeed, his words would have intensified her sorrow had she ever read them: "A powder mill is like a battlefield. A man drops: that is not an unexpected event: the ranks close up and march on."[3]

A private funeral service attended only by the family and a few intimate friends and relatives was held for Lammot at his home on Tuesday morning, April 1, with the Reverend Dr. Henry J. Morton of St. James Protestant Episcopal Church officiating. The body was taken by special train to Wilmington and thence to Sand Hole Woods, the du Pont family cemetery near the entrance to Eleutherian Mills. The day was raw and blustery with occasional snow squalls as the Right Reverend Alfred Lee, Episcopal Bishop of Delaware, conducted the service for the dead.

Many gathered round the grave to pay their last respects, du Ponts, Belins, Lammots, Kembles, and other relatives. To some of these Lammot had been advisor, confidant, "Uncle Big Man," and source of financial aid in time of need. There were close friends, neighbors, business associates, and a large gathering of workmen. The many workmen, Aunt Sophie noted in her diary, bore testimony to Lammot's goodness and generosity of heart, remembering him as "the poor men's friend." "Yes, *he* had that philanthropic spirit which characterized the preceding generation of du Ponts, alas! becoming rapidly extinct in the rising generation I fear—a sad, sad day for me."[4] If Aunt Sophie had had access to Lammot's personal correspondence her heart would have warmed to him all the more as she read the many letters thanking him for the counsel and financial assistance he had given to those seeking help. Some were from Brandywine workmen, from injured powdermen at Wapwallopen who could no longer work, and from destitute miners at Mocanaqua. Former tutors and governesses expressed their gratitude for gifts and for loans of money made to them after they had left Mary's and Lammot's employ. The elderly widow of his Penn tutor, Dr. John Robertson, ill and near destitute, received funds from Lammot to pay for medical and nursing care and to meet the mortgage interest payments on her home.

In her own grief Mary did not forget that others had suffered from the Repauno explosion. Soon after Lammot's funeral she wrote a letter of sympathy to Mrs. Walter N. Hill. Mrs. Hill's reply, delayed by her inability to think and write clearly because of her sorrow, told Mary of her husband's strong attachment to Lammot: "He had been so kind a friend to my husband that he was most anxious to satisfy and please your husband. It was only rarely that Mr. Hill gave his affection as he did to your husband." She expressed a wish to call upon Mary sometime soon. "My heart goes out towards you and your children," and closed with grateful acknowledgment of the generous check that had accompanied Mary's letter to her.[5]

Mary poured out her heart in replying to one of several comforting notes Aunt Sophie had written in the days following the funeral: "Oh! dear Aunt, to have your dearest on earth snatched from you in the midst of life and strength! It is so hard to realize I shall never see him again. But I must try to think with thankfulness of the eighteen happy years I spent with my dear husband, during which time I can never remember one unkind word from him. I hope that my children may inherit his lovely disposition and kindness of heart. . . . We expect to spend the Summer at Cape May. Lammot had engaged a cottage there, thinking the change would be good for me after my confinement."[6] The following spring she had a broken stone column, the customary type of marker for one whose life had tragically been cut short, placed on her husband's grave.

Uncle Henry took Lammot's death very hard. "I was shocked," his sister Sophie noted some days after the funeral, "to see how much he was changed and aged by this affliction, and how badly he looked. He talked to me a great deal of Lammot and showed me letters he had about him." One letter, from Brig. Gen. Stephen Vincent Benét, chief of ordnance, U.S. Army, expressed the government's regret at Lammot's death and praised him as a very capable man "to whose scientific investigations and uniform courtesy it is so greatly indebted. . . . The satisfactory connection existing between your works and the Ordnance Department during so many years brings vividly home to us the loss of one so estimable in all the relations of life, and so distinguished in affairs in which the nation has so much interest." The Gunpowder Trade Association expressed its sympathy to the bereaved family in a resolution engrossed on parchment which noted Lammot's role in establishing that organization and the able leadership he had given it. Uncle Henry forwarded such letters of condolence received at the office to Mary. After reading them she placed them in a portfolio for her children to read as they grew older so that they might become aware of their father's admirable qualities and the high esteem in which he was held by so many people. Their grandmother Meta believed that knowing more about their father "may be an inducement for some of the boys to try and do right, for among the five you may hope *one* will be influenced for good."[7]

Henry du Pont was in his seventy-second year. Thoughts of his own mortality surely vivified as he began to realize what the loss of Lammot meant to him personally and to the future of the enterprise in which they had worked together for over thirty years. During these days of mourning he reflected upon their long association which had placed the Du Pont Company at the head

of the nation's black powder industry and more recently had set
it on the way toward control of the high explosives industry.
Nationwide there were now eighty plants producing both types
of explosives. An inherent sense of family unity and loyalty to
the family business had kept uncle and nephew working together
despite their contrasting temperaments and personalities and their
differing attitudes as to how that business might best be conducted.

The immediate urgency was to have someone take charge of
Repauno. Two-thirds of Lammot's shares in the company were
promptly repurchased from his estate by the Du Pont Company
and Mary retained the remaining third. Control of Repauno was
thus assured the Du Pont Company. Briefly Solomon Turck acted
as president pro tem, but he was soon succeeded by Uncle Henry's younger son, William, who had been secretary and treasurer
during Lammot's presidency. William closed the office in Philadelphia and moved it to Wilmington. In announcing these changes
the Du Pont Company informed its correspondents that "Lammot du Pont's plans are being carried out just as he intended."[8]

Lammot had left no will, but, perhaps presciently, at the
beginning of 1884 he had listed his assets and liabilities in a
financial statement that showed his total net worth to have been
$1,044,000. There is little likelihood this figure changed appre-
ciably in the three months before his death. An account of the
explosion at Repauno that appeared in the *Philadelphia Record*
put his fortune at thirteen million dollars, a figure most likely
confused with the total assets of the Du Pont Company.[9]

Mary's brother, Henry Belin, Jr., and Lammot's brother
Bidermann were named administrators of his estate, and brother
Fred, the Louisville bachelor, became the guardian of the children. Since 1877 Uncle Fred had also been the guardian of his
brother Irénée's children, a situation that led one of the du Pont
women to remark: "Fred, the bachelor, will have more children
to care for than many husbands and heads of families. It is a great
blessing for those orphans to have such a sensible man to watch
over them."[10]

The greater part of Lammot's wealth consisted of investments in firms in which he had been the key figure either as

founder, reorganizer, or instrumental in effecting a merger. These were:

Repauno Chemical Co.	$212,000
Hamilton Powder Co.	211,000
Atlantic Dynamite Co.	178,525
Acadia Powder Manufacturing Co.	37,640
Hercules Powder Co.	33,400
Hecla Powder Manufacturing Co.	20,800
Torpedo Powder Manufacturing Co.	10,300

His earlier forays into railroading and coal mining had not entirely disillusioned him about their potential as good investments, for he held a total interest of $130,000 in several railroad and mining companies. Whatever investment he had had in the Wilmington and Northern Railroad had been disposed of, most likely to Col. Henry A. du Pont, its president at the time of Lammot's death. His equity in the Wyoming soda lakes he had optimistically estimated at $50,000. The two Philadelphia properties at 35th Street and Powelton Avenue were valued at $110,000, against which there were mortgages totalling $25,000, and his bank account had a balance of $31,000. The individual most heavily in debt to Lammot was Thomas C. Brainerd, president of the Hamilton Powder Company, who had repeatedly borrowed money and now owed his estate $44,000.

Mary and her children were left comfortably well off by this inheritance of over a million dollars. Her brother Henry and Lammot's brother Bidermann carefully administered the one-third share she received as a widow, and Uncle Fred was an astute guardian of the children's legacies. A baby sister, the tenth child, tentatively called "Decima," was born to Mary on May 12 and named Margaretta Elizabeth Lammot after Lammot's mother. At times the responsibility of raising such a large family without her husband overwhelmed Mary. But her children were a great comfort to her, the two older ones, Louisa ("Loulie") and Pierre, helping with the younger ones, getting them ready for school in the morning, going over lessons with them, and playing with them. The younger children, Mary regretted, would have only "an indistinct remembrance of their Father, and will lose much in never having had the advantage of his conversation and ex-

Mrs. Lammot du Pont and family, photographed at their Powelton Avenue house in Philadelphia in 1886. Pierre, eldest son, at far right, was surrogate father to the younger children, who called him Dad.

ample. My five oldest, I am sure, will never forget him." An enlarged, tinted photograph of Lammot, a birthday gift from her brother Henry, she hoped would "help the little children to remember their father's face."[11]

Had Lammot survived his Uncle Henry, who died in August 1889 at the age of seventy-seven, he would have been the obvious successor as senior partner and head of the family. This might have been disputed by cousin Henry Algernon on the grounds that he, as the elder son and principal heir, should assume his father's role. But he would have stood alone in this, for the other junior partners, Eugene, Frank, and even his younger brother William, recognized Lammot's greater experience and competence, which would make him the logical person to be entrusted with these responsibilities.

When it came time to decide upon a successor, a serious rift developed between Uncle Henry's two sons. William asserted that his greater practical experience in explosives, most recently as secretary, then head of Repauno, better qualified him for this position. Henry Algernon, claiming primogeniture and seniority, believed these should endow him with leadership of the company and family, although his experience in the business had been largely confined to transportation matters. The conflict was resolved when Eugene, next to Lammot the junior partner with most experience, was selected to head the firm. As time and events demonstrated, Eugene lacked the innovative mentality, the drive, and the imagination to provide the executive ability needed to insure the Du Pont Company's paramount position in the industry. Henry A. and William withdrew from active participation in the firm, the former expanding his railroad and real estate interests, developing his Winterthur estate, and cultivating a penchant for family genealogy and history. He involved himself in state and national politics and in 1906 was elected to the U.S. Senate. William, embittered by the feud with his brother and ostracized by the family for divorcing his wife, May, who was also his cousin (the first divorce in the family), resigned as head of the Repauno Company and took up the life of a country gentleman at his Montpelier estate in Orange, Virginia.

Early in his administration Eugene invited Lammot's eldest

son, Pierre, recently graduated from the Massachusetts Institute of Technology, to enter the company's employ. An interest in chemistry, first aroused by his father, and the recommendation of his guardian, Uncle Fred, that M.I.T. would provide the best preparation for a young man entering industry, had influenced his choice of school. Pierre accepted Eugene's offer and began working in the refinery and laboratory in September 1890, following in his father's footsteps, working on assignments similar to those Lammot had performed at the beginning of his career.

Following Eugene's death in 1902, when it appeared the Du Pont Company would be dissolved or pass into other hands, Pierre and his cousins, Alfred I. and T. Coleman du Pont, by a daring gamble acquired control of the firm. Its revitalization assured its control of the explosives industry, but it soon expanded into the manufacture of many other commodities, the products of chemical experimentation and engineering. These innovative ventures, directed by Pierre, his cousins and younger brothers, were to lead to the Du Pont Company becoming one of the largest diversified corporations of this century.[12]

LAMMOT'S LEGACY: NEW DIRECTIONS

In an industrializing and urbanizing America the manufacture of explosives was an essential business. They helped to change the face of the land by excavating canal and railroad beds, boring tunnels, removing obstacles in road construction, deepening river and harbor channels, and in the construction of dams, reservoirs, and viaducts to supply cities with water. Deep excavations for the foundations of larger buildings were dug with explosives. They made it economically feasible to extract from the earth all types of minerals, metals, ores, coal, and oil, and the quarrying of stone would have remained a physically laborious enterprise without the enormously added force that explosives supplied.

In a century when guns were commonplace in many households for either hunting, target shooting, or protection against animals and hostile individuals, there was a continuing demand for various kinds of gunpowder for such firearms. And the government relied upon the producers of explosives to supply the armed forces with rifle, small arms, and cannon powder during the nation's wars and for the pacification of the Indians who resisted the seizure of their lands by the expanding civilization of the white man.

At midpoint in the nineteenth century the Du Pont Company was one of several larger companies engaged in the hazardous business of making explosives. Its history during the next thirty years can be clearly discerned in this biography of Lammot du Pont, a grandson of the founder of the company. His qualities of mind, inventive and innovative in powdermaking technology, made Du Pont the leading producer in the industry. His organization of the powder companies into an association seeking to promote their best interests through self-regulation and cooperation earned him recognition as its chosen leader and spokesman. A believer that a few larger producers were preferable to a large number of sharply competing smaller companies, Lammot planned and directed a program of consolidation that gave his firm domination of the industry by the time he left it. This creation of the Powder Trust came to be regarded as a restraint of trade a generation later when federal law forced its dissolution.

As did other manufacturers, Lammot sought greater control over the sources of the raw materials needed by his firm. Concomitant with this was a desire to find substitute materials that through chemistry could be transformed to perform as well, or better, than the traditional materials. His interest and investment in the Wyoming soda lakes and sulphur beds evidence an awareness of the newly developing mineral and mining frontiers of the Rocky Mountain region.

Lammot's assignments included the establishment of sales agencies in newly developing markets and in the acquisition or construction of new powder mills closer to the principal markets. This expansive outlook led him across the border to Canada where vast railroading, canal construction, and mining projects were underway. His acquisition of the only two Canadian companies manufacturing explosives was the first step that set a pattern of subsequent overseas expansion by the family firm.

The growth in size and complexity of operations made it apparent to Lammot that the management of the company needed to be changed. Decisions on policies, the distribution of responsibilities and compensation, and planning for the future demanded a managerial structure, infused by some outside blood, which the senior partner and company head, Henry du Pont, adamantly refused to accept. This determination to cling to an outmoded anachronistic form of management, paralleled by a refusal to take the Du Pont Company into the manufacture of the new high explosives that were seriously challenging the dominance of black powder, finally forced Lammot to sever his connections with the family firm.

The year 1850 when Lammot had resisted the temptation to "Go West" in search of his fortune in the gold fields of California and stayed home to enter the family business can be regarded as a pivotal year in his life. The year 1880 when he founded the Repauno Chemical Company can be viewed as the other year most significant in his career. Repauno was to give an altogether new direction to the future of the Du Pont Company with a consequent vast increase in the fortunes of the du Pont family. The venture into the production of high explosives with chemical components and the manufacture of the basic industrial chemicals, nitric and sulfuric acids, coincided with the advent of a surging interest in chemical education and engineering. New theories tested with old and newer methods and substances and varying formulations in laboratory and workshop led sometimes to anticipated results, but often to startling new discoveries. These were applied to the manufacture of an ever increasing range of products upon which new industries were founded and the marketplace vastly enlarged.

Lammot du Pont, the "life" of the Du Pont black powder business in an earlier time, in 1880 opened the door onto a new vista of opportunity that his sons and nephews utilized to create the Du Pont Company of the twentieth century.

Genealogical Table

Notes

Note on Sources

Index

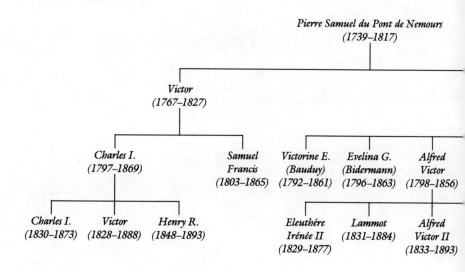

Pierre Samuel du Pont de Nemours
(1739–1817)

Victor
(1767–1827)

Charles I.
(1797–1869)

Samuel
Francis
(1803–1865)

Victorine E.
(Bauduy)
(1792–1861)

Evelina G.
(Bidermann)
(1796–1863)

Alfred
Victor
(1798–1856)

Charles I.
(1830–1873)

Victor
(1828–1888)

Henry R.
(1848–1893)

Eleuthére
Irénée II
(1829–1877)

Lammot
(1831–1884)

Alfred
Victor II
(1833–1893)

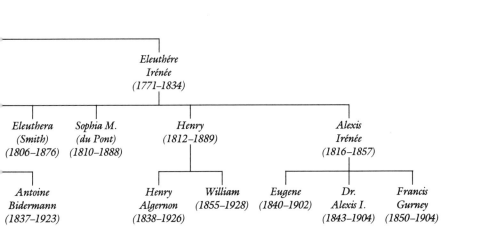

Eleuthére
Irénée
(1771–1834)

Eleuthera
(Smith)
(1806–1876)

Sophia M.
(du Pont)
(1810–1888)

Henry
(1812–1889)

Alexis
Irénée
(1816–1857)

Antoine
Bidermann
(1837–1923)

Henry
Algernon
(1838–1926)

William
(1855–1928)

Eugene
(1840–1902)

Dr.
Alexis I.
(1843–1904)

Francis
Gurney
(1850–1904)

Notes

Chapter I. As the Twig Is Bent

1. Lammot du Pont (LDP) Diary, Lammot du Pont Papers, Accession 384 Box 32 (hereafter Acc. 384/32, e.g.); "My Father," notes by Pierre S. du Pont on the life of his father (1948), Longwood Manuscripts, Group 10, Series B, Files 1–8 (hereafter LMSS, 10/B/1–8, e.g.). These and all other manuscript citations are from the collections in the Eleutherian Mills Historical Library, Greenville, Delaware, unless otherwise noted.

2. Victorine E. (du Pont) Bauduy to Margaretta E. du Pont, Mar. 13, 1833, Acc. 384/38.

3. E. I. du Pont to F. G. Smith, June 23, 1834, Letter Book, 1831–34, E. I. du Pont de Nemours & Company, Acc. 500; *American Watchman*, June 23, 1834.

4. LDP, "Notes on Accidents," memorandum, 1859, Acc. 384/48.

5. B. G. du Pont Notes, LMSS 7/A. As Irénée entered the powder yard on the day he began work, a rolling mill blew up, hurting no one. His Uncle Alexis facetiously remarked, "Why, it is a salute in your honor!" In a notation of much later date LDP added the comment, "Poor fellow, he heard a good many more before he died" (Acc. 384/48).

6. Victorine E. (du Pont) Bauduy to Evelina (du Pont) Bidermann, Jan. 15, Aug. 28, 1838, The Henry Francis du Pont Collection of Winterthur Manuscripts (hereafter WMSS), 6/4.

7. LDP to E. I. du Pont II, Aug. 3, 1843, Acc. 384/38.

8. Notes on the education of LDP compiled by his son Pierre S. du Pont and Margaret L. Kane, LMSS 10/C; Anne E. Mayer, "The Education of Lammot du Pont: Training for Industrial Leadership," 1970, Hagley Museum Research Report.

9. "Samuel Maxwell Gayley," *Presbyterian Historical Almanac and Annual Remembrancer of the Church for 1864* 6 (1864): 151–59.

10. *Delaware County Republican*, Nov. 3, 1854.

11. *Emporium of Arts and Sciences*, n.s., 1 (1813): 18; Dumas Malone, *The Public Life of Thomas Cooper, 1783–1839* (New Haven, 1926).

12. Edward P. Cheyney, *History of the University of Pennsylvania, 1740–1940* (Philadelphia, 1940), pp. 202–5.

13. Ibid., pp. 237–39.

14. *Mc Elroy's Philadelphia Directory, 1845–1846.*

15. Mrs. A. V. du Pont to E. I. du Pont II, n.d., [1845], Acc. 384/38.

16. *University of Pennsylvania Catalogue, 1845–1846*, p. 33; University of Pennsylvania Archives, Philadelphia, MSS Files, Box 1846.

17. John Robertson to Alfred V. du Pont, Nov. [n.d.], Acc. 384–47.

18. Minutes of the Zelosophic Society, 1847–48, University of Pennsylvania Archives.

19. Mrs. A. V. du Pont to E. I. du Pont II, Apr. 14, 1847, Acc. 384/38.

20. Alfred V. du Pont to E. I. du Pont II, Apr. [14?], 1847, Acc. 384/38.

21. Mrs. A. V. du Pont to E. I. du Pont II, Sept. 7, 1847, Acc. 384/38. Lex was their youngest uncle, Alexis I. du Pont.

22. Course descriptions are found in University of Pennsylvania catalogues, 1845–49; LDP's grades and class standing at graduation are in the Archives of the University of Pennsylvania, Students Files, 1846–49. More details of his years at the university are found in Mayer's "The Education of Lammot du Pont: Training for Industrial Leadership."

23. Commencement Program, University of Pennsylvania, July 2, 1852, Archives General, University of Pennsylvania, 1852.

24. "My Father," LMSS, 10/B/1–8.

25. Ibid.

26. Mrs. S. F. du Pont to S. F. du Pont, June 4, 1862, WMSS 9/D/105.

27. *Scientific American* 5 (July 20, 1850):347.

28. Ralph Andreano, ed., *The Economic Impact of the Civil War* (Cambridge, 1962), pp. 186–87, 189; Joseph C. G. Kennedy, ed., *Preliminary Report of the Eighth Census* (Washington, D.C., 1862), p. 173.

29. Ledgers, A, B, 1850–55, Acc. 500. Production figures are from LDP, "Powder Made by E. I. du Pont de Nemours & Company, 1803–1856," memorandum, Acc. 384/33.

30. Du Pont Company to Vital Lapeyre, Rio de Janeiro, Brazil, Dec. 4, 1851; and to Charles I. and Alfred Victor du Pont, Louisville, Sept. 12, 1855, both in Letter Books, 1851, 1855, Acc. 500.

31. "My Father," LMSS, 10/B/1–8; LDP, Diary, Acc. 384/32.

32. Alfred V. du Pont to John S. Twells, Apr. 24, 1850, LMSS 5/A/2.

33. Alfred V. du Pont to George W. Smith, July 20, 1850, Acc. 384/47.

34. Technical memoranda, notes by LDP, Acc. 384/31; LDP, "Report to father," Aug. 15, 1850, LMSS 5/A/2; LDP to "Fred" du Pont, c. 1851, Acc. 761/4.

35. Mrs. A. V. du Pont to Sophie du Pont, Oct. 13, 1850, Acc. 384/48. Victorine, his eldest sister, exclaimed she "never saw anything so gigantic as Sol [one of Lammot's several nicknames], he must soon stop his growing . . . else he won't have room to turn around" (to sister Sophie, n.d., Acc. 384/48).

36. Eleuthera (du Pont) Smith to Lt. Richard S. Smith, Aug. 10, 1850, Acc. 384/38.

37. Eleuthera (du Pont) Smith to Mrs. James I. Bidermann, Jan. 6, 1848, Acc. 761/17; LMSS 10/Kane File.

Chapter II. An Ultimatum and Reorganization

1. E. I. du Pont de Nemours & Company, Co-partnership Agreement, 1837, Pierre S. du Pont Office Collection, Acc. 501, D/8; Ledgers 1837–49, Acc. 500.

2. Henry A. du Pont to B. G. du Pont, Nov. 7, 1917, B. G. du Pont Notes, LMSS 7/A.

3. Alexis I. du Pont to Dr. Thomas M. Smith, Jan. 24, 1847, WMSS 7/C/22.

4. To Alfred V. du Pont, [July?] 1850, in handwriting of James A. Bidermann (copy), LMSS 5/A/2.

5. Eleuthera (du Pont) Smith to Leonie Bienaymé, Jan. 15, 1850, Eleuthera Bradford du Pont Collection, Acc. 146.

6. Mrs. A. V. du Pont to daughter Sophie, n.d., 1850, Acc. 384/48.

7. Ibid., Oct. 13, 1850, Acc. 384/48.

8. Eleuthera (du Pont) Smith to Lilia Bienaymé, Jan. 7, 1851, Acc. 146; LDP, "Powder Made by E. I. du Pont de Nemours & Company, 1803–1856," memorandum, updated to 1879, Acc. 384/33.

9. Francis Gurney du Pont Collection, Acc. 504/16.

10. Partnership Agreement, Jan. 1, 1851, Acc. 501, D/8.

11. Memorandum, Aflred V. du Pont to LDP, Nov. 1851, replying to his proposals, LMSS 5/A/2.

12. Mrs. A. V. du Pont to daughter Sophie, n.d., Acc. 384/48.

13. Charles I. du Pont to LDP, Sept. 8, 1854; copy of LDP's letter and analysis report, n.d., Acc. 384/47.

14. Mrs. A. V. du Pont to daughter Sophie, n.d., Acc. 384/48. Labels for powder kegs and canisters were multiply printed on large sheets and had to be individually cut.

15. Mrs. A. V. du Pont to daughter Sophie, Mar. 2, 1856, Acc. 384/48.

16. Ibid., Mar. 23, 1851, Acc. 384/48.

17. LDP, "Notes on Accidents in Powder Mills," 1859, Acc. 384/27. This summary listed 69 accidents between 1805 and 1859. In 1879 he extended the chronology to that year, concluding, "This furnishes a long list of explosions to this date, most of which could have been avoided." Newspaper accounts of the wagon disaster appeared in the *Philadelphia Evening Bulletin*, June 1, 1854, and in the *Delaware Gazette* and *Delaware State Journal*, June 2, 1854.

18. Letter Book, 1855–56, Acc. 500; Grinnell, Minturn & Company to

Du Pont Company, letters 1/22/55 to 7/30/56, Acc. 500/127; Hazard Powder Company to Du Pont Company (telegram), Jan. 29, 1855, LMSS 10/C.

19. LDP, "Powder Made by E. I. du Pont de Nemours & Company, 1803–1856," memorandum, updated to 1879, Acc. 384/33. The *Albany Journal*, Oct. 13, 1855, noted that two clipper ships of Grinnell, Minturn & Company had sailed for the Crimea during the summer laden with full cargoes of powder.

20. *Every Evening* (Wilmington), Apr. 2, 1884, and *Philadelphia Record*, Apr. 2, 1884.

21. LDP, Journal of a trip to Europe, 1858, LMSS 5/A/2; see also LMSS 10/C/49, Kane Files.

Chapter III. First Patent: "An Improvement in Gunpowder"

1. Du Pont Company to Brown, Shipley & Company, Liverpool, Oct. 13, 1855, Letter Book, 1855, Acc. 500.

2. LDP to H. M. Boies, Nov. 1, 1869, LMSS 5/A/2. LDP believed the first attempt in the United States to substitute sodium nitrate for potassium nitrate in black powder had been made by his grandfather, E. I. du Pont, in 1822.

3. Alfred V. du Pont, memorandum, Sept. 22, 1855, Acc. 384/47.

4. Mrs. Evelina (du Pont) Bidermann to LDP, Oct. 10, 1856, Acc. 384/8.

5. B. G. du Pont Notes, LMSS 7/A/1; Letters Patent No. 17,321, May 19, 1857, U.S. Patent Office.

6. Mrs. A. V. du Pont to "My dear girls," Aug. 31, 1857, Acc. 761; Eleuthera (du Pont) Smith to Lilia Bienaymé, Oct. 13, 1857, Acc. 150. See also Allen J. Henry, ed., *The Life of Alexis Irénée du Pont*, 2 vols. (Philadelphia, 1945), 1:1–2.

7. Pierre S. du Pont Papers, LMSS 10/C/49; Du Pont Company Journal, 1859, Acc. 500; LDP's yearly balances of accounts with the Du Pont Company, Acc. 384/29.

8. LDP to Edward C. Darling, n.d. (copy), Acc. 384/7.

9. Eleuthera (du Pont) Smith to Lilia Bienaymé, July 6, 1857, Acc. 521/19.

10. LDP, European Travels, Acc. 384/37.

11. LDP, "Memoranda on Powder Mills, 1857–1873," Acc. 384/38.

12. Norman B. Wilkinson, "Brandywine Borrowings from European Technology," *Technology and Culture*, 4, no. 1 (1963): 1–13.

13. LDP, "History of Mamouth [*sic*] Powder," undated memorandum, Acc. 384/30.

14. Peter Kemble to LDP, Feb. 12, 1858, Acc. 384/37.

15. Mrs. A. V. du Pont to LDP, Feb. 21, 1858, Acc. 384/37.

16. LDP, Journal of a Trip to Europe, Feb.-May 1858, LMSS 5/A/2. This account of his stay abroad is from his journal unless otherwise noted.

17. LDP (London) to Henry du Pont, Mar. 16, 1858, LMSS 5/A/2.

18. Sarah A. Wallace and Frances E. Gillespie, eds., *The Journal of Benjamin Moran*, 2 vols., (Chicago, 1949), 1:266.

19. *Delaware Gazette*, July 13, 1858.

20. Several attempts had recently been made on the emperor's life by Italian patriots for his interference in Italian governmental affairs. The most recent had been a bomb explosion near the Paris Opera on Jan. 14, 1858, where the emperor escaped death but others died. Napoleon III promptly suspended civil law throughout the country and placed it under military authority. LDP's detention and search occurred in this atmosphere of crisis and suspicion.

21. Alfred V. du Pont to LDP, Aug. 19, 1857, Acc. 384/37.

22. Sir Thomas Tobin (1807–1881) visited the United States in 1862. Enroute from Philadelphia to Washington he noted in his journal: "I knew that Du Pont's powder mills were on Brandywine Creek, and like the old hunter who loved the crack of the whip, I must see them" (MS 4110, National Library of Ireland, Dublin). It is likely Tobin was responding to an invitation extended by LDP. Acknowledgment is made to George D. Kelleher, Inniscarra, County Cork, for calling my attention to the Tobin journal.

23. Eleuthera (du Pont) Smith to Lilia Bienaymé, May 26, 1858, Acc. 521/1.

24. Du Pont Company to Lt. John C. Symmes, June 11, 1858, B. G. du Pont notes, LMSS 7/A.

25. LDP, "History of Mamouth Powder," Acc. 384/30; Thomas J. Rodman, *Properties of Metals for Cannon and Qualities of Cannon Powder* (Boston, 1861), pp. 217–74.

26. LDP, "Memorandum on Specific Gravity," n.d., Acc. 384/34.

27. LDP, "Accidents," memorandum, [1859], Acc. 384/27.

28. LDP, "Notes of Plans of Powder Mills and Machinery of E. I. du Pont de Nemours & Company, 1858," memorandum, Acc. 1600/8–13. Soon after beginning work in the mills LDP had made this note on Mar. 13, 1850: "I have thought of writing a history of the Brandywine. For this purpose I have commenced to gather all the information that I can. Today I walked down through the Upper Yard with Papa and as far as I could understand him I put down the rough plat that is on the other side." His rough plat resembles very closely a survey made of the property in 1802 when his grandfather had purchased it from Jacob Broom (Acc. 384/32).

29. LDP, "A summary of Water Wheels and Steam Engines in the Du Pont Powder Mills, 1874," memorandum, Acc. 384/33.

30. Francis G. du Pont, "Explosion of the Nitro-glycerine House of the Repauno Chemical Company," 1884. This account of the explosion in which

LDP lost his life includes an enumeration of his technical contributions to the Du Pont Company, LMSS 5/C/52.

31. U.S. Patents Nos. 50,104, Sept. 26, 1865, and 50,568, Oct. 24, 1865.

32. LDP, Untitled and undated memorandum, Acc. 384/32.

33. Charles B. Drake, attorney in Wilkes-Barre, to Du Pont Company, Apr. 13, 1859, Acc. 500/83.

34. C. A. Belin to Du Pont Company, Oct. 6, 1859, June 2, 1860, Acc. 500/16. The operations of the Wapwallopen plant for the next twenty years are told in Berlin's correspondence with the company and with LDP, the latter being in Acc. 384/3. LDP supervised Wapwallopen operations until his withdrawal from the Du Pont Company in 1880.

Chapter IV. Confidential Agent in Crisis

1. Bidermann du Pont to LDP, Dec. 15, 1860, Acc. 384/47.

2. Mrs. T. M. (Eleuthera du Pont) Smith to Lilia Bienaymé, Oct. 8, 1860, Acc. 521/30.

3. *Delaware Republican*, Apr. 25, 1861.

4. Mrs. Henry du Pont to Henry A. du Pont, Nov. 8, 1860, WMSS 8/A/100; *Delaware Republican*, Nov. 8, 1860.

5. Mrs. Henry du Pont to Henry A. du Pont, Nov. 8, 1860, and Ellen du Pont to same, Nov. 23, 1860, both WMSS 8/A/100.

6. Du Pont Company, Inventory no. 7, Dec. 31, 1861, Acc. 500/486.

7. Henry du Pont to Secretary of War Simon Cameron, Apr. 19, 1861, *War of the Rebellion*, ser. 1, vol. 51, pt. 1, pp. 328–29.

8. Mrs. S. F. du Pont to Henry W. Davis, U.S. representative from Maryland, Apr. 29, 1861, WMSS 9/D/100.

9. Mrs. Henry du Pont to Henry A. du Pont, Apr. 20, May 1, 1861, and Ellen E. du Pont to same, May 27, 1861, both WMSS 8/B/13.

10. Ellen E. du Pont to Henry A. du Pont, May 1, 1861, WMSS 8/B/13; Gen. Robert Patterson to Henry du Pont, Apr. 30, 1861, WMSS 7/B/5; *Delaware Republican* May 6, 1861.

11. Du Pont Company to Cabot and Pemberton, May 6, 1861, B. G. du Pont notes, LMSS 7/A/3.

12. Henry du Pont to S. F. du Pont, May 13, 1861, Letters Received (Powder), Apr. 14, 1861–Dec. 11, 1862, Navy Branch, National Archives; same to same, Nov. 18, 1861, WMSS 7/B/4.

13. William H. Seward, secretary of state, to Henry du Pont, Oct. 29, 1861, WMSS 7/B/8; LDP passport, Nov. 1, 1861, Acc. 384/37.

14. LDP to Mrs. A. V. du Pont, Nov. 30, 1861, Acc. 384/36; "An Incident of the Civil War," related by Samuel Bancroft, Jr., [1897] (typescript copy), Acc. 504 Add./42, hereafter cited as Bancroft, "Incident." Another version of

this incident told by LDP's brother Bidermann (Acc. 501) names the Anglo-American banking house of George Peabody & Company as the firm that granted him the large credit "on his face."

Both of these accounts of Lammot's saltpeter mission, Bancroft's and Bidermann's, were written long after the event and are without question apocryphal where they differ from the documented account given here. Not a scintilla of evidence in the du Pont papers, the voluminous records of Charles Francis Adams, or the relevant British archives can be found to support their colorful accounts of Lammot's activities in London.

15. *Times* (London), Nov. 28, 1861; J. Mackenzie to Lord Russell, Nov. 27, 1861, F.O. 5/806, 155, Foreign Office Records, Public Record Office, London.

16. Lord Palmerston Papers, National Register of Archives, London, courtesy the Earl Mountbatten of Burma; LDP to Henry du Pont, Nov. 30, 1861, Acc. 384/36.

17. Mrs. S. F. du Pont to S. F. du Pont, Dec. 29, 1861, WMSS 9/D/105, recounting a conversation with LDP upon his return home.

18. Mrs. S. F. du Pont to S. F. du Pont, Nov. 20 and Dec. 8, 1861, WMSS 9/D/105.

19. Du Pont Company [per LDP] to Seward, Dec. 26, 1861, Misc. Letters, Record Group 59, National Archives; Seward to Charles Francis Adams, Dec. 26, 1861 (Instructions, Great Britain), Record Group 59, XVIII, National Archives.

20. LDP to Henry du Pont, Jan. 18, 1862, Acc. 384/36.

21. Mrs. S. F. du Pont to S. F. du Pont, Apr. 29, 1862, WMSS 9/D/105.

22. J. W. Ripley to Edwin M. Stanton, May 3, 1862, Letters Received, Secretary of War, XIII, National Archives.

23. Serial no. 1123, Senate Executive Documents, 2d sess. 37th Cong. Case 92, p. 418, National Archives.

Chapter V. Captain Lammot du Pont

1. "Petition to Committee of Ways and Means of the House of Representatives," Mar. 18, 1862, Acc. 384/23; Representative George P. Fisher to Mrs. S. F. du Pont, Mar. 28, 1862, WMSS 9/E/133.

2. Sallie du Pont to Henry A. du Pont, Apr. 20, 1862, WMSS 8/B/100; Mrs. S. F. du Pont to S. F. du Pont, June 4, 1862, WMSS 9/D/105.

3. Mrs. S. F. du Pont to S. F. du Pont, June 8, 1862, WMSS 9/D/105.

4. S. F. du Pont to LDP, July 1, 1862, Acc. 384/8.

5. C. P. Buckingham to Henry du Pont, Aug. 16, 1862, *War of the Rebellion*, ser. 3, vol. 2, p. 398.

6. Mrs. S. F. du Pont to S. F. du Pont, Aug. 16, 1862, WMSS 9/D/106.

7. "Names of men who refused to join Lammot du Pont's Company B," Acc. 384/2.

8. Muster Roll, Company B, Fifth Regiment Delaware Volunteers, Acc. 384/2.

9. Mrs. Henry du Pont to Henry A. du Pont, Sept. 14, 1862, WMSS 8/B/100.

10. Mrs. S. F. du Pont to S. F. du Pont, Sept. 17, 1862, WMSS 9/D/106; Stanton to Halleck and Halleck to Reynolds, both Sept. 16, 1862, *War of the Rebellion*, ser. 1, vol. 19, pt. 2, p. 307; Lina du Pont to Henry A. du Pont, Sept. 19, 1862, WMSS 8/B/100.

11. Ellen du Pont to Henry A. du Pont, Nov. 9, 1862, WMSS 8/B/100.

12. *Delaware Gazette*, Sept. 23, Nov. 25, 1862; War Department, Adjutant-General's Office, Baker-Turner Papers, no. 230, Record Group 94, National Archives.

13. *Delaware Republican*, Oct. 2, Nov. 13, 1862; Internal Revenue Service receipts to LDP, Acc. 384/8; Ledgers C, D, 1862–64, Acc. 500.

14. *Delaware Republican*, Feb. 23, 1863; Henry du Pont to Henry A. du Pont, Feb. 22, 1863, WMSS 8/B/100.

15. *Delaware Republican*, Mar. 2, 1863; Mrs. S. F. du Pont to S. F. du Pont, Mar. 1 and 4, 1863, WMSS 9/D/106.

16. Mrs. S. F. du Pont to S. F. du Pont, June 20, 1863, WMSS 9/D/106; *Delaware Gazette*, June 23, 1863; LDP to Mrs. A. V. du Pont, June 23, 1863, Acc. 761/4.

17. Mrs. A. V. du Pont to LDP, June 1863, Acc. 384/2.

18. Papers of Delaware Volunteers, Company B, Fifth Regiment, LMSS 4/B/7; Mrs. Alexis I. du Pont to LDP, June 24, 1863, Acc. 384/2.

19. LDP to Mrs. A. V. du Pont, June 26, 1863, Acc. 761/4.

20. Mrs. S. F. du Pont to S. F. du Pont, June 25, 1863, WMSS 9/D/106.

21. Mrs. S. F. du Pont to S. F. du Pont, June 27, 29, 1863, WMSS, 9/D/106. Mrs. Alexis I. du Pont to Mrs. Leighton Coleman, July 1, 1863, Acc. 178/2; Ellen du Pont to Henry A. du Pont, June 29, 1863, WMSS 8/B/18.

22. Brig. A. F. Schoepf to LDP, July 6, 1863; LDP, "Condenser for Fort Delaware," memorandum, July 8, 1863, Acc. 384/35.

23. Lina du Pont to Henry A. du Pont, Aug. 23, 1863, WMSS 8/B/18.

24. *Delaware Republican*, July 16, 1863.

25. *Delaware Journal*, July 14, 1863.

26. Lina du Pont to Henry A. du Pont, Aug. 30, 1863, WMSS 8/B/15.

27. Mrs. Alexis I. du Pont to Mrs. Leighton Coleman, Sept. 4, 1863, Acc. 178/2.

28. Mrs. S. F. du Pont to S. F. du Pont, Oct. 11, 1863, WMSS 9/D/106.

29. C. A. Belin to LDP, Oct. 22, 1863, LMSS 4/B/8.

30. Du Pont Company to Comdr. H. A. Wise, Sept. 22, 1863, Letters received, United States Navy Ordnance Department, Book I, National Archives.

31. G. A. Lilliendahl to LDP, Oct. 19, 1863; LDP to G. A. Lilliendahl, Oct. 24, 1863, and G. A. Lilliendahl to LDP, Nov. 3, 1863, all Acc. 384/16.

32. LDP to G. A. Lilliendahl, Dec. 6, 1863, Acc. 384/16.

33. Gen. A. F. Schoepf to LDP, Nov. 6, 1863, LMSS 4/B/8; LDP to Gen. A. F. Schoepf (copy), n.d., 1863, LMSS 4/B/8.

34. "Settlement of Accounts, Co. B, 5th Reg't. Delaware Volunteers," LMSS 4/B/8; circular on "Home for Friendless and Destitute Children," LMSS 4/B/8.

35. Samuel B. Brown to LDP, n.d., 1863 or early 1864, LMSS 4/B/8. Brown soon left for Colorado, where he established a powder agency in the vicinity of the Pike's Peak goldfields.

36. Nicholas McCartney to LDP, Feb. 17, 1864, LMSS 4/B/8.

37. Peter Kemble to LDP, Nov. 27, 1863, LMSS 4/B/8; Lina du Pont to Henry A. du Pont, Dec. 20, 1863, WMSS 8/B/18.

38. Ledger C, 1861, 1862, 1863, Acc. 500.

39. *Delaware Republican*, Dec. 31, 1863.

40. John P. Hilyard to the Du Pont Company, Aug. 24, 1864, Acc. 500/150.

Chapter VI. *"Uncle Big Man"*

1. Lina du Pont to Henry A. du Pont, Jan. 3 and 30, July 2 and 12, 1864, WMSS 8/B/16.

2. T. T. S. Laidley to Du Pont Comany, Dec. 2 and 9, 1863, Acc. 501/7; same to same, Mar. 24, Nov. 6, 1863, Record Group 156, Ordnance Department, Class 8, Civil War Section, National Archives.

3. Lina du Pont to Henry A. du Pont, Jan. 30, Aug. 14, 1864, WMSS 8/B/16; S. V. Benét to the Du Pont Company, Dec. 6, 1864, Acc. 501/7.

4. Mrs. Henry du Pont to Henry A. du Pont, Apr. 2, 1864, WMSS 7/B/16.

5. Ibid., Jan. 25, 1868, WMSS 7/B/16; Marquis James, *Alfred I. du Pont, the Family Rebel* (Indianapolis, 1941), p. 55.

6. Mrs. T. M. (Eleuthera du Pont) Smith to Mrs. James I. Bidermann, May 14, 1864, WMSS 6/C/40; Mrs. Henry du Pont to Henry A. du Pont, May 18, 1864, WMSS 7/B/16.

7. LDP, Memorandum, specifications, and sketch of proposed bridge over the Brandywine, 1856, Acc. 384/55.

8. Mrs. Henry du Pont to Henry A. du Pont, May 1, 1864, WMSS 7/B/16.

9. Ibid., July 18, 1864, WMSS 7/B/16.

10. Lina du Pont to Henry A. du Pont, Aug. 14, 1864, WMSS 8/B/16; J. B. Fry, provost-marshall, to Henry du Pont, Aug. 10, 1864, *War of the Rebellion*, ser. 3, vol. 4, pp. 562–63.

11. *Delaware Republican*, Aug. 18, 1864; Lina du Pont to Henry A. du Pont, Aug. 30, 1864, WMSS 8/B/16. By late August the demand for substitutes so far exceeded the supply that the price shot up to $1,100 (*Delaware Republican*, Aug. 25, 1864).

12. Mrs. Henry du Pont to Mrs. S. F. du Pont, August 1864, and to Henry A. du Pont, Aug. 3, Sept. 5, 1864, WMSS 7/B/16.

13. Gen. A. F. Schoepf to LDP, June 9, Aug. 21, 1864, Acc. 384/51.

14. C. A. Belin to Du Pont Company, Aug. 18, Sept. 9, Oct. 22 and 28, 1864, and Jan. 2, 1865, Acc. 500/17; Sallie du Pont to Henry A. du Pont, Dec. 4, 1864, WMSS 8/B/16.

15. *Delaware Journal*, Nov. 4, and *Delaware Republican*, Nov. 7, 1864. For his role in the Virginia campaign Henry A. du Pont was awarded the Medal of Honor in 1898, thirty-four years later.

16. Du Pont Company to Leighton Coleman, Dec. 15, 1864, LMSS 5/A/2; Samuel Canby Diary, Dec. 18, 1864, Historical Society of Delaware, Wilmington; *Delaware Gazette*, Dec. 20, 1864.

17. Ellen du Pont to Henry A. du Pont, Jan. 1, 1865, WMSS 8/B/17; Mrs. Henry du Pont to same, Jan. 7, 1865, WMSS 7/B/16.

18. LDP, "Notes of Jobs on Hand," memorandum, Jan. 2, 1865, Acc. 384/30.

19. Mrs. Henry du Pont to Mrs. S. F. du Pont, Apr. 7, 1866, WMSS 7/B/16. A fire in the naphtha room which threatened her home provoked Aunt Louisa to protest, "These experiments of Lammot's might well be dispensed with—at least in such a place."

20. Mrs. Alexis I. du Pont to Mrs. Leighton Coleman, Apr. 10, 1865, Acc. 178/1; Mrs. Henry du Pont to Henry A. du Pont, Apr. 10, 1865, WMSS 7/B/16.

21. *Delaware Republican*, Apr. 13, 1865; Henry du Pont to Henry A. du Pont, Apr. 22, 1865, WMSS 8/A/101.

22. Charles I. du Pont, Jr., to LDP, Aug. 13, 1854, Acc. 384/8. It is not known whether LDP had ever met the young lady, member of a Beacon Hill family, daughter of Nathaniel Bradstreet Shurtleff, a wealthy physician, editor and author, an Overseer of Harvard College, and three-term mayor of Boston beginning in 1868 (Mrs. A. V. du Pont to Mary S. du Pont, n.d., Acc. 384/48).

23. LDP to Charles I. du Pont, Jr., July 19, 1854, Acc. 298/4; Petit Ledgers I & J, 1852–55, Acc. 501.

24. Charles I. du Pont, Jr., to LDP, Oct. 11, 1854, Acc. 384/47.

25. Ellen du Pont to Henry A. du Pont, July 3, 1859, Jan. 1, 1860, WMSS 8/B/12; Henry du Pont to LDP, Jan. 18, 1862, Acc. 384/8.

26. Mrs. A. V. du Pont to [Bidermann du Pont?] July 3, 1865, Acc. 761/2.

27. Mrs. Henry du Pont to Mrs. S. F. du Pont, July 3, 1865, WMSS 7/B/16.

28. Lina du Pont to Henry A. du Pont, July 3, 1865, WMSS 8/B/17; Mrs. T. M. (Eleuthera du Pont) Smith to Mrs. James I. Bidermann, n.d., 1865, WMSS 6/C/40. Lina had very firm ideas about marriage within the family or within the circle of long-standing friends: "I liked it well except for my dislike to marrying only in one's family or married circle, as we seem to be doing. I like new people and new ideas" (to Henry A. du Pont, Oct. 29, 1865, WMSS 8/B/17).

29. Charles A. Silliman, *The Story of Christ Church Christiana Hundred and Its People*, (Wilmington, 1960), p. 31.

30. Mrs. Alexis I. du Pont to Mrs. Leighton Coleman, Sept. 28, 1863, Acc. 178/1; Mrs. T. M. Smith (Eleuthera du Pont) Smith to [James A. Bidermann?] Sept. 26, 1864, WMSS 6/C/40; Mrs. Henry du Pont to Henry A. du Pont, Oct. 31, 1865, WMSS 7/B/16.

31. LDP to Mary Belin, July 24, 1862, Acc. 1597/1.

32. LDP to Mary Belin, May 20, 1864, Acc. 1597/1.

33. Mary Belin to LDP, July 1865, Acc. 384/48.

34. Lina du Pont to Henry A. du Pont, July 24, 1865, WMSS 8/B/17.

35. Mary Belin to LDP, July 24, 1865, Acc. 384/48.

36. Bidermann du Pont to LDP, Aug. 3, 1865, and Alfred V. du Pont to same, Aug. 27, 1865, both Acc. 384/8.

37. Mrs. T. M. (Eleuthera du Pont) Smith to Mrs. James I. Bidermann, Oct. 4, 1865, Acc. 761/17; Mrs. Henry du Pont to Henry A. du Pont, Oct. 3, 1865, WMSS 7/B/16.

38. Ellen du Pont to Henry A. du Pont, Oct. 25, 1865, WMSS 8/B/17. Ellen's implied wish was not fulfilled; marrying within the family continued in later generations.

39. Yearly Credit Balances of LDP's Accounts with the Du Pont Company, Acc. 384/27; Ledger C, 1863, Acc. 501.

Chapter VII. New Ventures

1. Arthur F. Burns, *Production Trends in the United States since 1870* (New York, 1934), p. 288; C. A. Ashburner in *Grand Atlas of the 2nd Penna. Geological Survey* (1884), gives production figures for 1870 as 16,182,191 tons and for 1879 as 26,142,689 tons.

2. Details of the agreement are found in a Luzerne County Court document filed Dec. 4, 1866, Acc. 384/41.

3. LDP to A. J. Cohen, July 16, 1867, Letter Book, LDP, president, Mocanaqua Coal Company, 1866–68, LMSS 4/B/8; George L. Breck and Mocanaqua Coal Company correspondence, Acc. 384/39.

4. Mocanaqua Coal Company Sales, 1867, Acc. 384/40; C. A. Belin to Du Pont Company, Feb. 22, 1867, Acc. 500/17; LDP Letter Book, 1866–68, LMSS 4/B/8; Ledger D, 1866–68, Acc. 500.

5. A. J. Cohen to LDP, Sept. 4, 1868, Acc. 384/39; LDP to Foxwell and Gallagher, Aug. 23, 1870, Acc. 384/40.

6. "The Welsh" to LDP, Dec. 16, 1868, Acc. 384/40.

7. William F. Lynch, oral interview transcript, 1956, Oral History File, Hagley Museum, Wilmington.

8. A. J. Cohen to LDP, Jan. 11, 1869, Acc. 384/39.

9. Ibid., June 12, 30, July 31, 1869, Acc. 384/39; Howard N. Eavenson, *First Century and a Quarter of American Coal Industry* (Pittsburgh, 1942), p. 151.

10. LDP to J. J. W. Wister, Pennsylvania Canal Company, Sept. 5, 1869 (copy), and Wister to LDP, Oct. 21, 1869, both Acc. 384/19.

11. LDP to Moses Taylor, Oct. 27, 1869, Acc. 384/23, to Robert Woolley, c. 1870, Acc. 384/25, and to Lewis Landmesser, Aug. 22, 1872, Acc. 384/40 (all copies); James E. Gowen to LDP, Apr. 23, 1873, Acc. 384/40.

12. George L. Breck to LDP, Feb. 14, 1871, Oct. 28, 1873, Acc. 384/39.

13. C. A. Belin to LDP, Dec. 6 and 12, 1872, Acc. 384/3.

14. C. H. Gallagher to LDP, Feb. 12, 1873, Acc. 384/40; legal papers bearing on this suit are in Acc. 384/46.

15. Ledgers E, 6, 1873–75, Acc. 500.

16. David L. Richards to LDP, Aug. 2, 1875, and Richard P. Rothwell to same, Dec. 9, 1871, both Acc. 384/20.

17. LDP to Charles Parrish, Mar. 26, 1876, Acc. 384/19; B. G. du Pont Notes, LMSS 7/A/2; Charles Parrish to LDP, Mar. 23, 1881 (telegram), Acc. 384/19; Ledger No. 7, 1879–82, Acc. 500.

18. *Wilmington and Reading Railroad Offer Their First Mortgage 7 Percent Interest Bonds* (Philadelphia, 1868); *From Coal to Tide* (Wilmington, 1870).

19. Ledger D, 1867–69, and Ledger 6, 1875–78, Acc. 500; Robert Frazer, president, Wilmington and Reading Railroad, to LDP, May 1, 1876, Acc. 384/43.

20. *Report of the Directors to the Stockholders of the Wilmington and Northern Railroad, 1873* (Coatesville, Pa., 1874).

21. Marvin W. Schlegel, *Ruler of the Reading: The Life of Franklin B. Gowen, 1836–1889* (Harrisburg, Pa., 1947), p. 50; Jon Clayton, "Railroad Building in Delaware," M.A. thesis, University of Delaware, 1948, p. 167.

22. Schlegel, *Ruler of the Reading*, p. 50.

23. *Justification for Foreclosing on the Wilmington and Reading Railroad by the First Mortgage Bondholders* (broadside), May 11, 1875, Acc. 384/44.

24. "List of first mortgage bondholders of the Wilmington and Reading Railroad showing amounts owned by each, 1876," Acc. 384/44. The Du Pont Company and family members together owned $88,300 worth of bonds, the largest single bloc.

25. Lewis W. Smith to LDP, Sept. 15, 1876, and *Report of the Purchasers of the Wilmington and Reading Railroad*, Jan. 23, 1877, both Acc. 384/44.

26. Lewis W. Smith to LDP, Jan. 17, Oct. 31, 1876, and *Report of the Purchasers of the Wilmington and Reading Railroad*, Jan. 23, 1877, both Acc. 384/44.

27. LDP's role in this reorganization struggle is evident in the notice of Attorney Lewis W. Smith of the date of the meeting establishing the new company: "Your presence is *absolutely necessary*" (Mar. 1, 1877, Acc. 384/44).

28. *April Sessions, 1878, Suit No. 16, in Equity, In the U.S. Circuit Court for the Eastern District of Pennsylvania* . . . Acc. 384/46.

29. T. O. Yarington to LDP, Sept. 2, 1878, Acc. 384/44.

30. LDP to Franklin B. Gowen, Mar. 22, 1879 (copy) and Franklin B. Gowen to LDP, Apr. 8, 1879, both Acc. 384/45.

31. LDP to Franklin B. Gowen, n.d. (copy), Acc. 384/45.

32. LDP to John R. Kaucher, May 17, 1879 (copy), Acc. 384/45.

33. LDP to C. A. Belin, May 2, 1880 (copy), Acc. 384/3.

34. Rodman W. Paul, *Mining Frontiers of the Far West, 1848-1880* (New York, 1963), pp. 109–96.

35. Cincinnati Chemical Laboratory to LDP, June 23, 1875, James Irwin and Company to Cincinnati Chemical Laboratory, July 26, 1875, and Mahla and Chappell to Cincinnati Chemical Laboratory, Aug. 3, 1875, all Acc. 384/42.

36. LDP, "Analysis of Soda, July 28, 1875," memorandum, July 28, 1875, Acc. 384/42.

37. Memorandum showing ownership in Wyoming soda lakes, Oct. 25, 1875, Acc. 384/42.

38. G. B. Graeff to LDP, Apr. 22, 1876, Acc. 384/42.

39. Lt. Joseph Kuffe, U.S. Fourth Infantry, to LDP, July 4, 1876, Acc. 384/42.

40. Henry Belin, Jr., to LDP, Aug. 14, 1876, Acc. 384/4.

41. LDP to Mary du Pont, Oct. 10, 1876, Acc. 1597/1.

42. Ibid., Oct. 17, 1876, Acc. 1597/1.

43. G. B. Graeff to LDP, Dec. 6, 1876, Mar. 5, 1877, Acc. 384/42. In 1967 the Tom Sun Ranch in central Wyoming was designated by the National

Park Service as a registered National Historic Landmark. See Robert G. Ferris, ed., *Prospector, Cowhand, and Sodbuster* (Washington, D.C., 1967), pp. 140–42.

44. Irving A. Stearns to LDP, Sept. 29, Oct. 1, 2, 12, and 17, 1879, Acc. 384/42.

45. "Expenditures on Soda Lakes," memorandum, Jan. 1, 1881, Acc. 384/42; Minute Books and Correspondence of the Natrona Alkali Company, 1899–1949, Acc. 228; interview with Irénée du Pont, Jr., July 19, 1977.

Chapter VIII. Upgrading Operations and Technological Triumphs

1. LDP, Abstract of information on the powder industry from the *United States Ninth Census Report, 1870,* 1872, Acc. 384/28.

2. Francis G. du Pont, "Reorganization of Hagley Yard," memorandum, 1872, Acc. 1600/26–11.

3. Joseph A. Litterer, "Systematic Management: The Search for Order and Integration," in *Business History Review* 35, no.4 (Winter 1961): 461–76. See also Litterer's "Systematic Management: Design for Organizational Recoupling in American Manufacturing Firms," in *The History of American Management,* ed. James P. Baughman (Englewood Cliffs, N.J., 1969), pp. 53–74.

4. LDP, "Labor Performed in Hagley as Organized in 1872," memorandum, Acc. 384/30. See also Norman B. Wilkinson, "In Anticipation of Frederick W. Taylor: A Study of Work by Lammot du Pont, 1872," *Technology and Culture* 6, no. 2 (1965): 208–21.

5. LDP, "A Summary of Water Wheels and Steam Engines in the Du Pont Powder Mills, 1874," Acc. 384/33.

6. "Reminiscences of Du Pont Company Employees," comp. Richard Stout, 1909, Oral History File, Hagley Museum, Wilmington.

7. LDP, "Accidents," memorandum, Acc. 384/27; Francis G. du Pont, "Rolling Mill Explosions, with their causes," 1871–1902, LMSS 5/C/52.

8. LDP, "History of Mamouth Powder," memorandum, n.d., Acc. 384/30.

9. Capt. William N. Jeffers to Du Pont Company, June 20 and 28, 1871, United States Navy Department, Records of Bureau of Ordnance, Record Group 74, National Archives.

10. J. D. Marvin to A. L. Case, Aug. 19, 1871, J. D. Marvin to William N. Jeffers, Sept. 2, 1871, and William N. Jeffers to J. D. Marvin Sept. 20, 1871, U.S. Navy, Ordnance, R.G. 74, NA.

11. J. D. Marvin to A. L. Case, Apr. 14, 1872, and J. D. Marvin to William N. Jeffers, Sept. 22, 1871, U.S. Navy, Ordnance, R.G. 74, NA.

12. Henry du Pont to Henry A. du Pont, May 28, 1872, WMSS 7/B/7.

13. Daniel Ammen, Ordnance Bureau, Navy Department, to Du Pont

Company, July 24, Aug. 1, 1872, Du Pont Company to Daniel Ammen, Aug. 3, 1872, and A. L. Case, Ordnance Bureau, Navy Department, to Du Pont Company, Aug. 15, 1872, U.S. Navy, Ordnance, R.G. 74, NA.

14. LDP, "Notes on Hexagonal Pellet Powder," memorandum, [1872–74], Acc. 384/34.

15. LDP, "Experiments on Drying," memorandum, Acc. 384/34.

16. Maj. T. G. Baylor, ordnance officer, Fortress Monroe, Va., to A. B. Dyer, chief of ordnance, War Department, Sept. 9, 1873 (copy), Acc. 384/30; William N. Jeffers to Du Pont Company, Nov. 18, 21, 1873, Jan. 8, 1874, U.S. Navy, Ordnance, RG 74, NA.

17. LDP to William Kemble, Mar. 19, Apr. 2, 1874, Acc. 384/40.

18. William N. Jeffers to Du Pont Company, July 8, 1875, May 3, 1876, U.S. Navy, Ordnance, R.G. 74, NA.

Chapter IX. Competition, Consolidation, and Control

1. C. A. Belin to LDP, Apr. 6, 1870, Acc. 384/3.

2. Henry A. Weldy to LDP, July 4, 1872, Acc. 384/24.

3. LDP, "Schuylkill Powder Trade," memorandum, July 1872, Acc. 384/31.

4. A. T. Rand to Du Pont Company, July 19, 23, 1872, Acc. 500/231.

5. Purchase Agreement between Du Pont Company and Conrad F. Shindel and Edward F. Shindel, May 5, 1871 (copy); LDP to Henry A. Weldy, May 18, 1871 (copy), Acc. 384/24; Henry A. Weldy to Du Pont Company, May 13, 1871, Acc. 500/413; Arthur P. Van Gelder and Hugo Schlatter, *History of the Explosives Industry in America* (New York, 1926), pp. 198–200.

6. Henry A. Weldy to Du Pont Company, Feb. 8, 1872, Acc. 500/413.

7. LDP to Solomon Turck, Oct. 13, 1873 (copy), Acc. 384/15. Solomon Turck had succeeded A. T. Rand as president of Laflin and Rand Company, and LDP is here reviewing for him the "understanding" made with his predecessor.

8. Henry A. Weldy to LDP, Feb. 14, 1876, Acc. 384/24.

9. Ibid., July 7, Sept. 9, 1872, Acc. 384/24.

10. LDP to A. T. Rand, Aug. 10, Sept. 15, 1872 (copies); A. T. Rand to LDP, Aug. 14, Sept. 18, 1872, Acc. 384/15.

11. Henry A. Weldy to LDP, Nov. 7, 12, 15, and 16, 1872, Acc. 384/24.

12. Henry A. Weldy to Du Pont Company, Sept. 11, 14, Oct. 6, 1873, Acc. 500/413; Weldy to LDP, Oct. 9, Nov. 10, 1873, and LDP to Weldy, Nov. 18, 1873 (copy), both Acc. 384/24.

13. Henry Dwight Laflin to LDP, Mar. 18, 1873, and LDP to Henry Dwight Laflin, Mar. 23, 1873 (copy), both Acc. 384/15.

14. LDP to Solomon Turck, Oct. 13, 1873 (copy), and Solomon Turck to LDP Oct. 22, 1873, both Acc. 384/15.

15. Henry A. Weldy to LDP, Sept. 15, 1874, Sept. 26, 1875, Acc. 384/24.

16. Solomon Turck to LDP, Nov. 26, 1875, Acc. 384/15.

17. Ibid., May 23, 1882, Acc. 284/15.

18. Idib., Dec. 23, 1875, Acc. 384/15.

19. Henry Dwight Laflin to LDP, Mar. 17, 1879, Acc. 384/15; Henry A. Weldy to LDP, June 1, 1882, Acc. 384/24; James Muir to LDP, June 28, 1882, Acc. 384/18.

20. Henry A. Weldy to Du Pont Company, Sept. 1, 1882, Acc. 500/414; Henry A. Weldy to LDP, Jan. 15 and 20, 1881, Acc. 384/24; Henry A. Weldy to Du Pont Company, Aug. 16, 1880, May 8, 1883, Acc. 500/414.

21. Henry A. Weldy to Du Pont Company, Dec. 23, 1883, Dec. 24, 1884, Acc. 500/414.

22 Ibid., Oct. 4, Nov. 25, 1879, Aug. 16, Sept. 16, 1880, Acc. 500/414.

23. Solomon Turck to LDP, Apr. 19, 1878, Acc. 384/15.

24. Henry A. Weldy to LDP, Jan. 21, 1881, Acc. 384/28; Henry A. Weldy to Du Pont Company, Jan. 6, 1882, Acc. 500/414.

25. LDP, Chronology of companies acquired and sketch of Du Pont Company "genealogical tree," memoranda, Acc. 384/30.

26. Henry A. Weldy to LDP, June 19, 1874, Acc. 384/24; Henry A. Weldy to Du Pont Company, Nov. 3, 1884, Acc. 500/414.

27. LDP to Paul A. Oliver, Jan. 6, 1876 (copy), Paul A. Oliver to LDP Feb. 29, 1876, and LDP to Paul A. Oliver, Mar. 3, 1876 (copy), all Acc. 384/18.

28. LDP to Furman L. Kneeland, Oct. 13, 21, and 26, 1877, Acc. 500/224. Lammot's memorandum, "Wapwallopen Mills, Costs of Powder, 1877," shows how he cut production costs, largely by reducing labor costs, to enable him to sell powder at $1.47 a keg, a price he believed would force Paul A. Oliver to sell (Acc. 384/30; Van Gelder and Schlatter, *History of the Explosives Industry in America*, pp. 213–14.

29. Furman L. Kneeland to Du Pont Company, Dec. 16, 1867, and correspondence between same, Jan. and Feb. 1868, Acc. 500/190; Furman L. Kneeland to Du Pont Company, May 15, 1867, Acc. 500/189.

30. Henry M. Boies to LDP, Aug. 5, 1868, and accompanying memorandum, Acc. 384/30.

31. Donald A. Grinde, Jr., "The Gunpowder Trade Association: A Search for Stability, 1872–1912," Ph.D. diss., University of Delaware, 1974.

32. Henry du Pont to Furman L. Kneeland, Apr. 4 and 21, 1872, Acc. 500/219.

33. Furman L. Kneeland to Henry du Pont, Apr. 6 and 10, 1872, Acc. 500/198.

34. Furman L. Kneeland to Du Pont Company, Apr. 8 and 18, 1872, Acc. 500/198.

35. Irénée du Pont to Furman L. Kneeland, Apr. 1872, Acc. 500/219.

36. LDP to Henry du Pont, Apr. 1872, WMSS 4/D/14; Henry du Pont to Furman L. Kneeland, Apr. 20, 1872, Acc. 500/219.

37. Minutes of the Gunpowder Trade Association of the United States (GTA), Apr. 23 and 29, 1872, et seq., Acc. 500/518.

38. Irénée du Pont to Furman L. Kneeland, Jan. 1873, Acc. 500/220; William S. Dutton, *Du Pont: One Hundred and Forty Years*, (New York, 1942), p. 120.

39. LDP, Memorandum of Address to Quarterly Meeting of GTA, Aug. 1872, Acc. 384/30.

40. Arthur Williams to Furman L. Kneeland, Dec. 26, 1874, Acc. 500/278.

41. GTA Minutes, Mar. 10, Apr. 12, 1876, Feb. 14, 1883, Acc. 500/518.

42. Furman L. Kneeland to Du Pont Company, Mar. 12, May 3, 1877, Acc. 500/207.

43. GTA Confidential Minutes, May 1, 1878, Acc. 500/534; "Lake Superior Agreement," Acc. 500/534; Solomon Turck, "Historical Report of the Laflin and Rand Powder Company," July 9, 1878, Acc. 501/18; LDP, to N. G. Kittle, Sept. 21, 1879, Acc. 384/6.

44. Bernard Peyton to Du Pont Company, July 16, 1876, Acc. 500/55; John F. Lohse to Du Pont Company, Feb. 19, 1877, Acc. 500/55; the California Powder Works Annual Report for 1872 shows total assets of $732,368, on which it earned profits of $89,310 and paid out $55,000 in dividends; in 1876, with assets over a million dollars, it paid out dividends amounting to $150,000 (Acc. 500/55).

45. "Neutral Belt Agreement," Feb. 11, 1875, Acc. 500/523; GTA Minutes, Mar. 17, 1875, Acc. 500/518; William S. Stevens, "The Powder Trust, 1872–1912," *Quarterly Journal of Economics*, 26, no. 3 (1912): 3–4.

46. LDP to N. G. Kittle, Sept. 21, 1879 (copy), Acc. 384/6. In this letter he reported that sales of Du Pont black powder in the Lake Michigan copper regions had dropped from 40,000 kegs in 1877 to an estimated 2,000 kegs by 1879.

47. Furman L. Kneeland to Du Pont Company, Dec. 12, 1868, Acc. 500/197. Kneeland wrote, "The death of Colonel Hazard has effected [*sic*] the standing of their Co. in the trade very seriously. It is reported that the Co. is falling to pieces, etc. I think they are badly in want of business ability" (ibid.). See also Van Gelder and Schlatter, *History of the Explosives Industry in America*, pp. 260–262.

48. LDP, Memoranda on purchase of Hazard Powder Company, May 8, 1876, Acc. 384/12, 31.

49. Solomon Turck to LDP, Dec. 24, 1874, Acc. 384/15.

50. Ibid., Feb. 14, 1876, Acc. 384/15.

51. Draft of LDP's Proposal to GTA, Mar. 10, 1876, Acc. 384/30; GTA Minutes, Mar. 10, 1876, Acc. 500/518; Dr. Thomas C. Brainerd to Solomon Turck, Jan. 15, 1877, Acc. 384/11.

52. Dr. Thomas C. Brainerd to LDP, Sept. 24, Oct. 16, 1877, Acc. 384/11.

53. Arthur Williams to LDP, Jan. 13, 1883, Acc. 384/18. The Oriental Powder Mills, in financial distress, had been taken over by the Big Three in 1879 but continued to operate as an independent company until 1903.

54. Hamilton Powder Company correspondence and business papers, 1876–83, Acc. 384/11, 18; Acadia Powder Company correspondence, 1882–83, Acc. 384/1; Inventory of Lammot du Pont's property, Jan. 1884, Acc. 1343/2; B. L. Turvolgi, *Evolution of a Canadian Company, Du Pont of Canada, 1862–1954* (Montreal, 1954), p. 2.

55. LDP to D. W. C. Bidwell (copy) c. 1881, Acc. 384/5.

56. LDP, Sketch of Du Pont company "genealogical tree" and chronology of companies acquired, Acc. 384/30.

57. Mrs. Henry du Pont to Mrs. S. F. du Pont, Jan. 16, 1880, WMSS 7/B/18.

Chapter X. Uncle Henry Challenged

1. LDP, "Criticism on the Articles of Co-Partnership of 1858," memorandum, Dec. 1877, Acc. 384/29.

2. LDP, Memorandum showing money withdrawn from Du Pont Company by its partners, 1873–77, 1877, Acc. 384/29.

3. LDP, "Criticism of Proposed Articles," memorandum, 1877, Acc. 384/29.

4. Henry du Pont to Henry A. du Pont, Aug. 28, 1858, WMSS 7/B.

5. Henry A. du Pont, as told to B. G. du Pont, c. 1915–16, in B. G. du Pont Notes, LMSS 7/A.

6. LDP to Henry du Pont, Dec. 6, 1877 (copy), Acc. 384/29.

7. Ibid., Apr. 7, 1878 (copy), Acc. 384/48.

8. Mrs. A. V. du Pont to LDP, Apr. 9, 1878, Acc. 384/48.

9. Henry du Pont to LDP, May 28, 1878, Acc. 384/48.

10. Ibid., Aug. 4, 1878, Acc. 384/48.

11. LDP to Henry du Pont, Aug. 6 and 8, 1878 (copies), Acc. 384/48.

12. Henry du Pont to LDP, Aug. 9, 1878, Acc. 384/48.

13. Ibid., Mar. 20, 1879, Acc. 384/48.

14. LDP to Henry du Pont, Apr. 4 and 30, 1879 (copies), Acc. 384/48.

15. LDP to N. G. Kittle, Sept. 21, 1879 (copy), Acc. 384/6.

Chapter XI. Repauno

1. Van Gelder and Schlatter, *History of the Explosives Industry in America*, pp. 402–8.

2. B. G. du Pont Notes, LMSS 7/A/2; LDP, "Comments on Inventory of E. I. du Pont de Nemours & Company, Dec. 31, 1881," LMSS 5/C/49; Bernard Peyton to Du Pont Company, Feb. 12, 1882, Acc. 500/55.

3. LDP, Notebook of experiments on acids and glycerine used in manufacture of dynamite, Acc. 384/44.

4. Bernard Peyton to Du Pont Company, July 21, 1876, Acc. 500/55.

5. J. W. Willard to Du Pont Company, Jan. 17, 1878, Acc. 500/55.

6. Bernard Peyton to Du Pont Company, Feb. 3, 1878; LDP to Bernard Peyton, Feb. 19, 1878, Acc. 384/6.

7. LDP to Sidney Dillon, [November?] 1876 (copy); Sidney Dillon to LDP Jan. 8, 1877; LDP to Sidney Dillon, Apr. 14, 1881 (copy), Acc. 384/20.

8. Solomon Turck to Du Pont Company, Nov. 11, 1879, Acc. 384/15.

9. Correspondence between LDP and Charles A. Morse, Nov. 1879–Apr. 1880, provides many details about plant construction. Morse was dismissed in March 1880 for running up expenses that Lammot considered excessive (Acc. 384/18).

10. Solomon Turck to LDP, Apr. 5 and 10, 1880, Acc. 384/15.

11. LDP to wife Mary, Feb. 25, 1880, Acc. 1597/1.

12. Van Gelder and Schlatter, *History of the Explosives Industry in America*, pp. 337, 490–91; LDP, Financial Statement, Jan.1, 1884, Acc. 1363/2.

13. LDP to C. A. Belin, May 2, 1880, Acc. 384/3.

14. LDP, "Comments on Inventory," LMSS 5/C/49; Van Gelder and Schlatter, *History of the Explosives Industry in America*, p. 568 n. 2, pp. 584–85.

15. Van Gelder and Schlatter, *History of the Explosives Industry in America*, pp. 567–68; Dutton, *Du Pont, One Hundred and Forty Years*, pp. 138–39.

16. Solomon Turck to LDP, May 22, 1880, Acc. 384/15.

17. John F. Lohse to LDP, Aug. 5 and 29, Sept. 6, 1881, Acc. 384/6; William du Pont to LDP, Mar. 14, 17, 1882, Acc. 384/8.

18. Mrs. A. V. du Pont to Mrs. S. F. du Pont, Dec. 1881, WMSS 7/A/4; Victorine (du Pont) Kemble to Mrs. S. F. du Pont, Dec. 1, 1881, WMSS 9/E.

19. Mrs. Lammot du Pont to Mrs. S. F. du Pont, Feb. 2, 1882, Feb. 13, 1883, WMSS 9/E.

20. Mrs. Lammot du Pont to Mrs. S. F. du Pont, July 22, 1882, WMSS 9/E.

21. "My Father," LMSS 10/B, 1–8.

22. Mrs. A. V. du Pont to Mrs. S. F. du Pont, Jan. 4, May 2, and Oct. 1882, WMSS 7/A/3.

23. Receipted Bills, June 1, 1878, 1881, Acc. 384/8, 24.

24. Reminiscences of George H. Kerr, Acc. 501/D/124. See also Kerr's *Du Pont Romance* (Wilmington, 1938), pp. 78–102.

25. LDP to Henry du Pont, Mar. 3, 1882 (copy), Acc. 384/8.

26. Henry du Pont to LDP, Mar. 4, 1882, Acc. 384/8.

27. LDP to Henry du Pont, Mar. 9 and 21, 1882 (copy), Acc. 384/8.

28. Ibid., Mar. 21 and 22, 1882(copies); Henry du Pont to LDP, Mar. 21, 1882, Acc. 384/8.

29. LDP to Henry du Pont, Mar. 22, 1882 (copy); Henry du Pont to LDP, Mar. 23 and 24, 1882, Acc. 384/8.

30. Henry Belin, Jr., to LDP, Mar. 24, 1882, Acc. 384/4; Alfred du Pont to LDP, Mar. 27, 1882, Acc. 384/8.

31. LDP to Henry Belin, Jr., Mar. 27, 1882 (copy), Acc. 384/4.

32. LDP to Furman L. Kneeland, June 5, 1870, Acc. 384/14.

33. Du Pont Company to LDP, Oct. 24, 1882, Acc. 384/8; Accounting record covering settlement of LDP's account with Du Pont Company, Acc. 384/8. See also Ledger no. 7, 1879–82, p. 1, Acc. 500.

34. Linus Austin to LDP, Dec. 9, 1881, Acc. 384/1.

35. Paul A. Oliver to LDP, Feb. 14 and 21, 1882, Acc. 384/18; Henry Belin, Jr., to LDP, May 13, 1882, Acc. 384/4.

36. Henry A. Weldy to LDP, Sept. 15, 1882, Acc. 384/24; Henry Dwight Laflin to LDP, Sept. 20, 1882, Acc. 384/15; C. A. Belin to LDP, Jan. 2, 1883, Acc. 384/3.

Chapter XII. A Broken Column

1. *Philadelphia Public Ledger*, Mar. 31, 1884.

2. Francis G. du Pont to Alexis I. du Pont, Apr. 1 and 7, 1884, Acc. 1597/1.

3. Bernard Peyton to Henry du Pont, Apr. 26, 1877, commenting on an explosion at the Santa Cruz plant of the California Powder Works, Acc. 500/55.

4. Mrs. S. F. du Pont Diary, Apr. 1, 1884, WMSS 9/F/182.

5. Mrs. Walter N. Hill to Mrs. Lammot du Pont, Apr. 12, 1884, LMSS 4/B/9.

6. Mrs. Lammot du Pont to Mrs. S. F. du Pont, Apr. 15, 1884, WMSS 9/E.

7. Mrs. S. F. du Pont Diary, Apr. 19, 1884, WMSS 9/F/182; Stephen Vincent Benét to Du Pont Company, Apr. 15, 1884, LMSS 4/B/9; Edmund Grace, secretary of GTA to Henry Belin, Jr., June 2, 1884, Acc. 1363/1; Mrs. A. V. du Pont to Mrs. S. F. du Pont, Apr. 30, 1884, WMSS 7/A/3.

8. Du Pont Company to Albert Dibblee, Apr. 17 and 21, 1884, B. G. du Pont Notes, LMSS 7/A/2.

9. LDP, Financial Statement, Jan. 1, 1884, Acc. 1363/2; *Philadelphia Record*, Apr. 2, 1884.

10. Mrs. Henry du Pont to Mrs. S. F. du Pont, Apr. 15, 1884, WMSS 7/B/19. Many years later, one of Uncle Fred's wards, Marguerite, a daughter of Irénée's, informed her cousin Pierre that Uncle Fred had been invited by Henry du Pont to succeed him as head of the Du Pont Company. Upon hearing of this, Meta, Uncle Fred's and LDP's mother, advised her son to stay in Louisville; she did not want him working himself to death as his brother Irénée had done "to put money into Henry's and Willie's pockets." Fred remained in Louisville and prospered (Marguerite du Pont to Pierre S. du Pont, Sept. 15, 1935, LMSS 10/file 328).

11. Mrs. Lammot du Pont to Mrs. S. F. du Pont, Oct. 20, 1884, Apr. 8, 1885, WMSS 9/E/166. The University of Pennsylvania at this time was setting up a new department of chemistry and considered naming it after Lammot. The Penn authorities wrote to his brother Fred, also a Penn alumnus, informing him of this and presumably seeking an endowment. Nothing further is known of the proposal (Mrs. A. V. du Pont to Mrs. S. F. du Pont, Apr. 1885, WMSS 7/A/3).

12. Two members of the trio who established the present E. I. du Pont de Nemours and Company, Pierre S. and Alfred I. du Pont, have been subjects of readable and perceptive biographies: Alfred D. Chandler and Stephen Salsbury, *Pierre S. du Pont and the Making of the Modern Corporation* (New York, 1971) and, cited earlier, Marquis James, *Alfred I. du Pont, the Family Rebel*.

Note on Sources

THE PRINCIPAL SOURCES of information for this biography are the Lammot du Pont Papers housed in the Hagley Museum and Library, Greenville, Delaware. Filling over sixty manuscript boxes, this collection is designated Accession 384. This collection (and items from other collections that bear accession numbers) are cited by accession and box numbers.

Papers of other du Pont family members who were contemporaries of Lammot du Pont are in the same repository in two major collections, the Longwood Manuscripts and the Winterthur Manuscripts. These collections are organized by group, series, box, file, or folder numbers and are cited accordingly.

The records of the Du Pont Company for the nineteenth century (until 1902), ledgers, journals, letter books, incoming correspondence, inventories, agreements, annual reports, and the like, are found in Accessions 500 and 501. Loose materials, such as incoming letters, fill over 600 file boxes and are cited by accession and box numbers.

Index

Du Pont, Francis Gurney (*cont.*)
powder mill explosions, record of, 174; and Repauno Chemical Company, equipment for, 257; and research, on military powder, 176

Du Pont, Henry (uncle): on Abraham Lincoln, 72, 123; and Brandywine powder mills, 43, 74, 90, 91, 98, 99, 101, 115, 169, 173; and children, 8, 26, 72, 87, 99–100, 106, 108, 233, 238, 250, 276, 289; in Civil War, 74, 92, 96; on competition, 209, 273; death of, 289; described, 131, 228–30, 259–60, 285; and Du Pont Company, changes in, 62, 66, 112–13, 231, 233–34, 235, 242–44, 292; and Du Pont Company, as junior partner, 24, 28, 31; and Du Pont Company, as senior partner and head, 30, 136, 141, 151, 166, 235–36, 237, 238, 261, 317 n. 10; and Gunpowder Trade Association, organization of, 203, 210, 211, 212; and high explosives, attitude towards, 250, 253; income of, 106; and LDP, over co-ownership of Repauno Chemical Company, 259, 273–75, 276; and LDP, relationship with, 39, 64, 67, 81, 90, 102, 106, 108, 116, 126–27, 173–74, 228, 230, 245; and Mocanaqua coal mines, 139; and politics, 71, 72; and saltpeter supplies, 76–77; and Wapwallopen powder mills, 88, 260

Du Pont, Mrs. Henry (Louisa) (aunt), 4, 99, 109, 111, 115–16, 122–23, 126–27, 306 n.19

Du Pont, Henry Algernon (cousin): described, 26, 156; and Du Pont Company, 233, 238–39, 289; and Du Pont Company, in LDP's plan for, 234, 238; military career of, 87, 94, 107, 118, 122, 306 n.15; and politics, 289; as railroad executive, 156–58, 239, 261, 289; and Repauno Chemical Company, 276; and Winterthur, 238, 253, 289

Du Pont, Henry B. (son), 161

Du Pont, Irene (cousin), 132

Du Pont, Irénée (son), 161, 226

Du Pont, Lammot (Motty): and black powder industry, consolidation of, 188–203; and black powder industry, as spokesman for, 86–87; and Canadian black powder market, 222–26; in Civil War, 74, 75, 90–94, 95, 96, 97–98, 99, 100–101, 104, 115, 116–17; death of, 282–83; described, 23, 77, 123–24, 268–69, 270–72; and Du Pont Company, duties in, 32, 35–36, 64, 65, 117–21, 165, 166, 174, 259, 260–61; and Du Pont Company, ideas for changes in, 61–65, 112–14, 120, 231–35, 236, 237, 238; and Du Pont Company, as junior partner, 41, 235, 236; and Du Pont Company, resignation from, 227, 241–43, 245, 259, 277–78; education of, 1, 9–10, 13, 14, 16–17; engagement and marriage of, 123, 126–27, 129–31, 132–34; experiments and patents, 22, 29, 32, 39–40, 63–64, 76, 104, 118–19, 122, 160, 175–76, 177–81, 251, 263, 281, 306 n.19; fights fire, 34; family of, 1–4, 5, 8, 109, 110, 119, 130, 134, 161, 265, 268–69, 277; finances and estate of, 95, 106, 134–36, 163–64, 234, 259, 286–87; and Gunpowder Trade Association, 212, 216–17, 220, 226–27; and high explosives industry, 219, 250–53, 254–55, 258, 259, 260–61, 265, 272–73, 274, 277–79, 291; health of, 21–22, 102–4, 107–8, 114, 115, 116, 119;

Gunpowder Export Company, 219, 223, 224
Gunpowder Trade Association (G.T.A.): Brainerd threat to, 222–23; and Canadian market, opening of, 222–24; Council on Prices of, 212, 216, 217; and Du Pont Company, domination by, 221, 226, 227; dynamite companies brought in, 259; LDP as president of, 212, 216, 226, 285; Neutral Belt agreement of, 220, 259; and nonmembers, treatment of, 217–19, 220; operations of, 216–17; organizational meetings for, 203, 211–12; structure of, 212–14

Halleck, Henry W., 91–92
Hamilton Powder Company, 223–24, 277, 287
Harding, George, 257
Hazard, Augustus G., 221
Hazard Powder Company: and association plans, 205, 210; and coal mining, 66; decline of, 221; and Du Pont Company, sale to, 219, 221–22; as Gunpowder Trade Association member, 211, 212, 214, 219, 220, 222, 223; in high explosives enterprise, 254; LDP and, 245, 277; wartime powder sales of, 35, 204
Hecla Powder Manufacturing Company, 287
Helmuth, George, 138
Henderson, Charlotte Shepard. See Du Pont, Mrs. Eleuthère Irénée, II (sister-in-law)
Henry, J. Buchanan, 42
Henry Clay Village, 75
Hercules dynamite, 249, 252, 264
Hercules dynamite plant, 221, 250, 253, 257, 264–65
Hercules Powder Company, 221, 265, 272, 274, 277, 287
Hexagonal powder, 181–83
High explosives industry: as future of explosives industry, 221, 247;

and patent infringement, 249–50, 252, 257, 258; stabilization of, 259. See also Dynamite; Nitroglycerine
Hill, Walter N., 256, 263, 280, 281, 282, 284
Hill, Mrs. Walter N., 284
Hilles, William H., 149
Hilyard, John P., 106
Homberg, Moses, 131
Hubert, M. de, 56
Hunter, Richard, 98
Hunting and sporting powder, 18, 40, 56, 167
Huston, Charles, 149
Home Guards. See Brandywine Home Guards
Hounsfield, Edgar, 132
Howder, James, 219, 249

Indian saltpeter. See Potassium nitrate
Indians (Native Americans), 161–62
Ingersoll, J. R., 12

Johnson, Mr. (Walter R.?), 12

Keating, William H., 11, 12
Kemble, Peter, 42, 44–45, 106
Kemble, Mrs. Peter. See Du Pont, Victorine (sister)
Kemble, William, 181
Kerr, George H., 270, 271–72
Kieselguhr, 248, 251
Kittle, N. G., 264
Kneeland, Furman L., 108, 209–10, 211–12, 220, 224, 228
Koch, Louis, 191, 193, 200

Lackawanna and Bloomsburg Railroad, 68
Laflin, Henry Dwight, 195, 198, 279
Laflin and Rand Company: in association plans, 205, 210; and black powder industry, consolidation in, 188–200; and coal mining, 186; and cooperation, 209, 254; and Du Pont Company, competitor with, 191, 196–97, 200, 208–9, 227; as